82T
ion

SUCCESSFUL SIGHT • SINGING, Book 2

A Creative, Step by Step Approach

By Nancy Telfer

© 1993 **Neil A. Kjos Music Company,** 4380 Jutland Drive, San Diego, California, 92117.
International copyright secured. All rights reserved. Printed U.S.A.
Warning! The contents of this publication are protected by copyright law. To copy or reproduce them by any method is an infringement of the copyright law. Anyone who reproduces copyrighted matter is subject to substantial penalties and assessments for each infringement.

Nancy Telfer is a Canadian composer who has been a choral clinician for many national and provincial organizations in Canada. Since 1979 she has composed over 250 works for soloists, chamber ensembles, orchestras, bands and choirs, many of which are published in Canada and the United States. Her music ranges from beginning to virtuoso levels and she has been commissioned to compose music for many very fine performers. She believes that all music (even sight-singing exercises!) should delight the ears, capture the imagination of the mind and feed the soul.

Contents

Page Number

Introduction

Everything in the arts begins with a dream. Then through expertise, hard work and a strong desire we, the artists, turn that dream into a reality.

Nancy Telfer

Nancy Telfer

For Whom is Book 2 of Successful Sight-Singing Designed?

Students and adults with unchanged, changing or changed voices who have completed Book 1:

1) Singers in **middle school, high school, university, community or church choirs**;

2) **Instrumental and choral music students at the university level** studying musicianship, ear-training, theory or sight-singing;

3) **Private instrumental, vocal or piano students** who wish to review skills learned in Book 1 and continue ear-training at a more advanced level.

Gifted students in accelerated programs may be able to use Book 2 without preliminary work in Book 1.

At the **university** level, all first year music students can be tested with some of the final exercises from the last milestones of Books 1 and 2. Then divide the students into three groups:

1) No sight-singing skills – Start at the beginning of Book 1; complete Books 1 and 2

2) Some sight-singing skills – Start at the beginning of Book 2; complete Book 2

3) Excellent sight-singing skills - Exemption from sight-singing classes

All university music students should reach the competency level of Milestone 8 before they graduate.

Exercises in three parts may be sung:

1) Each part separately;
2) Parts 1 and 2 alone;
3) Parts 1 and 3 alone;
4) All three parts together.

Which Features are Continued From Book 1?

- lyrics and dynamics;
- contemporary musical elements;
- unaccompanied exercises;
- well-crafted, original music;
- limited ranges whenever possible;
- variety of styles of music;
- technical pitfalls;
- color-coded information;
- choral publishing format;
- 5-10 minute sessions at least once a week;
- exercises that are fun to sing.

What New Features are Included in Book 2?

- a quick review of all elements presented in Book 1;
- old skills continued on to more advanced levels;
- new sight-singing tips;
- exercises with three independent parts;
- more practice with bass clef;
- extensive use of modulations, advanced interval training and atonal music;
- new activities for problem areas;
- problem-solving chart for singers;
- quick diagnostic chart for teachers;
- "In Rehearsal" suggestions for reinforcement and transferral to concert repertoire.

Teaching Sight-Singing

Should All Singers Learn to Sight-Sing in Both Treble and Bass Clefs?

Yes, but they should spend most of their time using the clef suitable for their own voices. The important sight-singing skills are the same whether you are reading in treble or bass clef; these skills transfer fairly easily between the two clefs.

All singers need to learn to sing from both treble and bass clefs to be able to read their cues from other vocal parts or the piano accompaniment. Basses need treble clef skills to read unison sections. Tenor parts may be in treble clef or in bass clef (i.e. when they are on the same staff as the bass part).

Is it Important to Use the Lessons in Order?

The singers should have a strong sense of the rhythm framework and the pitch framework before continuing on to more difficult exercises. Then it is possible to skip ahead to a later lesson to teach a rhythm, pitch or concept which is used frequently in the singers' current repertoire. It is more meaningful for the singers if the information in the sight-singing lessons relates directly to problems in current repertoire. The teacher can systematically cover the missing lessons later.

How Many Exercises Should I Do in a Session?

It depends on the individual choir. In one session you may do only one exercise or perhaps two or three if the singers learn those particular skills quickly.

Should I do All the Exercises and Activities with Each Choir?

No. Each choir has different strengths and weaknesses. Conductors should use their own common sense to move at a pace which will encourage and challenge the singers.

Because of the unexpected rhythms and pitches, the music in the exercises is not very memorable. If a choir needs to repeat a lesson, it is unlikely that the singers will remember the music exactly from a previous session.

Boosting the Success Rate

Singers who are naturally good at sight-singing learn differently (not better) than the vast majority of singers. They have taught themselves certain skills and habits which help them to be successful at sight-singing. These skills and habits are introduced systematically in detail in the lesson plans in the Teacher's Edition and are described briefly in the following paragraphs:

◆ **Posture:**

The success rate for keeping a steady beat and singing accurate rhythms is much higher if the body is evenly balanced. The very last thing singers should do before sight-singing is to position their bodies properly. **The success rate for accurate pitches and leaps is much higher if the head is in a proper position for singing.**

◆ **The Lyrics:**

Sight-singing is being able to sing a new piece of music accurately with the lyrics the first time through. Singers may have difficulty using the lyrics with the music at first but they quickly improve and the lyrics become a natural part of sight-singing.

If these exercises are sung to a neutral syllable, sol-fah syllables, time names or numbers the first time through, the singers never have an opportunity to practice real sight-singing with these exercises. It is particularly important that the singers practice fitting the words with the music in the first few exercises. This gives them an opportunity to let their eyes develop the skills needed to read words and music at the same time before the exercises become more difficult.

After the singers have sight-sung an exercise, some teachers may wish to go back over the exercise to analyze or make corrections using any skills the singers have with sol-fah syllables, time names or numbers.

Teachers who do not use sol-fah syllables, time names or numbers can get excellent results just by following the lessons plans in the Teacher's Edition. Sol-fah syllables, time names or numbers are not necessary for a successful sight-singing program.

◆ **Precision:**

Singers who lag slightly behind never have any practice in sight-singing because they always hear the correct pitches and rhythms from the good sight-singers just a fraction of a second before they sing.

Similarly, singers who glide into the correct pitch hear the correct pitch and tuning from the good sight-singers before they reach the center of the pitch themselves. The only way to learn to sight-sing is to sing with precision in tune.

◆ **Frequent Pitches:**

When a pitch appears frequently in a piece, the singers should memorize that pitch. Each time it appears, they can use it as a check to make sure that it still sounds at the same pitch. This acts as a continual reinforcement for the singer's confidence.

NOTE: Many singers know this concept intellectually but do not use this information when sight-singing. They may not sing the F at the end of a line at the same pitch as the F at the beginning of the line.

◆ **Using A Framework:**

For Pitches

Good sight-singers memorize the sound and sight of the tonic and dominant. Then they **fit the other pitches within the framework of the tonic and dominant** (above, below or between the pitches of the framework):

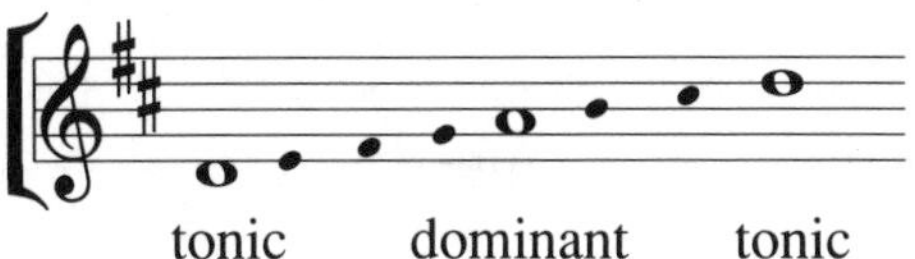

As the singers become more experienced, the pitches within the framework will become more accurate so that the singers always know exactly what each pitch sounds like. However, the skill of using a pitch framework continues to be valuable as the singer works with more and more difficult music.

For Rhythms

Good sight-singers fit the rhythms within the framework of the beat:

They use a strong sense of eighth-note pulse to divide the quarter-note beat for changing meters:

◆ **Silent Singing**

The singers must learn to hear each pitch and rhythm in the mind before singing aloud. Silent singing is one of the best ways for each singer to:

i) Improve the skill of hearing and singing accurate rhythms and pitches;
ii) To monitor their own individual progress. When an exercise is repeated aloud, the singer determines:
  1) Where they made the errors;
  2) Why they made these errors;
  3) What strategies will help them with this problem.

◆ **The Eyes**

When the singer's eyes are trained to move continuously from left to right in a bouncing motion, **there is a higher success rate for keeping a steady beat and singing accurate rhythms.**

◆ **Marking Scores:**

Good sight-singers use markings to clarify the score and to create signposts to assure themselves that they are sight-singing correctly. A pencil is one of the most useful tools for a singer.

◆ **Unaccompanied Sight-Singing:**

With a cappella sight-singing:

i) No one can inadvertantly receive help from the piano part;
ii) The singers can hear their own voices more clearly so that each singer can monitor individual progress.

An accompaniment should be used for sight-singing only when the teacher is demonstrating specific skills in how to find cues in the accompaniment.

◆ **Acoustical Situations:**

Good sight-singers adapt quickly to different acoustical situations and still sight-sing accurately under adverse conditions. When the singers are given a variety of acoustical situations during sight-singing sessions:

i) They become more independent;
ii) Their sense of pitch and rhythm becomes much stronger;
iii) They are able to concentrate better on their own part.

◆ **Reading Full Scores:**

When a singer learns to scan the eyes over other parts of the score, they can spot information which can be helpful to them (texture changes, cues from other vocal parts, etc.).

NOTE: Make sure you have the necessary equipment before you begin:
i) Good lighting;
ii) A copy of the music and a pencil for each individual singer;
iii) A piano, tuning fork or pitch pipe for the true beginning pitch of each exercise.

How Do You Transfer the Skills to Rehearsal Repertoire?

After each sight-singing session, keep your Teacher's Edition open on your music stand for the rehearsal. Use the information in the "In Rehearsal" section for reinforcement and transferral of the skills and habits you have just taught in that lesson.

As the singers are taught the skills and habits of successful sight-singers in their sight-singing sessions, they will be eager to transfer this knowledge to rehearsal repertoire because they can see quite clearly how it will help them. They are developing habits which will last them a lifetime.

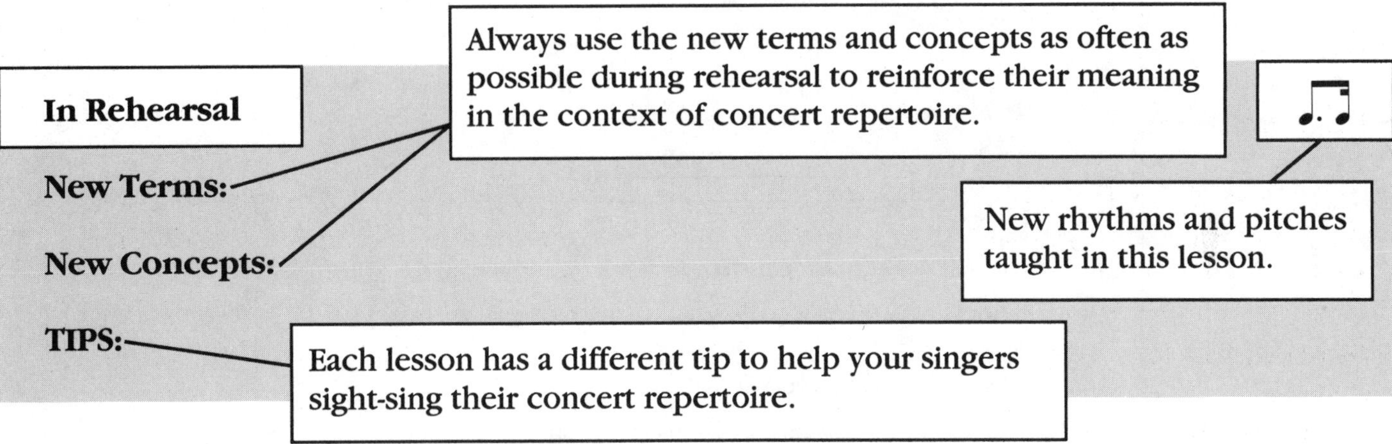

NOTE: For teachers with more than one choir or choral class, this feature acts as a reminder as to which terms and concepts have been covered with each group.

A Philosophy of Learning

Think of music as a life-long activity. Sight-singing sessions should be of immediate help to the singers in their everyday repertoire, but the sessions should also be preparing the singers for the skills needed in more advanced repertoire (i.e. when the singers are only singing in unison or two parts, they should be experiencing "readiness" skills for three and four part music).

Encourage your singers to:
i) Sing each exercise musically. There is no market for "singing robots" no matter how well they can sight-sing;

ii) Be brave in trying out each new skill;
iii) Monitor their own progress as individuals within the group;
iv) Determine the strategies which work best for them individually.

When singers learn to sight-sing, it changes the whole atmosphere in the choral rehearsal. What a delight to be able to make music together from the first read-through!

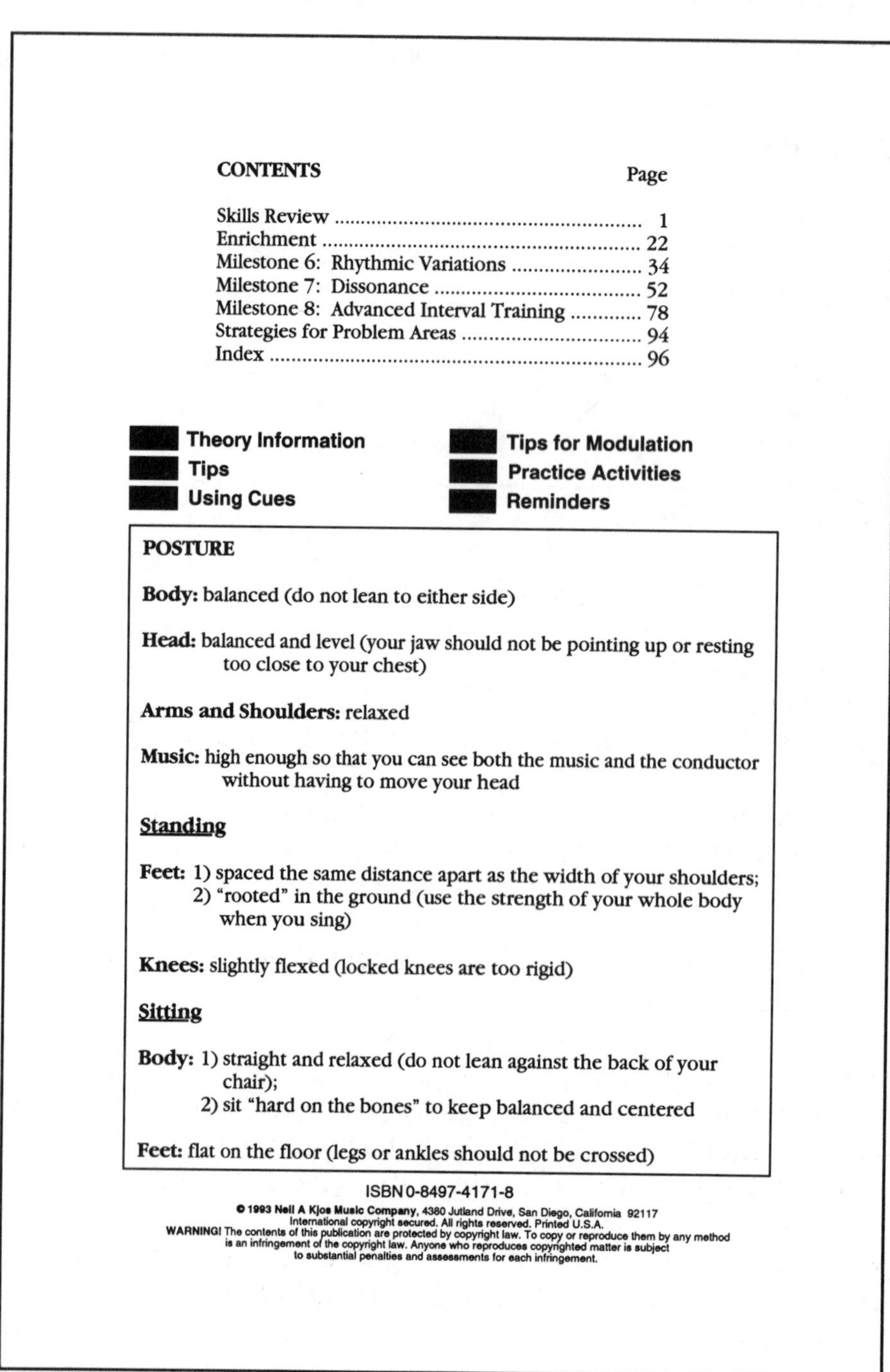

CONTENTS — Page

Theory Information
Tips
Using Cues
Tips for Modulation
Practice Activities
Reminders

POSTURE

Body: balanced (do not lean to either side)

Head: balanced and level (your jaw should not be pointing up or resting too close to your chest)

Arms and Shoulders: relaxed

Music: high enough so that you can see both the music and the conductor without having to move your head

Standing

Feet: 1) spaced the same distance apart as the width of your shoulders;
2) "rooted" in the ground (use the strength of your whole body when you sing)

Knees: slightly flexed (locked knees are too rigid)

Sitting

Body: 1) straight and relaxed (do not lean against the back of your chair);
2) sit "hard on the bones" to keep balanced and centered

Feet: flat on the floor (legs or ankles should not be crossed)

ISBN 0-8497-4171-8

© 1993 Neil A Kjos Music Company, 4380 Jutland Drive, San Diego, California 92117
International copyright secured. All rights reserved. Printed U.S.A.
WARNING! The contents of this publication are protected by copyright law. To copy or reproduce them by any method is an infringement of the copyright law. Anyone who reproduces copyrighted matter is subject to substantial penalties and assessments for each infringement.

Color Coding

Research indicates that the brain is stimulated by the use of color on the page: the singers will learn more quickly and have better retention of skills.

Posture

Singers who have difficulty with sight-singing tend to go into a "contorted fetal position" as soon as they know they are going to sight-sing. And they stay in this position until they know the music well! Because they are afraid of sight-singing, they lean to one side, scrunch their heads down and forward and twist their bodies into protective positions. What a handicap!

Good sight-singers go into correct posture just before they begin to sight-sing and maintain this posture throughout the music.

Activities for Balanced Posture

i) To help singers understand the importance of balanced posture:
   1) Have Part 1 singers balance their weight on one foot; Part 2 singers lean their head to one side.
   2) Sing an easy exercise (i.e. Exercise 4).
   3) Switch parts and REPEAT with the body balanced on two feet and the head balanced.
   4) Notice how much easier it is to sing the beat and the rhythms with precision when the posture is correct. Think how much difference posture would make if the exercise were difficult!

ii) At the beginning of each rehearsal, have the singers:
   1) Stand;
   2) Shift their weight to the right foot;
   3) Shift their weight to the left foot;
   4) Balance their weight steadily in the center; flex the knees slightly.

   NOTE: Sometimes singers think they are balanced when they are actually tilting to one side. When they must shift the weight from foot to foot first, then it is easier for them to find the balanced position in the middle.

iii) During rehearsal, occasionally have the singers check their balance. Eventually they will balance automatically.

iv) When the singers are suddenly faced with very difficult music, the old posture may return. Remind them not to handicap themselves; they will need all the help they can get for sight-singing difficult music. Have them do a quick relaxation exercise before they begin (i.e. a few deep breaths, rotation of the shoulders, etc.).

With younger singers, it is more common to see the entire weight shifted to one leg. With older singers, it is more common to see the head tilted to one side (a more sophisticated version of the entire body being off-balance).

With a balanced posture:

- The body is steady;
- The singer can use the strength of the whole body to help them to sing;
- The body is psychologically in a position of confidence;
- There is a noticeable improvement in the quality of tone, the control over musical phrasing and dynamics, the tuning and the precision;
- Less energy is required from the singer.

The balanced position is a position of power. The success rate for beat and rhythms is much higher if the body is balanced.

Activities for Proper Head Position

i) Have the singers sing while holding their music on their knees. To be able to see the music, the singers will have their heads down.

REPEAT with the music up at a proper level where the singers can see the music and the conductor without moving their heads up and down.

Notice how much easier it is to sing the correct pitches when the head is in a proper position. This is particularly obvious when the music has octave leaps.

ii) During rehearsal, occasionally have the singers check the position of their music. **Make sure that the singers do not set their music on their desks while they are singing.**

NOTE: When the music is down, the head is down. The success rate for correct pitches and leaps is much higher when the head is in the proper position.

When the head is down, the pitch is affected in three ways:

1) Vocally: It is much more difficult to produce any pitches because the throat is tight and the chin has nowhere to fall.

2) Kinesthetically: When the head is up in a proper position, high pitches have a certain feeling in the head, middle pitches feel different and low pitches create yet another sensation.When the head is down, all pitches feel more alike; they are harder to “find.” The singers think they are going to sing a high pitch, but a middle or a low pitch may come out instead.

3) Psychologically: When the head is up, the singer is in a position of confidence. This helps them to sight-sing more accurately.

TIP: The very last thing singers should do before sight-singing is to check their posture for balance and head position.

Sight-Singing Lessons

◆ ◆ SKILLS REVIEW ◆ ◆

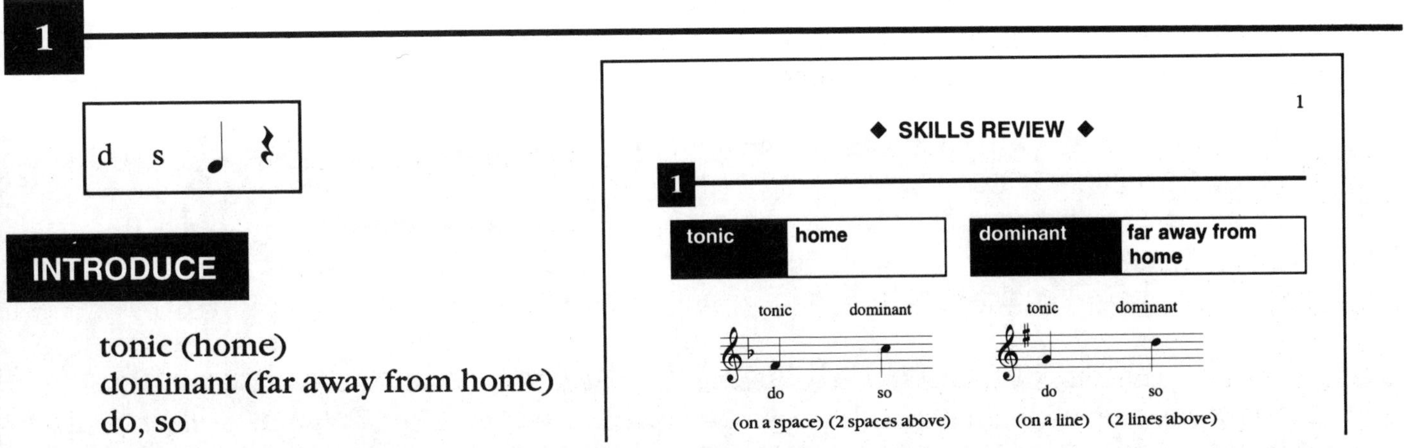

tonic (home)
dominant (far away from home)
do, so

Teachers who use numbers instead of sol-fah syllables may wish to continue using numbers.

EXPLAIN: The higher the note is on the staff, the higher in pitch it will sound. Let the notes show your voice whether to go higher or lower in pitch.

Sing as a chant:

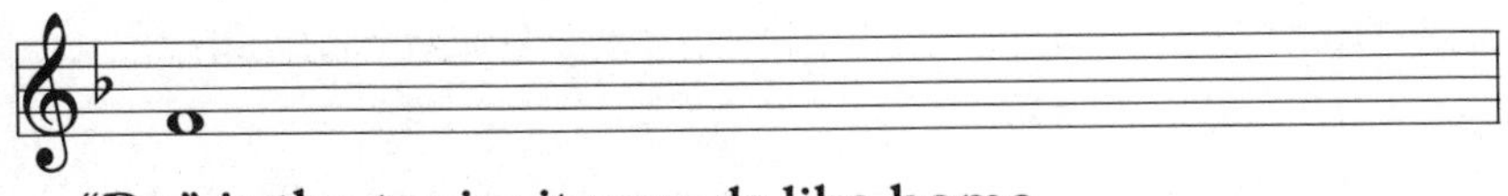

"Do" is the tonic; it sounds like home.

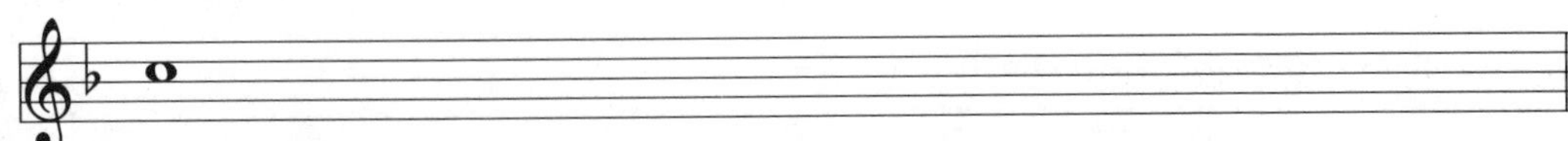

"So" is the dominant; it sounds far away from home.

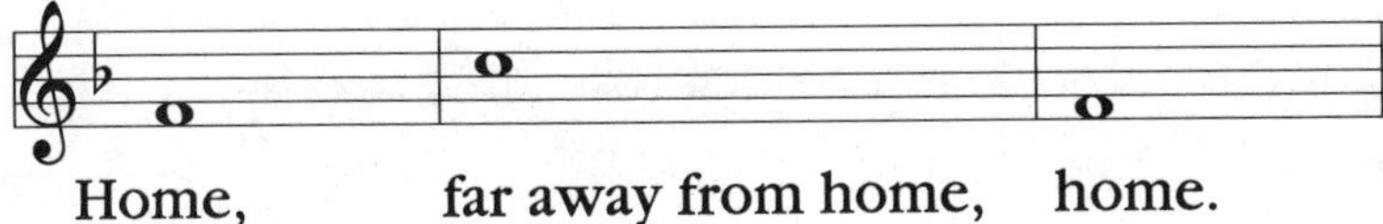

Home, far away from home, home.

NOTE: Whenever the "home" tone is sung, it should sound solid and strong. "Far away from home" should sound less settled. The tonic and dominant are used more often than any other pitches in concert repertoire. The singers should memorize:

i) The sound of the pitches "do so do";
ii) The feeling of the "home" tone.

Ask the singers to sing "do so do" in F major, then in G major, then in F major again.

See page 179 in the Teacher's edition for an activity to memorize the interval of a fifth.

INTRODUCE

fifth

SING Exercise 1:

In two parts with the lyrics the first time through.
(Tenors and basses will sound an octave lower than the written music.)

NOTE: Sight-singing is being able to sing a new piece of music accurately with the lyrics the first time through. Singers may have difficulty using the lyrics with the music at first but they quickly improve and the lyrics become a natural part of sight-singing.

<u>If these exercises are sung to a neutral syllable, sol-fah syllables, numbers or time names the first time through, the singers never have an opportunity to practice real sight-singing with these exercises.</u> It is particularly important that the singers practice fitting the words with the music at this very easy level in the first few exercises. This gives them an opportunity to let their eyes develop the skills needed to read words and music at the same time before the exercises become more difficult.

After the singers have sight-sung an exercise, you may wish to go back over the exercise with them to analyze or make corrections using any skills they have with sol-fah syllables, time names or numbers.

REPEAT Exercise 1:

Encouraging the singers to sing:

precisely together and *exactly in tune.*

Commend their courage in attempting the right pitches and rhythms without waiting to hear their neighbors' voices first. Mistakes are permissible.

Each singer should monitor their own progress and take pride in being responsible for their own achievements in sight-singing. If singers start to lag behind on each note, remind them to be brave.

NOTE: <u>Singers who lag slightly behind never have any practice in sight-singing because they always hear the correct pitches and rhythms from the good sight-singers just a fraction of a second before they sing.</u>

Similarly, singers who glide into the correct pitch hear the correct pitch and tuning from the good sight-singers before they reach the center of the pitch themselves. Tell your singers that <u>the only way to learn to sight-sing is to sing with precision in tune.</u>

See page 183 in the Teacher's Edition for activities for precision. **See pages 193 and 195** for activities for tuning.

READ the TIP under the music in the Vocal Edition.

NOTE: The success rate for keeping a steady beat and singing accurate rhythms is much higher if the body is evenly balanced. **See page 11** in the Teacher's Edition for activities for balanced posture.

REPEAT Exercise 1:

Switch parts. Pay special attention to the tuning on repeated pitches. Be aware of the feeling of "home" every time you sing the tonic.

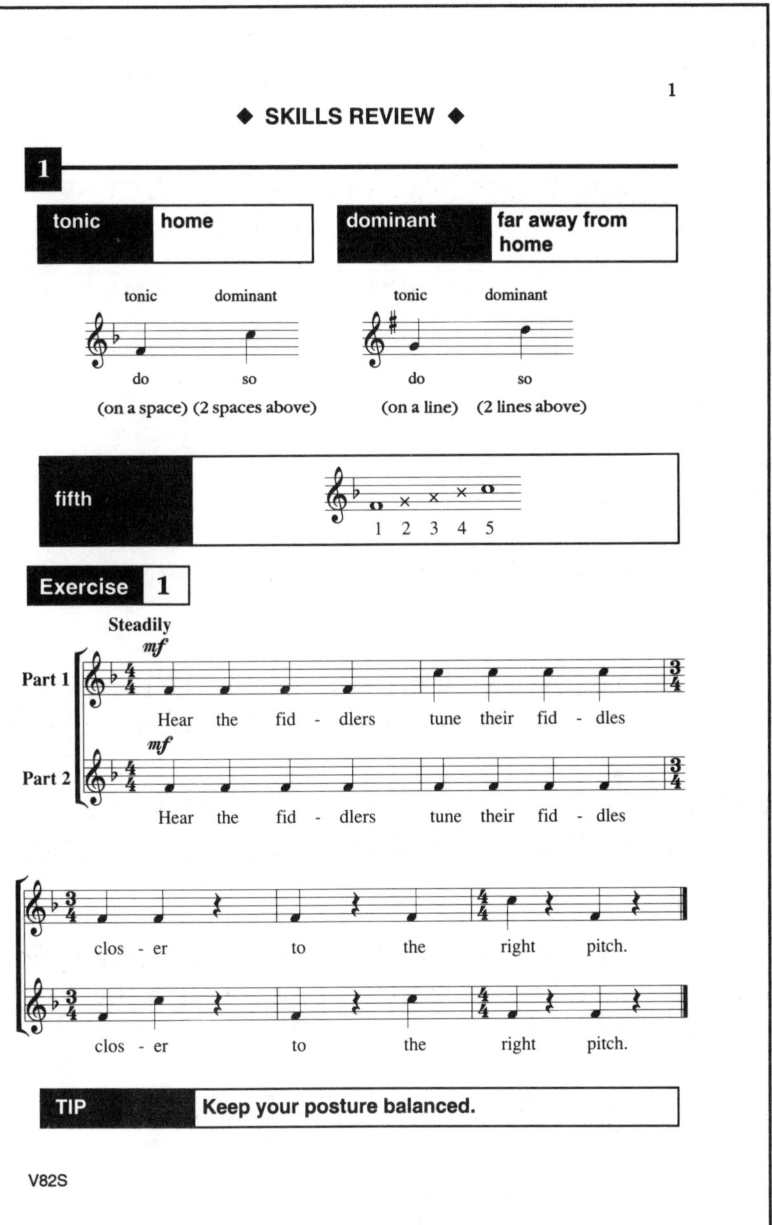

1

◆ SKILLS REVIEW ◆

1

tonic	home

dominant	far away from home

tonic dominant
do so
(on a space) (2 spaces above)

tonic dominant
do so
(on a line) (2 lines above)

fifth 1 2 3 4 5

Exercise 1

Steadily
mf
Part 1: Hear the fid - dlers tune their fid - dles
Part 2: Hear the fid - dlers tune their fid - dles

clos - er to the right pitch.
clos - er to the right pitch.

TIP	Keep your posture balanced.

V82S

IN REHEARSAL

do so

New Terms: tonic, dominant, fifth

New Concepts: precision, tuning, balanced posture, follow the direction of the pitches as they move higher and lower, feeling of "home" tone

TIPS:

i) Sight-sing concert music with the lyrics the first time through.
ii) Before beginning each piece:

- If any singers are unsure how to find the tonic on the staff, at this stage simply tell them:
  "The tonic is on the bottom line for sopranos, altos and tenors; the second space from the top for basses."
  (In Lesson 7, key signatures will be reviewed.)
- Sing "do so do" (minor keys: "tonic dominant tonic").
- Check for balanced posture.

2

INTRODUCE

quarter note (one beat)
quarter rest (one beat)
marking tonic at the beginning of the music

SING Exercise 2:

Singers on the right: Part 1.
Singers on the left: Part 2.

2

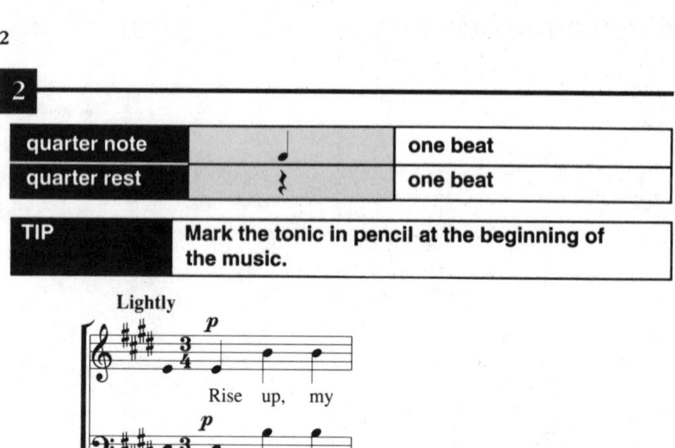

Always know where the tonic sits on the staff in every piece of music. Each time you see the tonic, sing the same pitch.

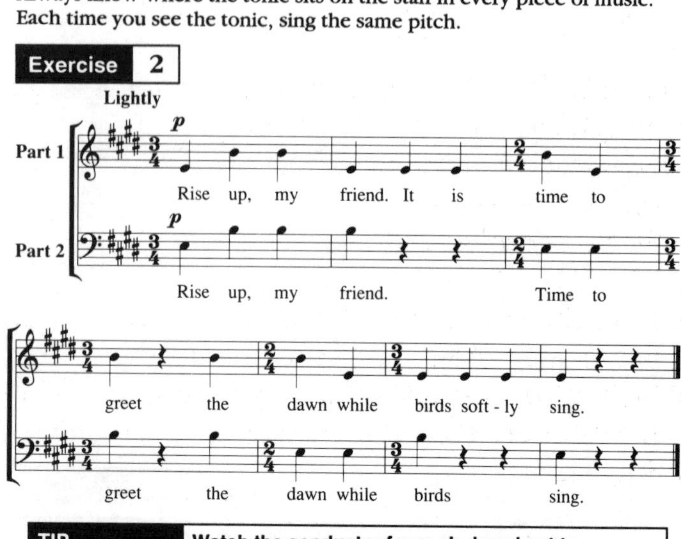

V82S

NOTE: If the singers do not keep a steady beat, the conductor may tap the beat. It is essential for the singers to have a strong sense of beat before they concentrate on more difficult rhythms. See the Teacher's Edition of Book 1 of **Successful Sight-Singing** for activities to improve the sense of beat.

EXPLAIN: There is a vertical line at the end of each measure. These barlines divide each line of music into sections. The first measure has three notes with the words "Rise up, my."

Ask the singers:

"How many notes are there in the second measure of Part 1 (3 notes)? . . . the fifth measure of Part 2 (2 notes)?"

READ the TIP under the music in the Vocal Edition.

EXPLAIN: The barlines look like the downbeats of the conductor.

Conduct a few measures of Exercise 2 as you speak the words of Part 1. The downbeat should be bigger than the other beats. Ask the singers to notice how the barlines correspond with the conductor's downbeat:

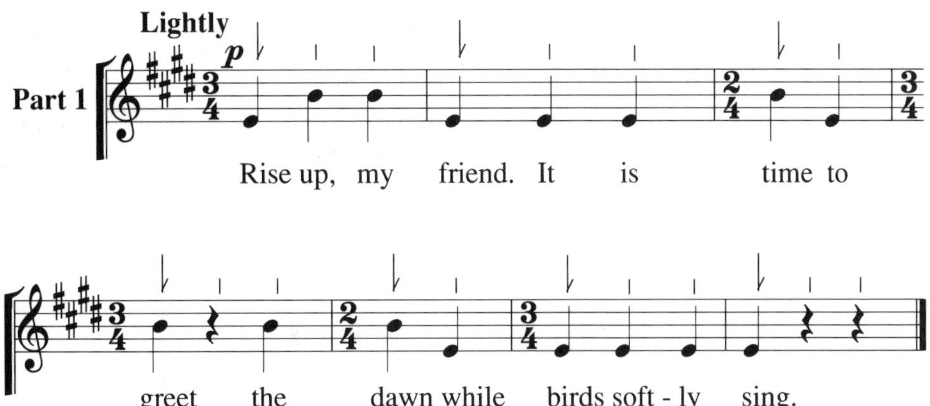

NOTE: If the conductor is also the accompanist and never actually "conducts" the choir, the conductor may tap the beat clearly instead of conducting. When the singers have learned to sing with a steady beat, omit the tapping.

REPEAT Exercise 2:

i) Have the singers watch for the conductor's downbeats as they sing. Did anyone in Part 1 pause after "friend"? Encourage the singers to keep a steady beat.
ii) Switch parts and sing silently. The singers should try to imagine the music inside their own heads; there should be no sound of singing or humming in the room.
iii) Sing aloud.

NOTE: In sight-singing, the singer must be able to hear each pitch and rhythm in the mind before singing aloud. Silent singing is one of the best ways for singers to become more independent with this skill. It takes concentration and develops keen hearing. Every singer has an opportunity to develop sight-singing skills without "leaning" on someone else.

At first the singers may not hear any music in their own minds. To the conductor, it will seem as if there is a great vacuum in the room. Gradually the singers will start to hear shapes of sound moving up and down, then definite pitches and rhythms and finally an accurate sound of the music (complete with lyrics and dynamics). Then the conductor may notice that the rehearsal room, although silent, has a sense of music flowing through it.

Immediately after each attempt at silent singing, ask the singers to sing the same exercise aloud so that they will:

i) know how well they have done and will be encouraged by any success;
ii) note the specific problems they have experienced;
iii) determine strategies to correct the problems.

IN REHEARSAL

New Terms: barline, measure

New Concepts: marking the tonic, measure number, barline corresponding to conductor's downbeat, silent singing

NOTE: Always use new terms and concepts as often as possible during rehearsal to reinforce their meaning in the context of concert repertoire.

TIPS:

i) At the beginning of each rehearsal, check that every singer has a pencil.
ii) Before beginning each new piece, have the singers mark the tonic in pencil and sing "do so do" (minor keys: "tonic dominant tonic").
iii) When you stop the choir in the middle of a piece to work out a problem, first take a few seconds to ask the singers to think "tonic" and then, on cue, sing the tonic. Emphasize the feeling of "home." Ask them where the tonic is on the staff. Then continue on with the rehearsal.

REPEAT several times with different pieces in each rehearsal.

After a few weeks, they will be able to hear and see the tonic quickly and easily in any piece. The singers should check that they are on the correct pitch every time they see the tonic.

3

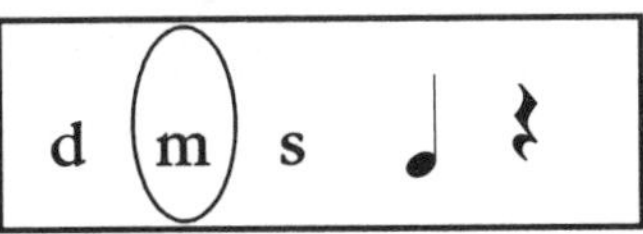

Have the singers mark the tonic in Exercise 3:

Firmly

INTRODUCE

mi
third
major triad

3

3

mi — between do and so

do mi so
(the line between)

do mi so
(the space between)

third

do mi
1 2 3

Memorize the sound of a major triad:

do mi so mi do

Sing on "dah":

Exercise 3

Firmly

Part 1

Wish-es three would I make all for the

Part 2

Wish-es three would I make for the

sake of the fu - ture. Wish-es three: one, two, three.

sake of the fu - ture. Wish-es three: one, two, three.

V82S

SING the practice example above the music in the Vocal Edition.

SING Exercise 3:

Singers in the front: Part 1.
Singers in the back: Part 2.

TIP: In the third measure of Part 2, the singers will know their first pitch by remembering it from the preceding measures.

REPEAT Exercise 3:

i) Standing. Sing each phrase musically. In today's world, there is no market for the mechanical sound of "singing robots"; every moment in the music class or rehearsal should be a musical experience. Are some singers pausing at the end of measure 6?
ii) Switch parts. Sing the first measure aloud, second measure silently, etc.
iii) Sing entire exercise aloud.

NOTE: Lesson 3 is continued on page 20.

NOTE: When alternate measures are sung silently, the singers learn different sight-singing skills than they would if they sang the entire exercise silently. It is helpful to use many variations of silent singing to improve different types of skills. **See page 186** in the Teacher's Edition for variations of silent singing.

INTRODUCE

letter names for treble clef

Have the singers say the letter names for Part 1 of Exercise 32, 46 or 91.

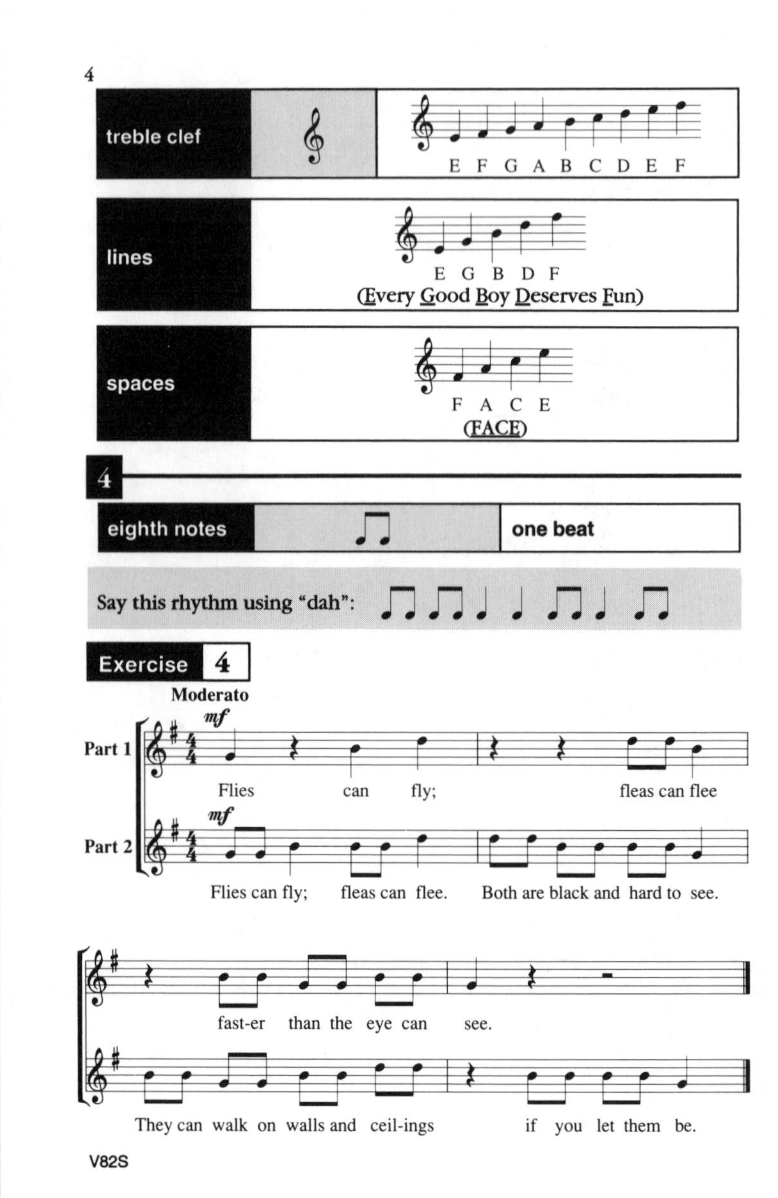

IN REHEARSAL | **mi**

New Terms: third, major triad, letter names for treble clef

New Concepts: remembering a previous pitch, alternating measures aloud and silent

TIPS:

i) Before beginning each familiar piece, check for the tonic the singers have already marked on the staff. Then sing the major triad. Memorize the sight and sound of tonic in each piece.

ii) Memorize any pitches which are frequently used in a piece. If the highest pitches in the soprano and tenor parts are repeated in several places, these pitches are fairly easy to memorize and may be useful to the singer.

iii) When you give instructions, use treble clef letter names to identify pitches:

- the starting and ending pitches of each part;
- the climax note of a phrase;
- out of tune notes;
- any other notes you wish to name.

For a few rehearsals, identify pitches by the letter name and the lyrics:
"In measure 6, the G on the word "sun" is not high enough."

As the singers become used to the letter names, remove the reference to the lyrics:
"In measure 6, the G is not high enough."

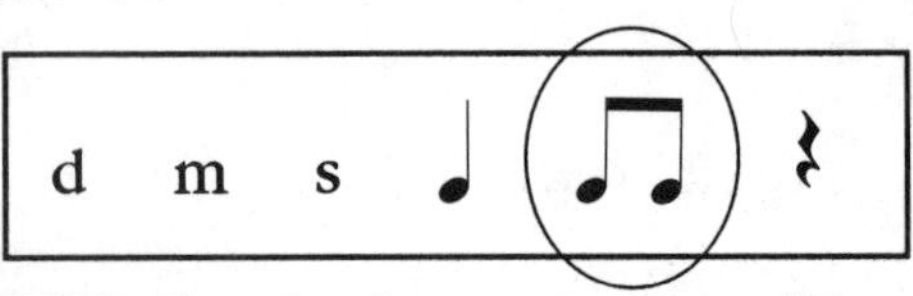

REVIEW: Say the letter names of Exercise 4.

INTRODUCE

eighth notes

SPEAK the practice example above the music in the Vocal Edition.

Have the singers count the eighth notes in the second measure (Part 1: two eighth notes; Part 2: six eighth notes).

SING Exercise 4

REPEAT Exercise 4:

Concentrate on singing all eighth notes steadily.

See page 182 in the Teacher's Edition for activities with eighth note pulse.

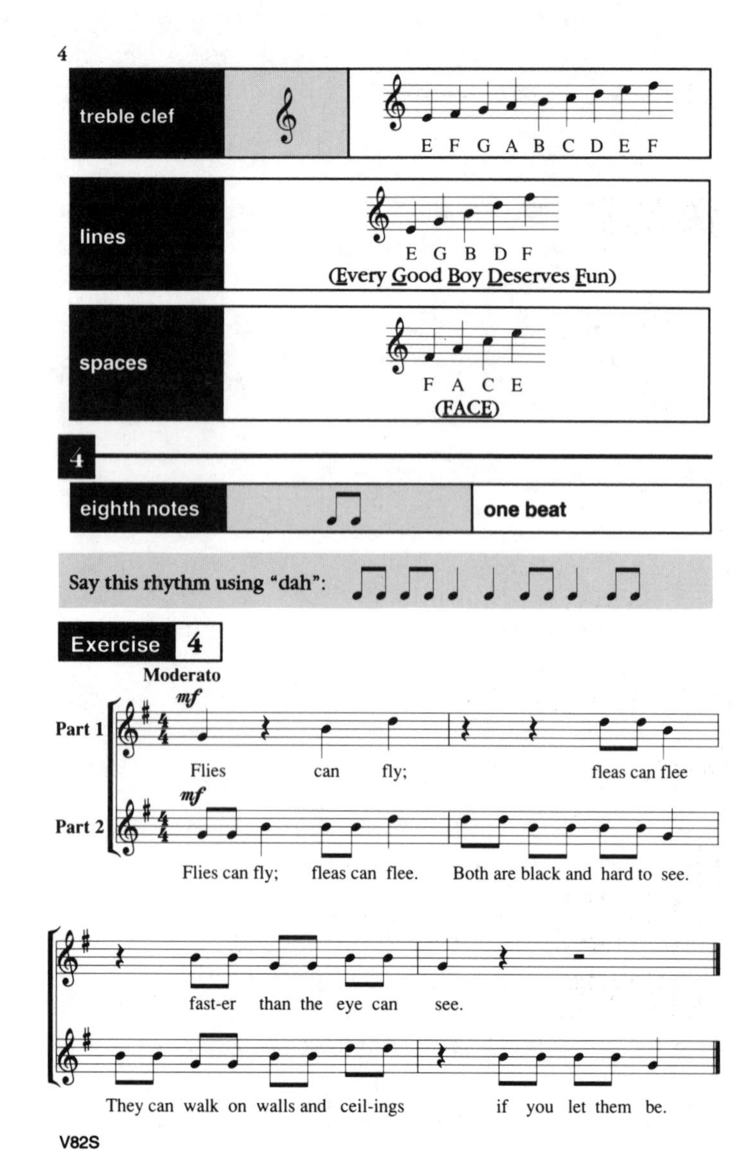

IN REHEARSAL

TIPS:

i) Refer to eighth notes and quarter notes by letter and rhythm names:
"In measure 57, make sure that the eighth notes on D are in tune."

ii) If the singers are confident at hearing the tonic in every piece of music, start reinforcing the sound of the dominant.

When the choir stops in the middle of a piece to work on a problem, ask the singers to think "dominant" and then, on cue, sing the dominant. Ask them where the dominant is on the staff.

REPEAT several times in each rehearsal.

5

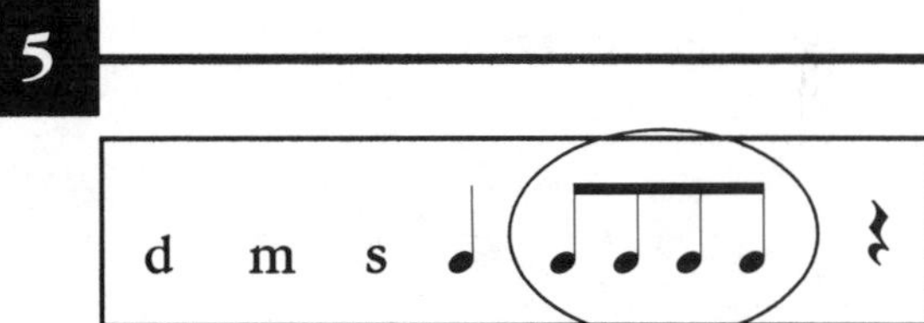

NOTE: Each group of eighth notes may include more than one pitch.

INTRODUCE

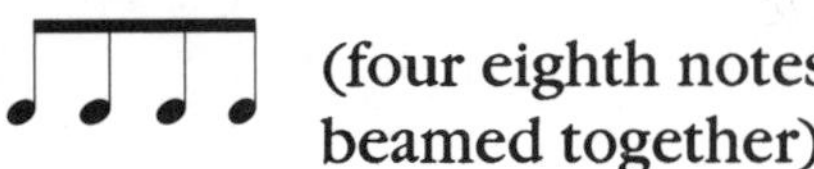
(four eighth notes beamed together)

PREVIEW TIP: Have the singers read through the nonsense lyrics silently.

NOTE: Lesson 5 is continued on page 24.

SING Exercise 5

NOTE: Whenever the singers have difficulty with an exercise, give them a few moments afterwards so that each singer can determine where they had difficulty and decide on a strategy to correct the problem. Then repeat the exercise.

TIP: At the end of each line, whip your eyes quickly down to the beginning of the next line.

REPEAT Exercise 5:

i) Switch parts. Sing the first system (measures 1-2) aloud, second system silently, third system aloud.
ii) Sing the entire exercise aloud.

IN REHEARSAL

TIP: If the measures are numbered, refer to those numbers when you are giving any instructions to the singers.

If the measures are not numbered, refer to the measures by system:
"Let's begin on page 3, second system, second measure."

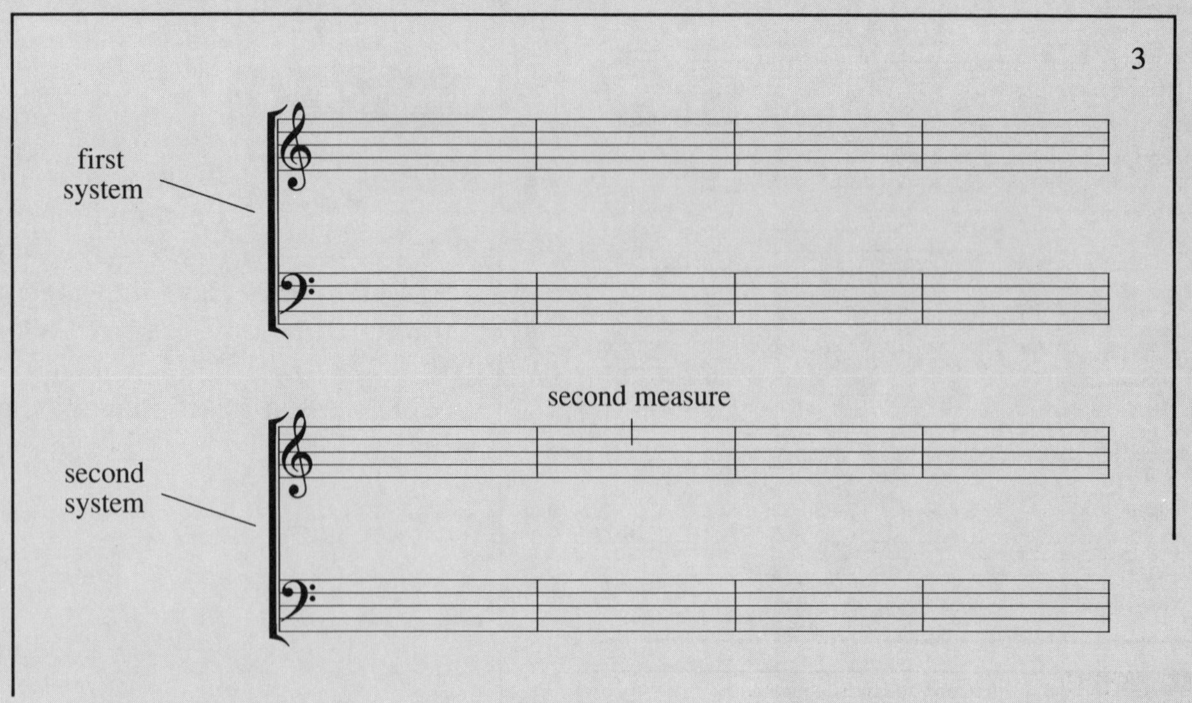

6

INTRODUCE

time signature in simple time

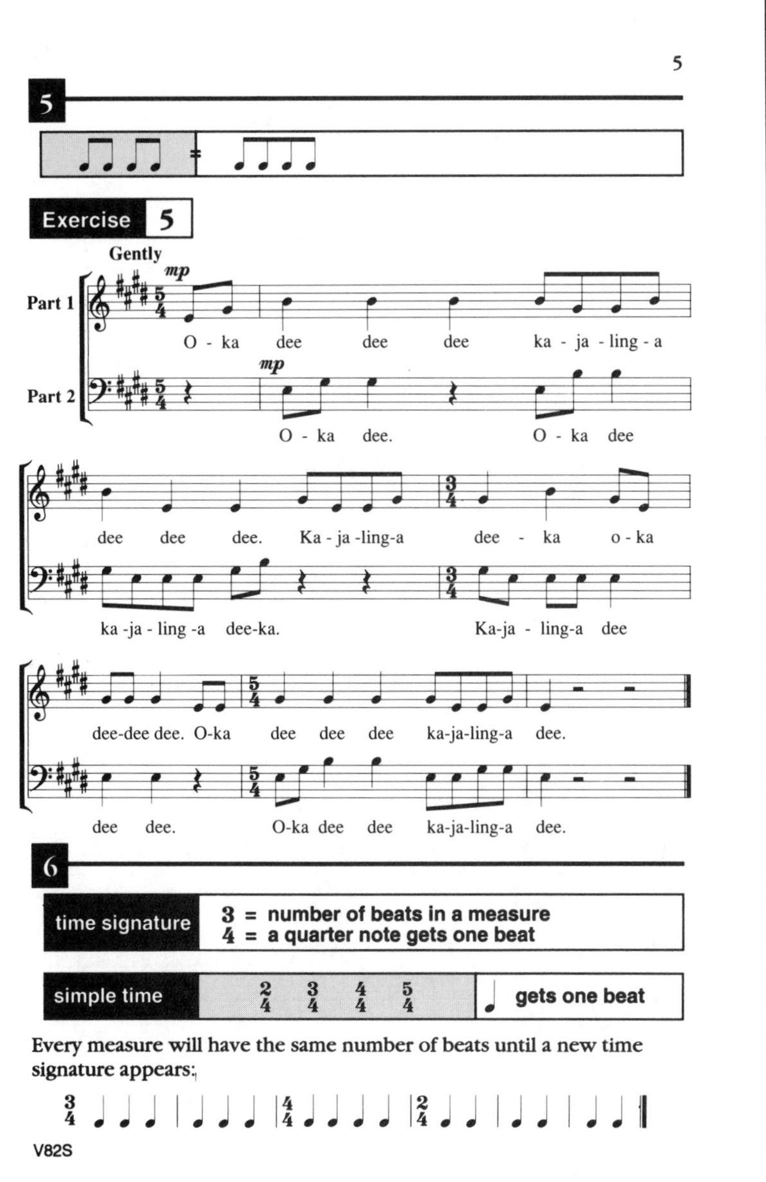

5

5

Exercise 5

Gently

Part 1 (*mp*): O - ka dee dee dee ka - ja - ling - a dee dee dee. Ka - ja -ling-a dee - ka o - ka dee-dee dee. O-ka dee dee dee ka-ja-ling-a dee.

Part 2 (*mp*): O - ka dee. O - ka dee ka -ja - ling -a dee-ka. Ka-ja - ling-a dee dee dee. O-ka dee dee ka-ja-ling-a dee.

6

time signature
3 = number of beats in a measure
4 = a quarter note gets one beat

simple time 2/4 3/4 4/4 5/4 — quarter note gets one beat

Every measure will have the same number of beats until a new time signature appears.

V82S

INTRODUCE

half note in simple time (two beats)
half rest in simple time (two beats)

SPEAK the practice example above the music in the Vocal Edition. The vertical lines above the rhythms show the beat.

SING Exercise 6:

Read beat by beat but sing the phrase.

NOTE: It is very important to be able to ignore the time signatures and read beat by beat so that the singer will develop a strong sense of beat that may be used as a framework for rhythms.

The important part of the time signature at this stage is the number which shows what kind of a note gets one beat. Later the singer will learn to sight-sing with an awareness of the number of beats in each measure. However, experienced sight-singers still continue to sing beat by beat when they sing difficult passages of music.

REPEAT Exercise 6:

i) Be careful to sing every note in tune.
ii) Switch parts.

IN REHEARSAL

New Terms: time signature, simple time

New Concept: reading beat by beat

TIP: In difficult rhythmic passages, encourage the singers to read beat by beat.

7

INTRODUCE

bass clef letter names

INTRODUCE

key signature with flats (major keys)

REVIEW: Check the time signatures in Exercise 7.

NOTE: Unchanged voices will sing Part 2 an octave higher than written. All singers need to learn to sing from both treble and bass clefs. **See page 5** in the Teacher's Edition for a full explanation.

SING Exercise 7

NOTE: The conductor should try to remain neutral; do not show when each entry comes by your breath or any other movement. Use a large downbeat and clear intermediary beats and look supportive! When the singers see the conductor using neutral conducting, they quickly realize that they must learn to rely on their own skills to sight-sing.

REPEAT Exercise 7:

i) Facing the side of the room. Be ready to whip the eyes down to the third line.
ii) Switch parts. Face the back of the room.

NOTE: When you change the direction the singers are facing, the acoustics for each singer changes. Good sight-singers react quickly and easily to the change. The other singers must work hard to sing the right pitches and rhythms despite a change in acoustics. This helps them to become more independent. The more practice they have with changing acoustics, the better they become at sight-singing.

See page 190 for activities with changing acoustics.

IN REHEARSAL

New Terms: bass clef letter names

New Concepts: key signature with flats (major keys), changing acoustics

TIP: Occasionally have the choir face another direction in the rehearsal room for a short period of time or for an entire rehearsal.

Key Signatures With Flats

Find the flat farthest to the right in the key signature:

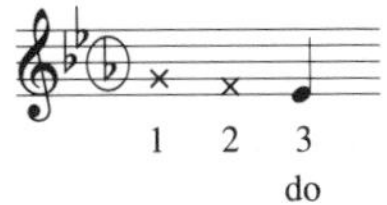

"Do" is three notes below this flat.

Because the first flat in the key signature is B flat, every B in the music will be called a "B flat."

8

INTRODUCE

time signature in duple time
marking duple time

NOTE: The singer's eyes should move continuously from left to right across the page in a bouncing motion. At first the eyes learn to bounce beat by beat and then word by word, measure by measure or phrase by phrase. Gradually the eyes begin to move ahead of the voice to spot problems.

Many singers let their eyes get stuck on long notes or difficult rhythms. When the eyes stop moving, the singer loses all sense of time and space. Then their eyes suddenly move on to the next note but it often takes them a measure or two to regain a steady beat and accurate rhythms. As long as the eyes keep moving steadily, the singer can keep the sense of beat.

See page 187 in the Teacher's Edition for activities to train eye movement.

PREVIEW TIP: Ask the singers to check the key signature in Exercise 8:

SING Exercise 8

INTRODUCE

ledger line names

Say the letter names in Part 2 of Exercise 8 in rhythm. **REPEAT** with Part 1.

8

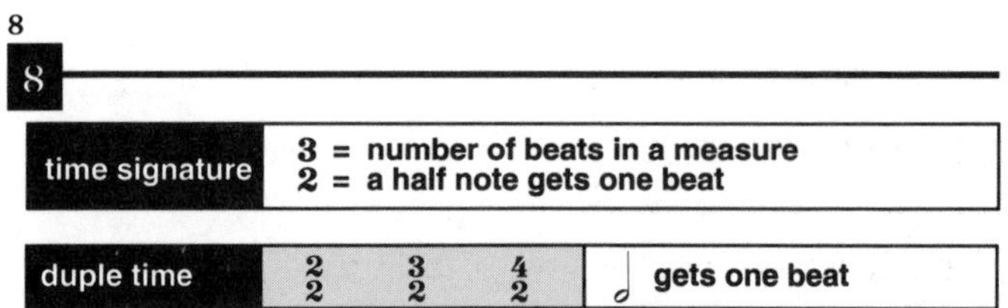

Circle the bottom 2 in the time signature to remind you to think a half note for each beat. Mark a vertical line in pencil above each beat:

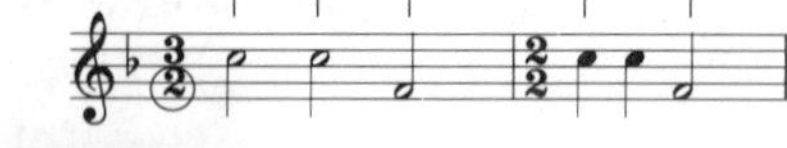

Exercise 8

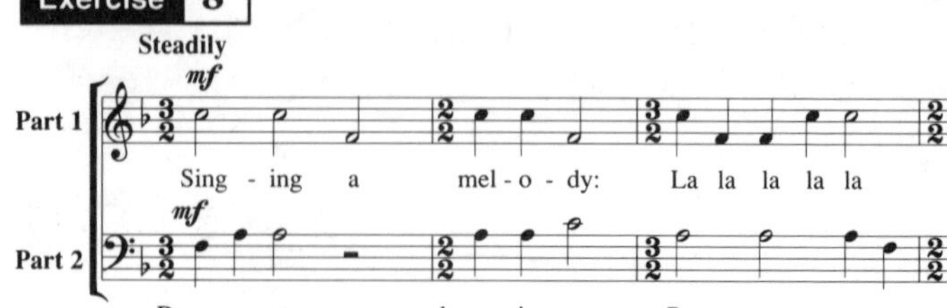

Extra pitches above and below the staff sit on ledger lines and continue with the alphabet:

V82S

REPEAT Exercise 8:

i) Switch parts.
ii) Two singers sing Parts 1 and 2 as a duet.
iii) All singers sing.

NOTE: The use of solos or duets encourages independence. Even the other singers listening to the solos start to be more aware of themselves as distinct individuals. They start to realize that the conductor listens to all the voices individually while the choir is singing as an ensemble.

As one singer sings solo, the others sing along silently (in their own hearts, they "know" they could do better than the soloist if they were only given a chance!). Everyone else has intense practice at silent solo singing while the real soloist continues singing aloud. Because they are not under stress and because they are dreaming they are doing their very best work as soloists, the silent singers may very well be getting better practice at sight-singing than the real soloist.

Include solo singers with mediocre voices who would not have other opportunities to do solos.

IN REHEARSAL

New Terms: duple time, ledger line

New Concepts: marking time signatures, eye movement, solos and duets for independence

TIPS:

i) Before starting a piece in duple time, ask the singers to notice that the half note gets one beat. If singers have difficulty remembering, have them draw half notes (instead of vertical lines) over the first two beats in each system:

ii) While you are rehearsing with one vocal part, ask the other singers to determine the names of any pitches on ledger lines in their music.

9

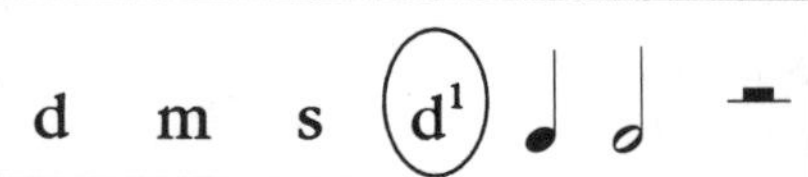

INTRODUCE

key signature with sharps (major keys)
octave "do"
marking the tonic in octaves
pitch framework

NOTE: At first the singers learn to determine new pitches as being higher or lower than one of the pitches of the framework. Later they will learn exactly how all the pitches should sound. However, the skill of using a pitch framework continues to be valuable as the singer works with more and more difficult music.

See pages 179 and 180 in the Teacher's Edition for an activity to memorize the interval of an octave.

PREVIEW TIP: Circle the bottom 2 in the time signature.

SING Exercise 9

NOTE: Each singer should be encouraged to work at their own ability level, sight-singing as much as they are able with each exercise. Some singers will read the pitches well, others the rhythms; others will read the dynamics, phrasing, rhythms and pitches. Within the group, each singer continues to progress at their own individual pace. Each singer should monitor their own progress.

REVIEW: Ask the singers to state the letter names for the first four pitches in the bass clef in Exercise 9 (D F♯ A D).

9

Key Signatures With Sharps

Find the sharp farthest to the right in the key signature:

"Do" is one note above this sharp.

Because the first sharp in the key signature is F sharp, every F in the music will be called an "F sharp."

octave

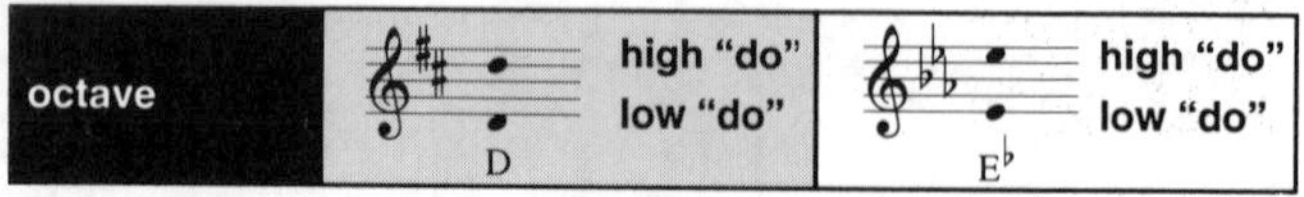

One note of the octave is always on a line and the other note is on a space. Both notes have the same letter name.

Mark the tonic in octaves in pencil at the beginning of each piece:

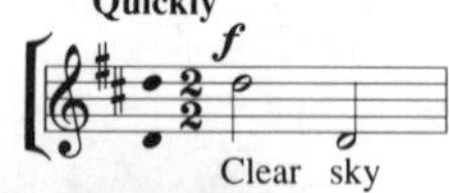

TIP Use the three most important pitches (do, so and high do) as the framework. Fit the other pitches within the framework.

Exercise 9

READ the TIP below the music in the Vocal Edition. Sing measures 3-5 several times to practice a quick page turn.

REPEAT Exercise 9:

i) Switch parts. Sing the first measure silently, second measure aloud, etc.
ii) Sing entire exercise aloud.

IN REHEARSAL — high do

New Term: octave "do"

New Concepts: key signature with sharps (major keys), marking the tonic in octaves, "do, so, high do" as the pitch framework, marking a page turn

TIPS:

i) Ask the singers to see if any parts begin or end a piece on pitches one octave apart.
ii) Encourage the singers to use "do, so, high do" as a framework for finding other pitches.

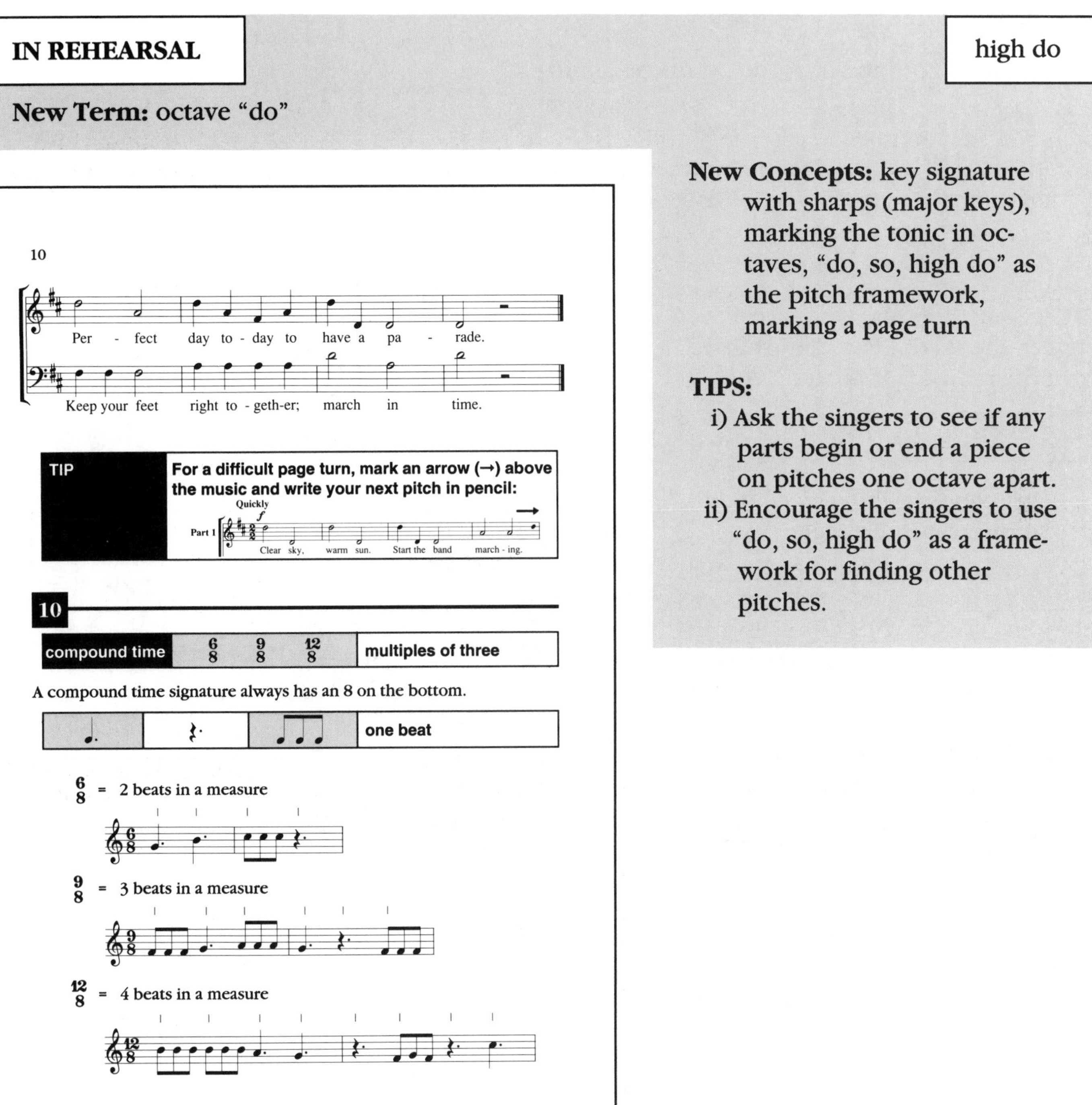

10

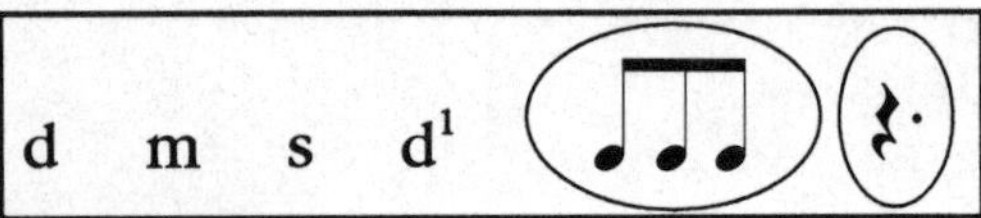

INTRODUCE

time signatures in compound time

♩. 𝄽. ♪♪♪ in compound time

key signature with no sharps or flats

REVIEW: Mark low and high "do" at the beginning:

NOTE: Sometimes the lyrics are placed between the staves. Part 2 must look above their music for the lyrics.

SING Exercise 10:

Let your eyes bounce continuously across the page.

REVIEW:

i) Ask the singers which measures are in octaves (measures 1, 2 and 6).

ii) Say the letter names in Exercise 10 in rhythm.

NOTE: The success rate for pitches and leaps is much higher when the singers have their heads in a proper position. **See page 12** in the Teacher's Edition for more information.

REPEAT Exercise 10:

Switch parts. Choose a singer to conduct.

10

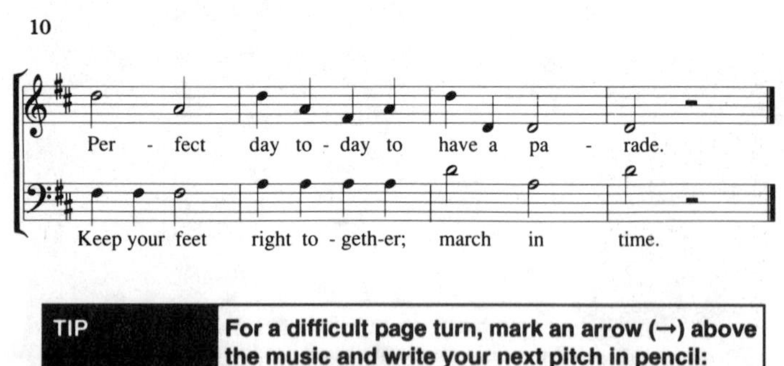

10

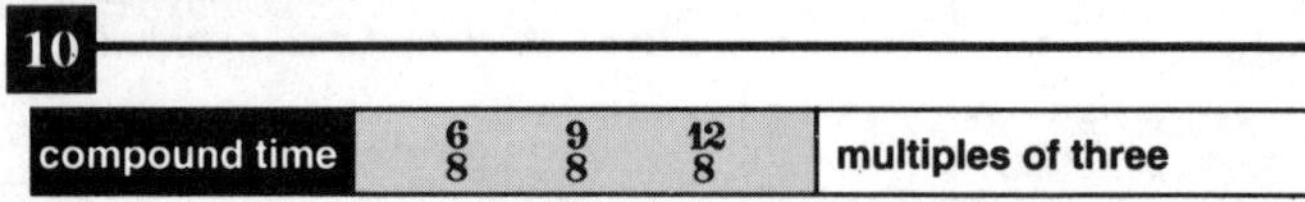

A compound time signature always has an 8 on the bottom.

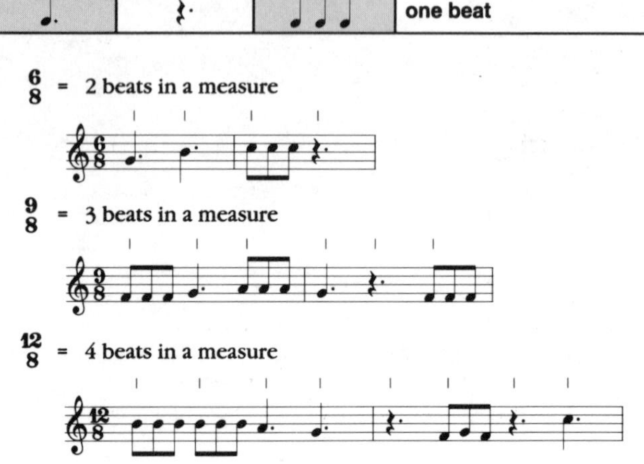

IN REHEARSAL

New Term: compound time

New Concepts: key signature with no sharps or flats, lyrics between the staves, proper head position

TIPS:

i) Before starting a piece in compound time, ask the singers to notice the number of beats in a measure and the dotted quarter note as the beat.

ii) Check proper head position.

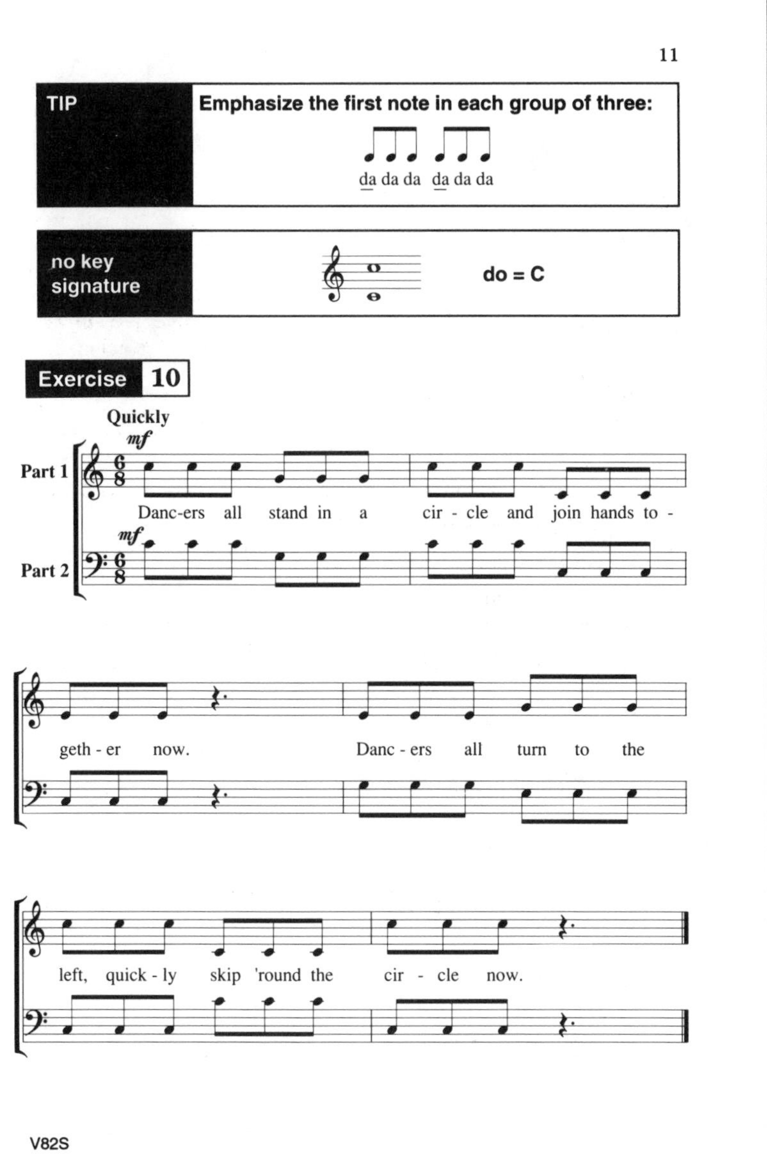

11

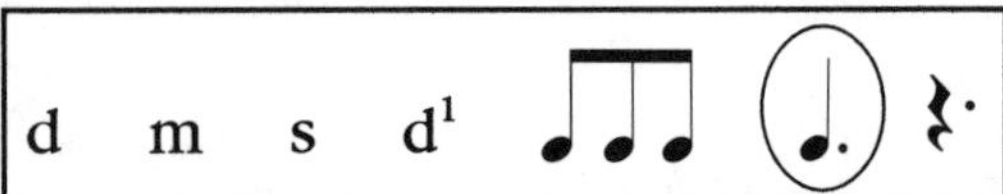

NOTE: Each group of three eighth notes may include more than one pitch.

INTRODUCE

tempo

PREVIEW TIPS:

i) Check the time signatures.
ii) Mark the tonic in Exercise 11:

iii) Be ready to whip your eyes down to the next line.

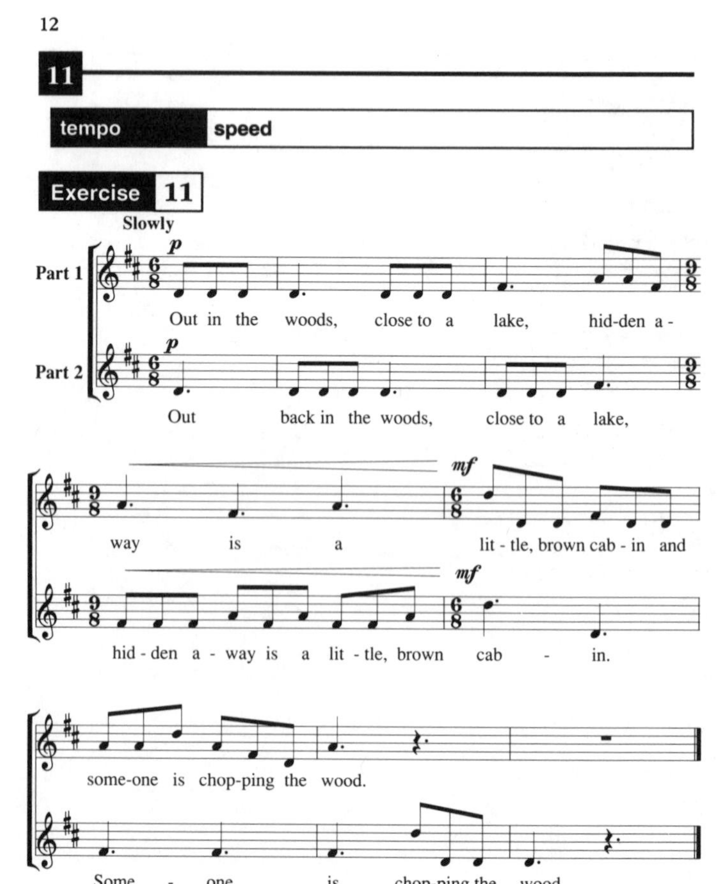

Use vertical lines above the music when:

i) The beat is not easy to see;
ii) The rhythms are difficult;
iii) Your eyes need help to keep moving continuously to the right.

The vertical lines act as a framework for the rhythms. Fit the rhythms within the framework.

V82S

SING Exercise 11:

First and third rows: Part 1.
Second and fourth rows: Part 2.

NOTE: When the parts are divided row by row rather than side to side, it changes the acoustics for the singers. Whenever you change the acoustics, it is more difficult for the singers to inadvertantly follow along with someone singing their own part; they know if they are trying to listen for someone else on their own part. Encourage them to sight-sing independently.

INTRODUCE

using vertical lines
rhythm framework

NOTE: Each singer should mark in vertical lines only when they need them. Some singers will need the vertical lines frequently at first but less often as their skills improve. These markings continue to be a valuable aid as the singers work with more and more difficult music.

See page 187 in the Teacher's Edition for activities with eye movement.

REPEAT Exercise 11:

i) At a different tempo. Emphasize the first eighth note in each grouping of three eighths.
ii) At a different tempo; switch parts. Sing the first measure silently, second measure aloud, etc.
iii) Sing entire exercise aloud.

IN REHEARSAL

♩.

New Terms: tempo, rhythm framework

New Concept: using vertical lines

TIPS:
i) In compound time, some singers may wish to mark the beat with a vertical line in the first few measures to help them remember that a dotted quarter note gets one beat.
ii) Encourage the singers to mark their scores carefully in pencil and use these markings later. Vertical lines may be used as a framework whenever needed.

12

INTRODUCE

same-pitch cue right before an entry
fourth
low "so"

EXPLAIN: The interval from low "so" to "do" sounds the same as the interval from "so" to high "do":

REMINDER: Sight-sing each exercise with the lyrics (not neutral syllables, time names, numbers or sol-fah syllables) the first time through.

SING Exercise 12:

Musically.

REMINDER: Encourage the singers to let their eyes bounce continuously across the page.

REPEAT Exercise 12:

i) Switch parts. Sing silently.
ii) Sing aloud.

IN REHEARSAL

low so

New Terms: low "so," fourth

New Concept: same-pitch cue

TIP: Whenever a singer misses an entry, they should mark the cue.

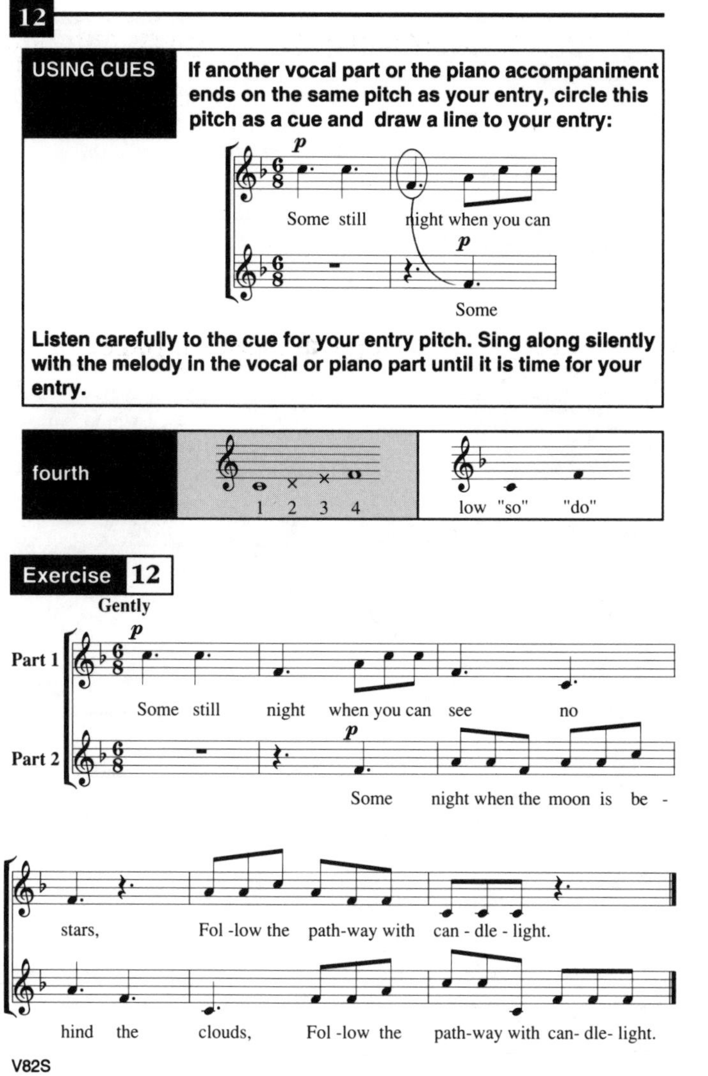

13

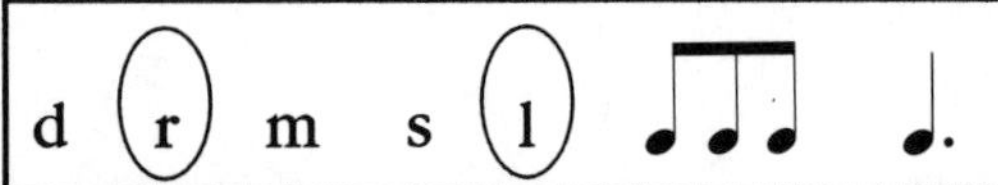

INTRODUCE

re
la
major second (whole tone)

SING the practice example above the music in the Vocal Edition.

See page 179 in the Teacher's Edition for an activity to memorize the interval of a major second.

PREVIEW TIP: Have the singers check the key signature in Exercise 13:

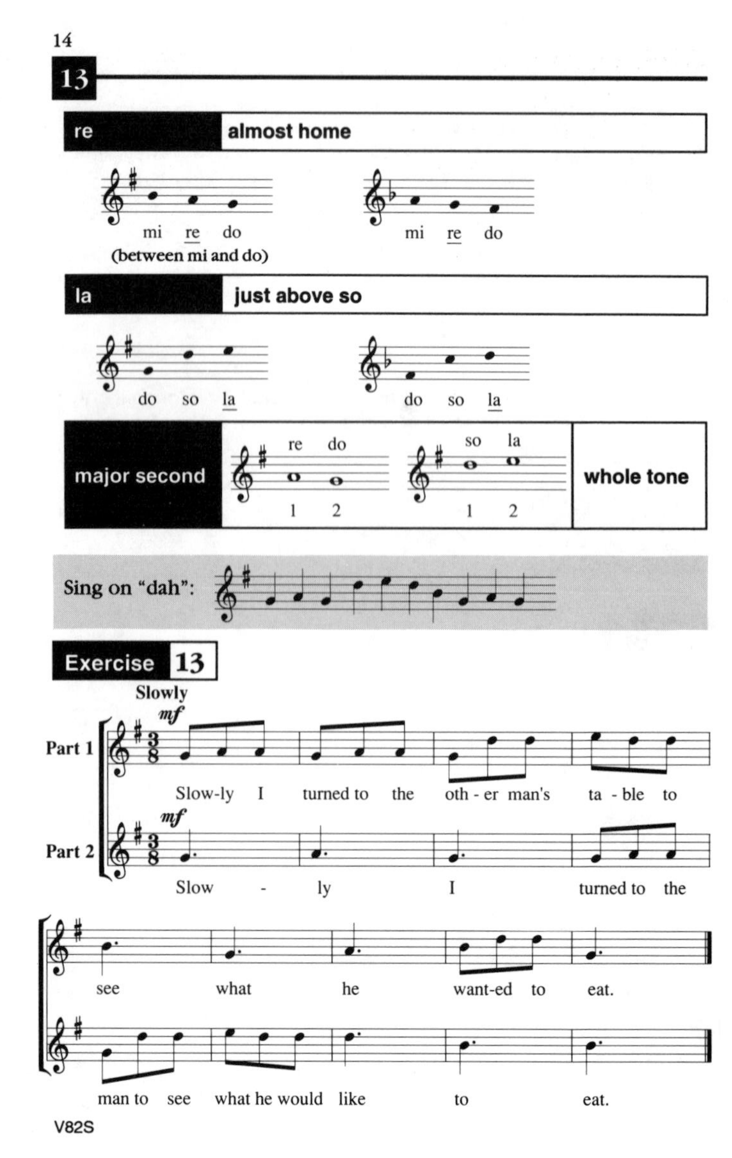

SING Exercise 13:

Singers in the middle of the choir: Part 1.
Singers at the sides: Part 2.

REVIEW: Pitch framework.

REPEAT Exercise 13:

i) Switch parts. Part 1 sings aloud while Part 2 sings silently.
ii) Both parts aloud. Encourage the singers to sing in tune.

IN REHEARSAL

re la

New Terms: major second, whole tone

TIPS: When you stop at the end of a phrase to work out problems, ask the singers to notice:

- any "re" which leads to a "do"
- any "la" which leads to a "so"

14

INTRODUCE

whole rest

TIP: Have the singers circle the time signature each time it changes:

or mark vertical lines above the beats:

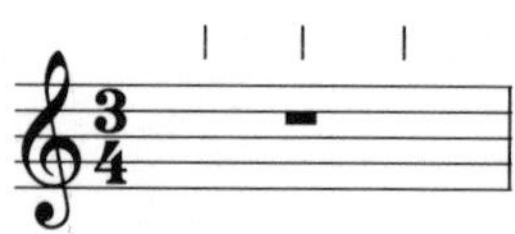

INTRODUCE

cues from memory

NOTE: Most singers are fine as long as they are singing continuously, but if they have a few measures or a page rest, they have great difficulty with the next entry. It takes them several measures before they start singing musically again. It is important for singers to feel confident with entries after rests.

PREVIEW TIPS:

i) Have the singers check the key signature in Exercise 14:

ii) Have the singers mark the cue for each entry after a rest in Exercise 14. For the entry in the fifth measure, singers may use the B♭ from either measure 2 or 4.

SING Exercise 14:

Silently.

REPEAT Exercise 14:

Aloud.

REVIEW: Have the singers give the letter names of the first four pitches in Part 2 of Exercise 14 (B♭ G B♭ C).

REPEAT Exercise 14:

i) Switch parts. Have a singer choose a tempo and conduct.
ii) Use a different tempo.

IN REHEARSAL

New Concepts: marking measures of rests, cues from memory

TIP: Different singers may find different cues for the same entry. Each singer should decide which cue is most helpful for them.

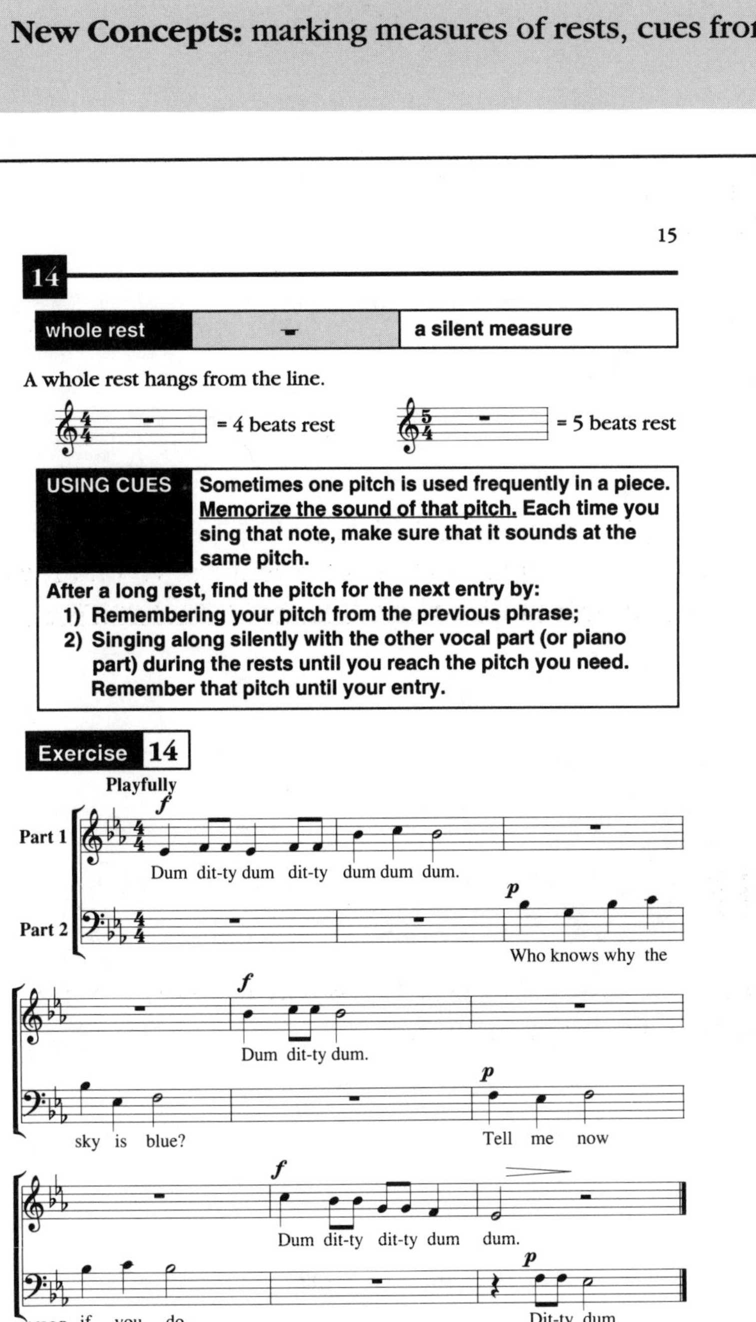

15

14

whole rest	𝄻	a silent measure

A whole rest hangs from the line.

4/4 𝄻 = 4 beats rest   5/4 𝄻 = 5 beats rest

USING CUES Sometimes one pitch is used frequently in a piece. Memorize the sound of that pitch. Each time you sing that note, make sure that it sounds at the same pitch.

After a long rest, find the pitch for the next entry by:
1) Remembering your pitch from the previous phrase;
2) Singing along silently with the other vocal part (or piano part) during the rests until you reach the pitch you need. Remember that pitch until your entry.

Exercise 14

V82S

15

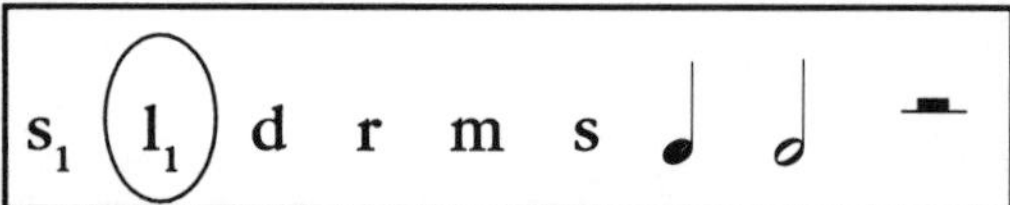

REVIEW: Circle the bottom 2 in the time signature.

PREVIEW TIP: Find a cue for Part 1 and mark it:

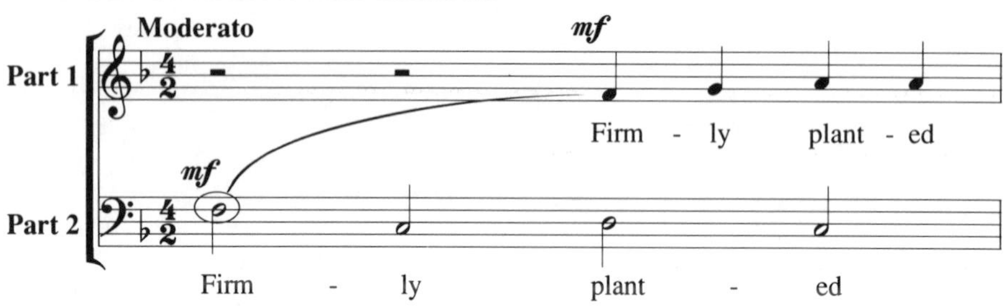

See page 180 in the Teacher's Edition for an activity for hearing a cue at the octave.

NOTE: Because this exercise has many seconds and fifths, it is excellent practice for a typical bass line found in traditional repertoire. The basses should have an opportunity to sight-sing both parts.

SING Exercise 15:

First and third rows: Part 1.
Second and fourth rows: Part 2.

REVIEW: Have the singers say the letter names in Part 2 in rhythm.

REMINDER: Check for balanced posture and head in proper position.

REPEAT Exercise 15:

Switch parts. Sing precisely together.

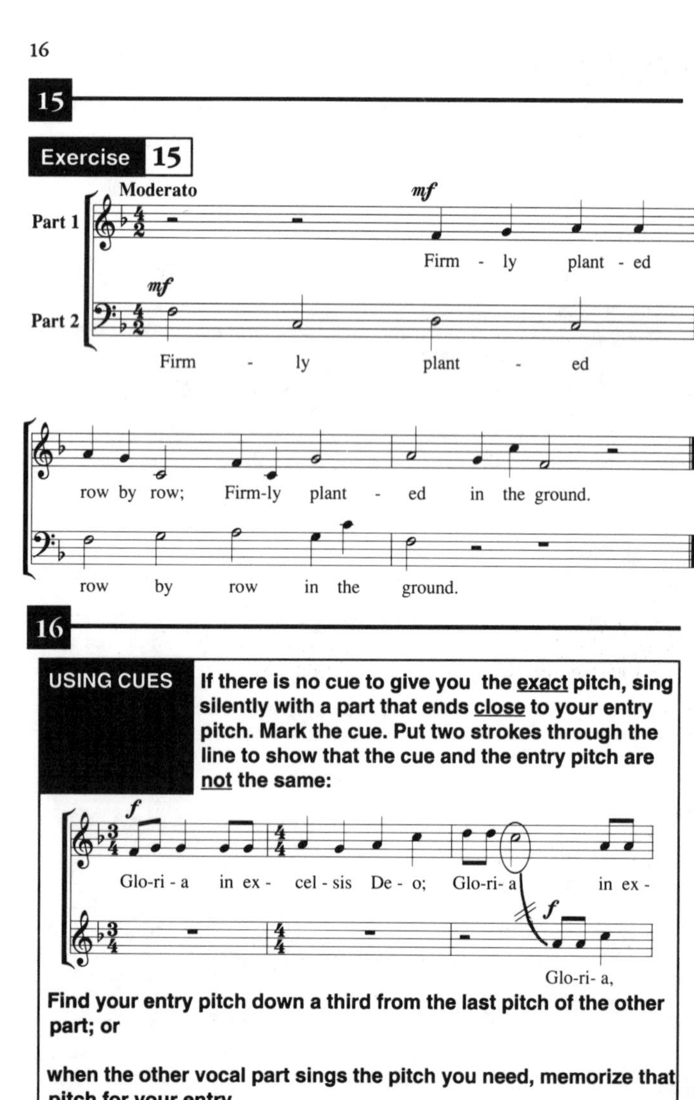

16

15

Exercise 15

16

USING CUES

If there is no cue to give you the exact pitch, sing silently with a part that ends close to your entry pitch. Mark the cue. Put two strokes through the line to show that the cue and the entry pitch are not the same:

Find your entry pitch down a third from the last pitch of the other part; or

when the other vocal part sings the pitch you need, memorize that pitch for your entry.

V82S

IN REHEARSAL

low la

New Concept: cue at the octave

TIP: When the music has a traditional bass line, have the basses notice the presence of seconds and fifths. If the alto or tenor is the lowest voice in the music, sometimes it will have a line which will sound very much like a traditional bass line.

16

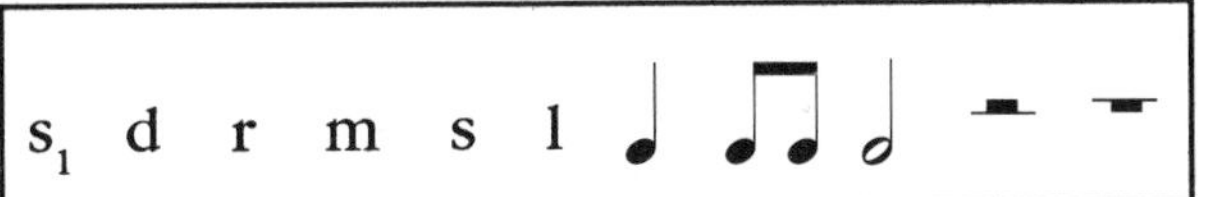

17

Exercise 16

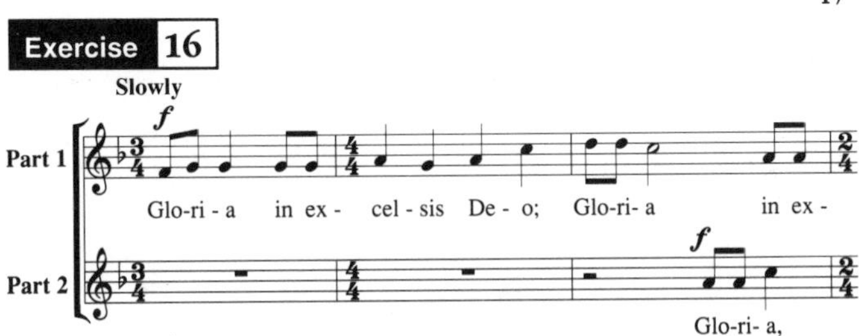

17

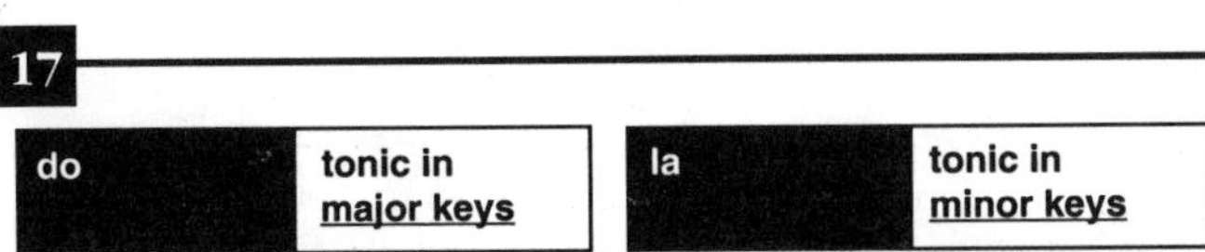

If one of the vocal parts or the accompaniment ends the piece on "la," then the tonic will be on "la." The music will sound minor or modal.

Mark low and high "la" at the beginning of the music:

But the other pitches will not sound the same.

V82S

REVIEW: Whole rest.

INTRODUCE

cue at a pitch different from the entry

SING Exercise 16:

Singers seated in the middle: Part 2.
Singers at the sides: Part 1. (Encourage Part 2 to find the entry down a third from Part 1.)

NOTE: If singers have difficulty with the A in the fifth measure of Part 1, have them remember that pitch from the third measure.

NOTE: Lesson 16 is continued on page 46.

REPEAT Exercise 16:

i) Encourage Part 2 to find their entry by memorizing the A in Part 1. Then each singer can decide which strategy works best for them.
ii) Switch parts. Encourage Part 2 to try the first strategy for their cue.
iii) Sing Part 1 aloud while Part 2 sings silently. Encourage Part 2 to try the second strategy for their cue. Then each singer can decide which strategy works best for them.
iv) Both parts aloud.

IN REHEARSAL

New Concept: cue at a pitch different from the entry

TIP: If the music is difficult to sight-sing, only sight-sing part of it. Teach part of it by rote or sight-sing more of it at a later rehearsal. Stop sight-singing while the singers are still feeling successful (before the singers become discouraged).

17

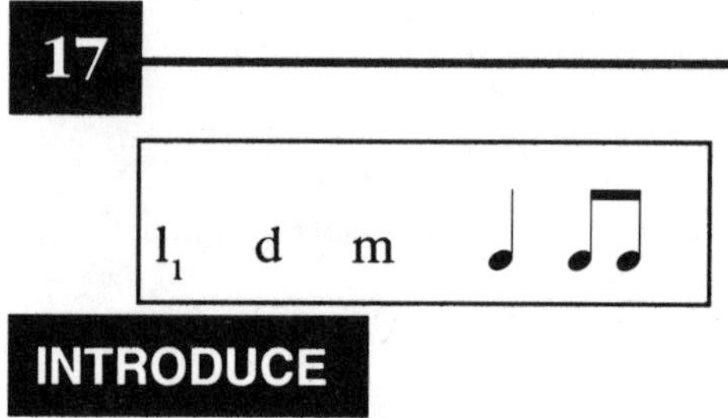

INTRODUCE

minor keys

EXPLAIN: If the music is in sections, check the end of each section for "la."

INTRODUCE

minor triad

NOTE: It is important for the singers to have a strong experience sight-singing in major keys first so that they will have the "sound" of major strong in their minds. Then it is easier to make the switch into the "sound" of minor keys.

17

If one of the vocal parts or the accompaniment ends the piece on "la," then the tonic will be on "la." The music will sound minor or modal.

Mark low and high "la" at the beginning of the music:

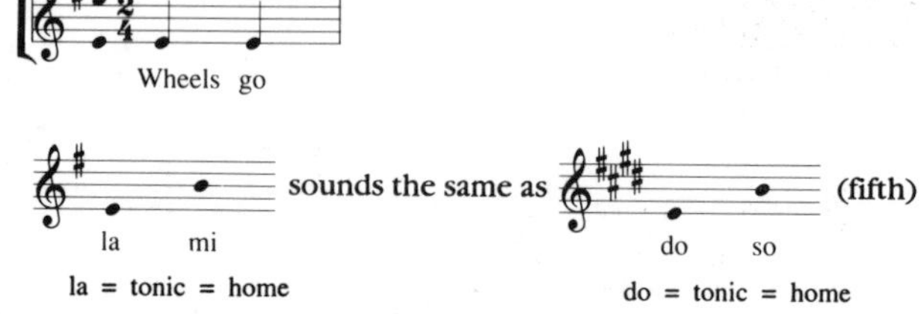

But the other pitches will not sound the same.

V82S

SING Exercise 17:

Standing. Sing musically.

TIP: Start encouraging the singers to keep their eyes moving continuously slightly ahead of the beat.

REPEAT Exercise 17:

i) Switch parts. Sing measures 1 and 2 aloud, 3 and 4 silently, etc.
ii) All measures aloud.

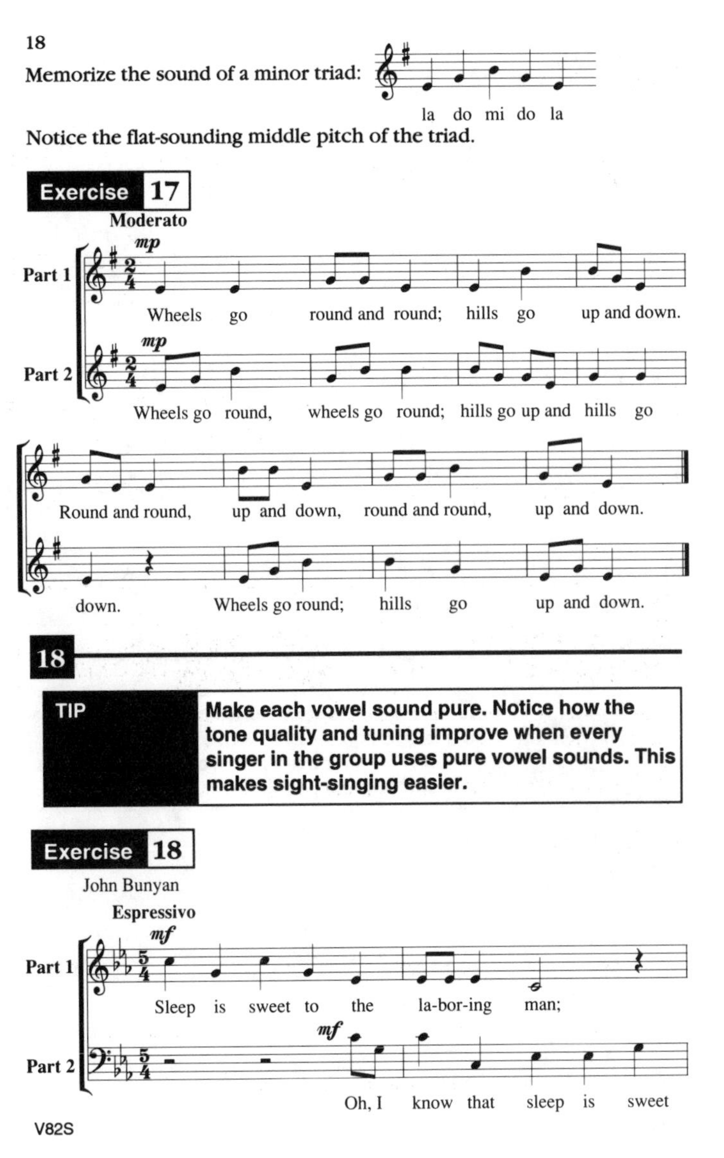

18

Memorize the sound of a minor triad:

Notice the flat-sounding middle pitch of the triad.

Exercise 17

Moderato

18

TIP Make each vowel sound pure. Notice how the tone quality and tuning improve when every singer in the group uses pure vowel sounds. This makes sight-singing easier.

Exercise 18

John Bunyan

Espressivo

V82S

IN REHEARSAL

New Terms: minor key, minor triad

New Concepts: finding tonic in minor keys, moving the eyes slightly ahead of the beat

TIP: Before beginning each piece in a minor key, have the singers mark the tonic and sing the minor triad, "la_1 do mi do la_1."

18

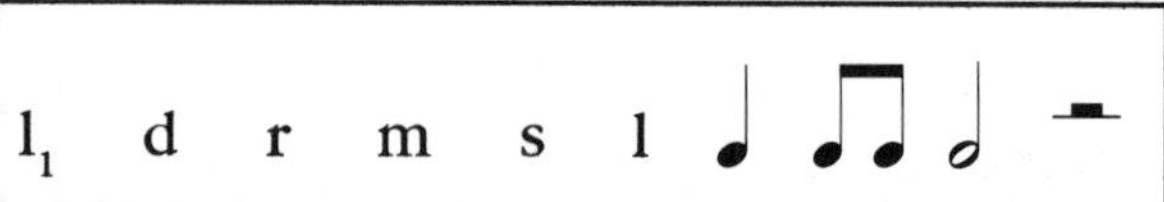

READ the TIP above the music in the Vocal Edition.

NOTE: When singers are instructed to make each vowel sound pure, they tend to unconsciously model their sound after the best natural (or trained) voices in the group. Even when the teacher is unable to demonstrate a good vowel sound, the singers will be able to improve the purity of their vowel sounds.

A teacher whose own voice is not "model" should not demonstrate a pure vowel sound. Use descriptive words or images instead.

When the vowel sounds are more uniform, the tuning improves and it is easier for the singers to tell quickly whether they are singing the right pitches.

PREVIEW TIPS:

i) Mark the tonic at the beginning of Exercise 18:

ii) Sing "la$_1$ do mi do la$_1$."

SING Exercise 18:

First and third rows: Part 2.
Second and fourth rows: Part 1.

TIPS:

<u>At the beginning of the music:</u>

Breathe in rhythm with the conductor's upbeat:

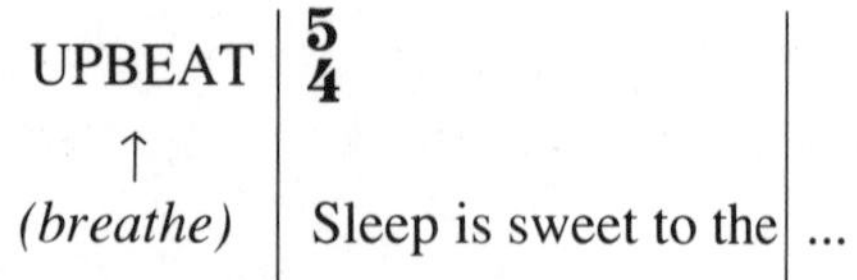

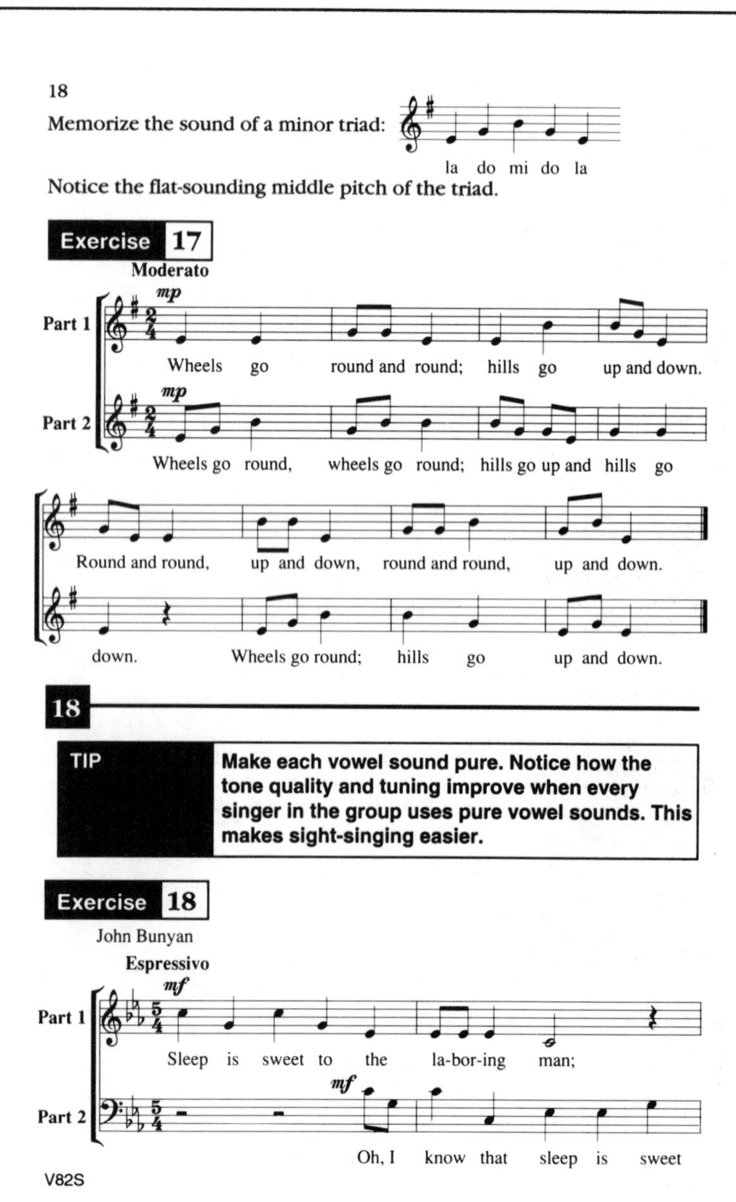

<u>After rests:</u>

Breathe in rhythm a few beats before the entry:

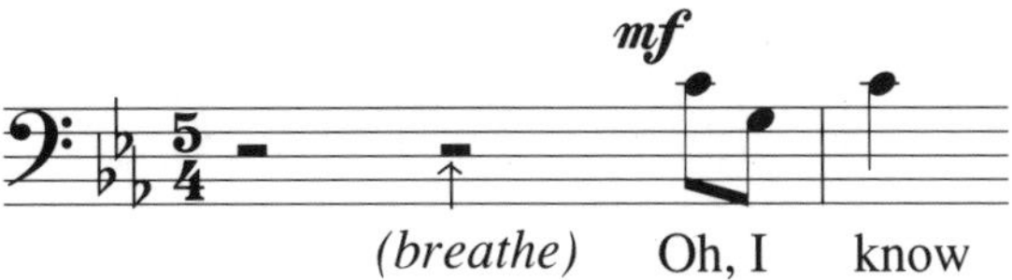

<u>Between phrases:</u>

Breathe quickly in rhythm with the music:

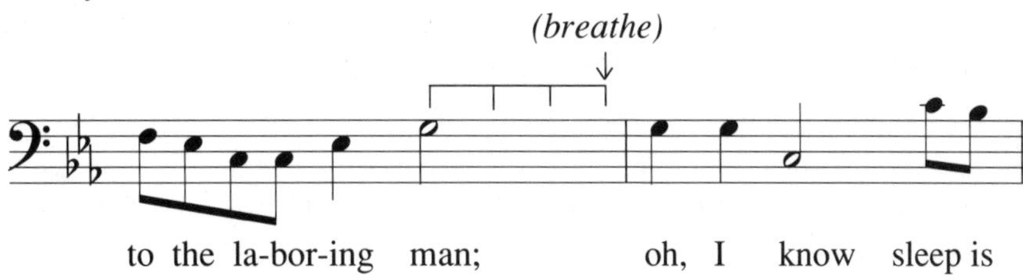

19

dotted half note	𝅗𝅥.	3 beats in simple time
dotted half rest	𝄼.	

A dot after a note makes the note 1 1/2 times as long as it would be without the dot.

Exercise 19

V82S

In some music the singers should take a full beat breath between phrases.

The singers should breathe through the mouth quietly; the first sound the audience should hear is the music. Noisy breathers are not listening.

<u>Good breathing habits steady the singer for sight-singing the correct pitches with a steady beat.</u>

REPEAT Exercise 18:

i) Switch parts. Part 1 sing silently, Part 2 aloud.

ii) Both parts aloud. Part 2 should be ready to move the eyes up quickly to the top of the next page.

NOTE: It is possible to skip ahead in the lessons to teach a rhythm, pitch or concept which is used frequently in the singers' current repertoire. Then go back to cover the missing lessons.

IN REHEARSAL

New Concepts: pure vowel sounds, good breathing habits

TIPS:

i) Ask the singers to concentrate on pure vowel sounds when working on pieces with:
   1) A slow tempo; or
   2) Long held notes.

The singers have more time to produce pure vowels in these types of music. The voice gets a better workout with sustained vowels and the singers will start to form a habit of using pure vowels all the time. This habit will gradually transfer to music with a faster tempo or short notes.

ii) During an introduction or interlude, show by your conducting when you want the singers to start breathing early (i.e. raise your left hand slowly with the palm up as they breathe in).

19

INTRODUCE

dotted half note in simple time
dotted half rest in simple time

REVIEW: i) Mark the tonic at the beginning of Exercise 19:

ii) Breathing.

SING Exercise 19:

Singers with birthdays from January to June: Part 1.
Rest of singers: Part 2.

REPEAT Exercise 19:

i) After the singers have had a moment to silently correct any problems.
ii) Switch parts.

IN REHEARSAL

TIP: Encourage the singers to determine the duration of any new kinds of dotted notes by themselves.

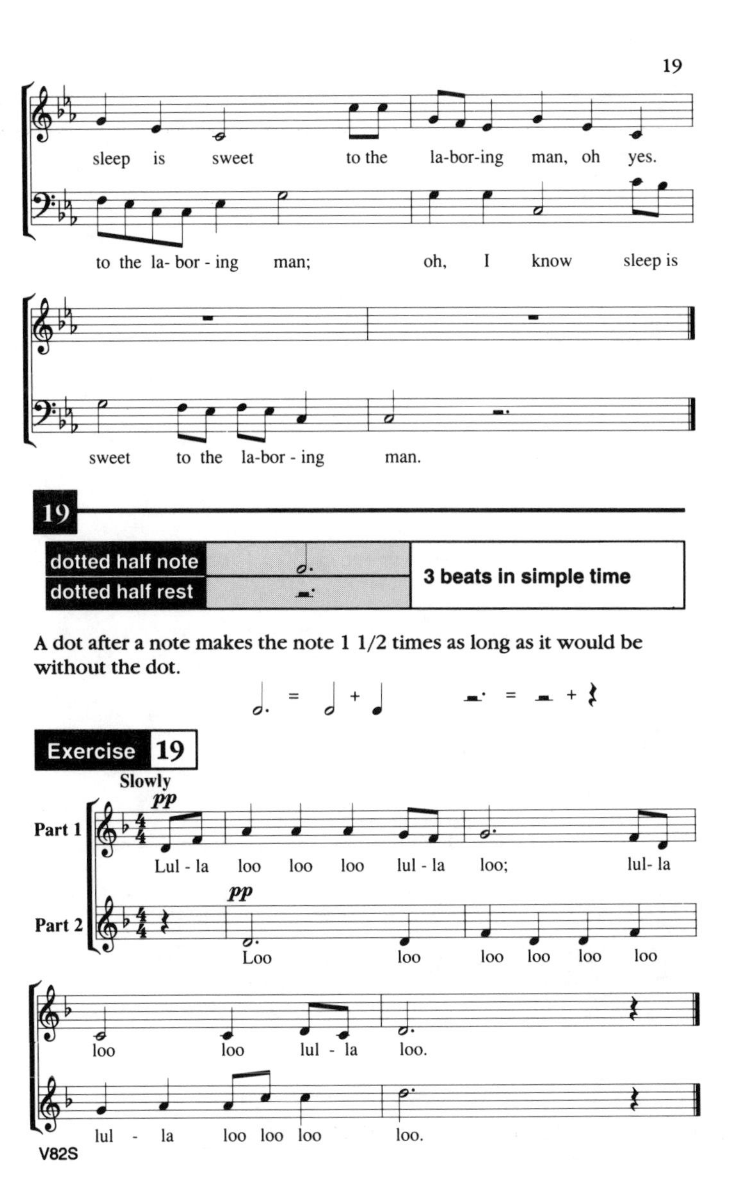

20

TIP: Check for imitation in the music:

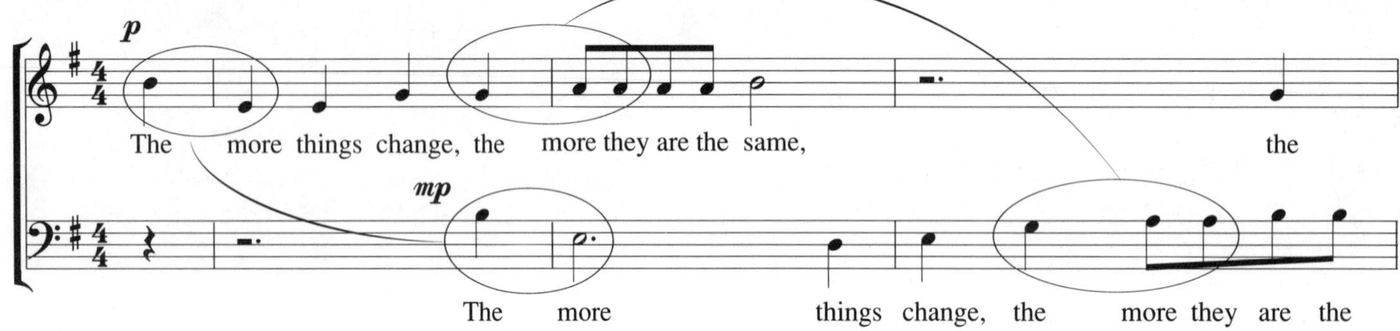

NOTE: As singers start to see that patterns of imitation are commonly found in music, it will be easier for them to sight-sing new music.

REVIEW: Ask the singers to mark the tonic at the beginning of Exercise 20:

SING Exercise 20:

Singers in the back: Part 1.
Singers in the front: Part 2.

INTRODUCE

REPEAT Exercise 20:

One singer as a solo: Part 1.
Rest of the singers: Part 2 (quietly).

IN REHEARSAL

New Concept: imitation

TIP: Whenever there is imitation in the music, notice whether the imitation is exact. In each case, determine whether the imitation should be performed as much like the original as possible or whether there should be some change (i.e. dynamics).

21

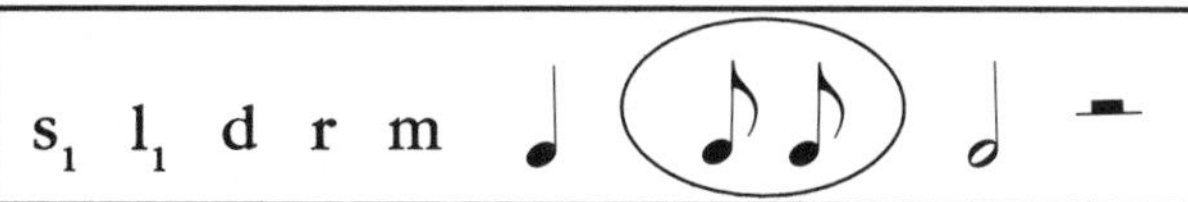

INTRODUCE

REVIEW: Ask the singers to check Exercise 21 for imitation:

SING Exercise 21:

First and third rows: Part 2.
Second and fourth rows: Part 1.

TIP: If Part 2 singers have difficulty with the A in the last measure, it may help to think of the A as being one pitch below the B they sang in the previous measure.

REVIEW: Encourage the singers to let their eyes bounce with the vertical lines across the page.

REPEAT Exercise 21:

Switch parts and face the back of the room.

IN REHEARSAL

New Concept: marking vertical lines for notes flagged separately

TIP: Some publishers print the eighth notes separately. Encourage the singers to mark vertical lines where needed in any music published in this way.

22

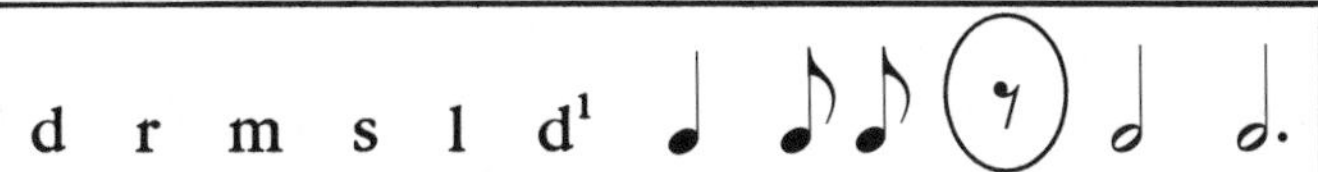

NOTE: Exercises in three parts may be sung:
i) Each part separately;
ii) Parts 1 and 2 together;
iii) Parts 1 and 3 together;
iv) All three parts together.

SING Exercise 22:

Sopranos: Part 1.
Altos: Part 2.
Baritones: Part 3.

REPEAT Exercise 22:

In the last measure, let the second word bounce in after the second beat.

REPEAT Exercise 22:

i) Three singers sing Parts 1, 2 and 3 as a trio.
ii) Singers on the right: Part 1.
Singers in the middle: Part 2.
Singers on the left: Part 3.

IN REHEARSAL

7

TIP: Regularly change the seating position of each singer within a vocal section (i.e. each alto). If they are sitting beside the same people all the time, they may become dependent in some way upon that particular situation.

◆ ◆ ENRICHMENT ◆ ◆

23

EXPLAIN: Part 1 sings the notes with stems up; Part 2 sings the notes with stems down.

INTRODUCE

modulation (D major to D minor to D major)

REVIEW: Major and minor triads.

Ask the singers to sing each triad several times to refresh their memories. Remind the singers to sing each note right in the middle of each pitch so that the sounds of major and minor will be clearly defined.

SING Exercise 23:

Musically.

INTRODUCE

rit., ritard., ritardando
a tempo

REPEAT Exercise 23:

i) With the ***rit.*** and ***a tempo*** as marked.
ii) Have a singer choose a different tempo and conduct with a ***ritard.*** somewhere else during the exercise.
iii) Switch parts. Use a different conductor.

IN REHEARSAL

New Terms: modulation, ***rit.***, ***a tempo***

New Concepts: two parts on a single staff, modulation (major to minor with same tonic)

TIPS:
i) Before beginning each new piece, have the singers mark the tonic for each key signature change.
ii) During warmups, use gradual tempo changes (i.e. conduct a ***ritard.*** or ***accel.***).

During whole notes, keep the eyes moving steadily to the right and feel the continuous beat. If necessary, mark the beats above the music:

Space the vertical lines to co-ordinate with the other vocal part.

V82S

24

INTRODUCE

whole note
co-ordinating the vocal parts

EXPLAIN: The beat is aligned vertically on the page:

You can quickly move your eyes up or down to another part to see what they are doing at the same time.

PREVIEW TIP: Check the modulations (F minor to F major to F minor).

REMINDER: Sight-sing each exercise with the lyrics (not neutral syllables, time names or sol-fah syllables) the first time through.

SING Exercise 24:

Standing.

INTRODUCE

dynamics

REPEAT Exercise 24:

i) Switch parts. Face one side of the room. Use the dynamics as indicated.
ii) Face the back of the room.

24

Exercise 24

dynamics	volume	
f	*forte*	loud
p	*piano*	soft
mp	*mezzo piano*	medium soft
(crescendo sign)	*crescendo*	gradually louder

V82S

IN REHEARSAL

low mi

New Concept: coordination of vocal parts

TIP: Each singer should take responsibility for singing the dynamics as marked. They should listen carefully to maintain a balance of dynamics with the rest of the choir.

25

INTRODUCE

slur

Ask the singers:

i) *In Part 1 measure 2, how many notes are there for the word "blue"? (4)*

ii) *In Part 2 measure 3, how many notes are there for the word "breeze"? (2)*

REMINDER: Check posture.

SING Exercise 25

REPEAT Exercise 25:

i) Sing the first measure aloud, second measure silently, etc.;

ii) Sing entire exercise aloud. Encourage each singer to monitor their own progress.

25

Continue to sing the same syllable for all the pitches within the curved line.

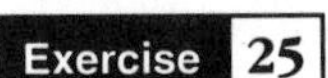

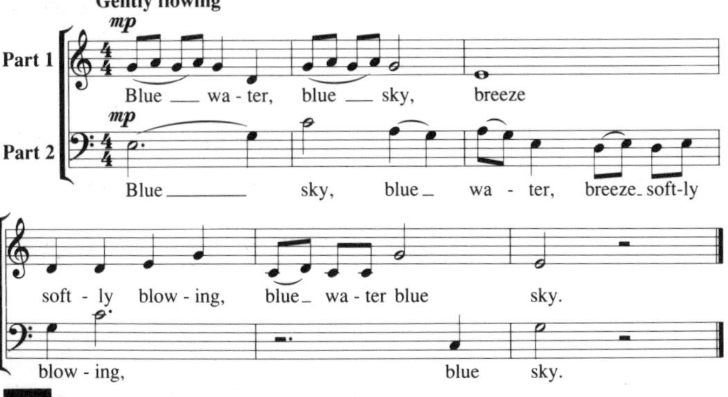

26

TIP While singing long notes, follow along with the beat in another vocal part or the piano accompaniment. Be ready to move your eyes quickly back to your own part for your next note.

Exercise 26

IN REHEARSAL

New Term: slur

TIP: Whenever the slurs are used in an unusual way, give the singers a few moments to determine how the words fit with the notes. Then have them sing that measure alone to make sure that it is correct.

26

READ the TIP above the music in the Vocal Edition.

SING Exercise 26

REVIEW: Mark the page turn with an arrow and the next pitch. SING measures 3-4 several times to practice a quick page turn.

REPEAT Exercise 26:

i) Singers with birthdays from January to June: Part 2. Rest of singers: Part 1.
ii) Add more details (i.e. dynamics, phrasing, etc.).

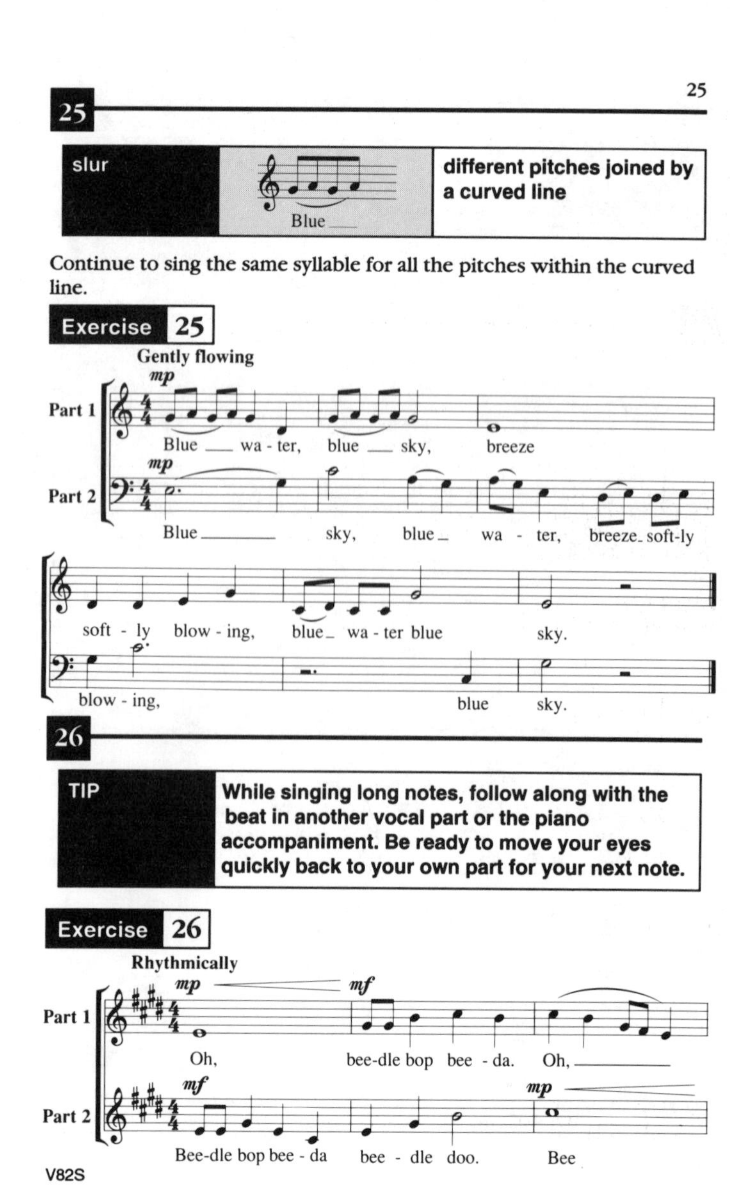
25

25

slur	Blue ___	different pitches joined by a curved line

Continue to sing the same syllable for all the pitches within the curved line.

Exercise 25

Gently flowing

26

TIP	While singing long notes, follow along with the beat in another vocal part or the piano accompaniment. Be ready to move your eyes quickly back to your own part for your next note.

Exercise 26

Rhythmically

V82S

IN REHEARSAL

New Concept: watching other parts while singing long notes

TIP: Encourage the singers to let their eyes quickly scan the other parts while they sing their own part.

27

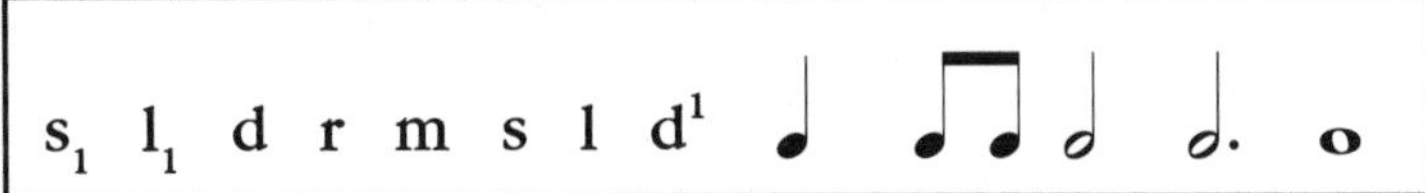

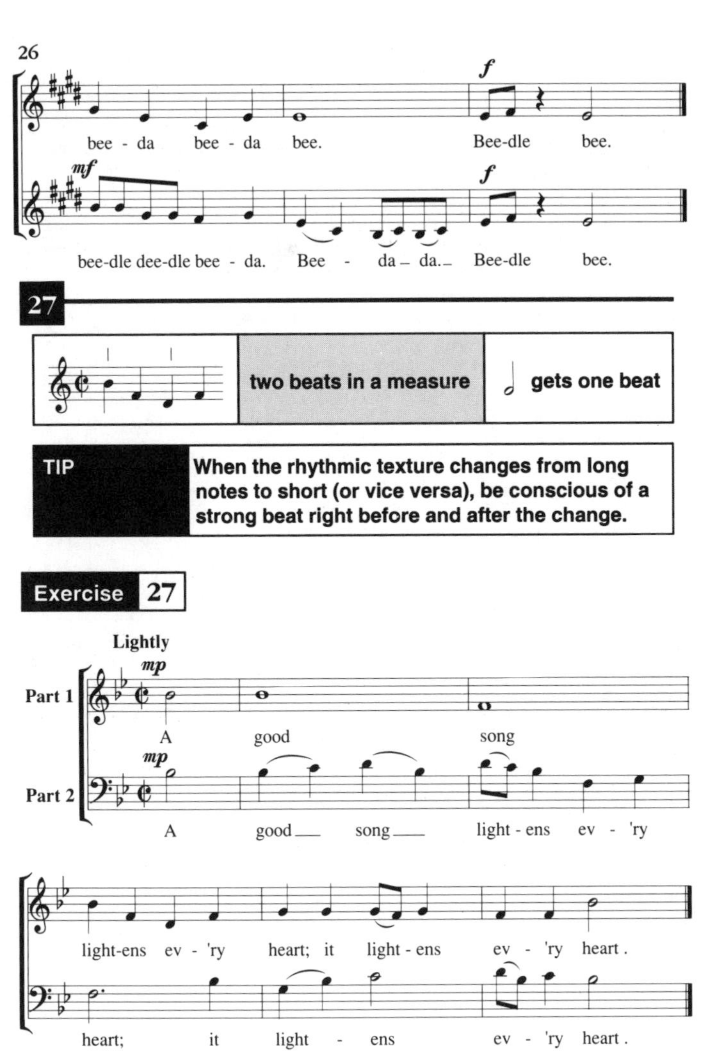

INTRODUCE

cut time (𝄵)

READ the TIP above the music in the Vocal Edition.

SING Exercise 27:

Standing.

REPEAT Exercise 27:

i) Facing the back of the room.
ii) Switch parts.

Have the singers read the **REMINDER** below the music in the Vocal Edition.

IN REHEARSAL

¢

New Term: cut time

New Concept: change of rhythmic texture

TIP: When the singers become more competent at sight-singing, give only the tonic pitch before you begin a new piece.

28

USING CUES When you cannot sing along silently with another part to get your cue:

i) Mark the beat with vertical lines;
ii) Follow the beat with your eyes and ignore the sounds of the pitches until you reach the cue. Start a long, slow breath a few beats before your entry;
iii) Quickly focus your ear on the pitch of the cue and remember that pitch until your entry.

Exercise 28

Adagio

Part 1

Part 2

Part 3

Adagio

pp

Key - board

28

INTRODUCE

cues in non-melodic music

The music always begins with the first sound, whether it is the sound of the piano or the singers. The singing should naturally continue on from the introduction. Encourage the singers to think of music as a total art form.

SING Exercise 28

28
p
Morn-ing comes.
Ros - y dawn
p
Morn-ing, morn-ing
p
Morn-ing comes
p
beck-ons us.
Morn-ing comes.
comes,
beck-ons us.
Morn-ing comes.
so ear-ly.
Morn-ing comes.
V82S

REVIEW: i) Quickly scan the eyes over the full score as you sing.
ii) Check for imitation:

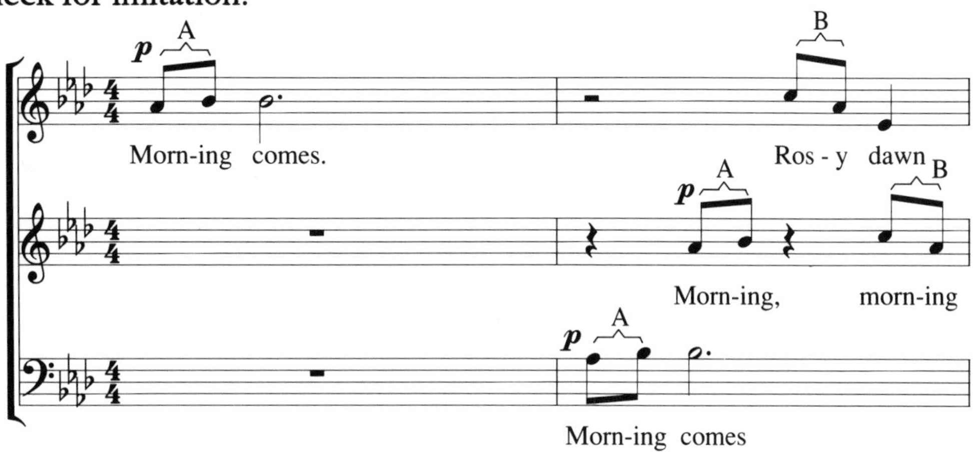

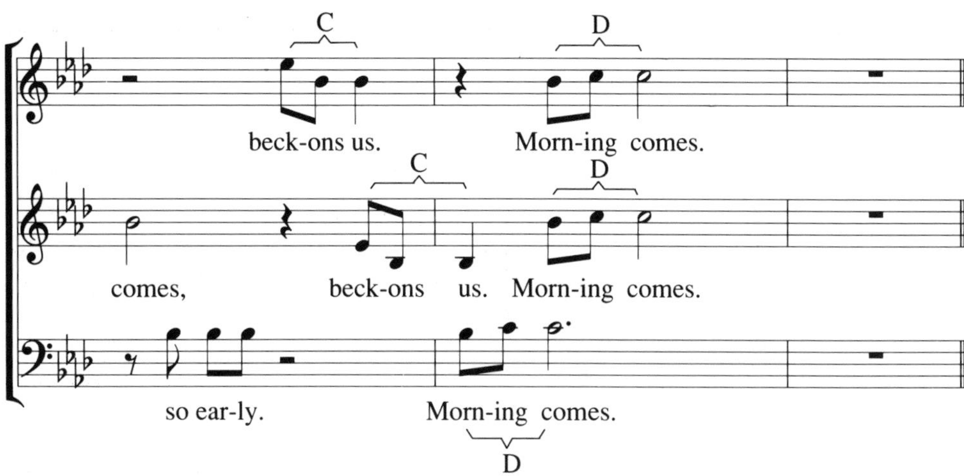

REPEAT Exercise 28:

i) Silently (with piano accompaniment).
ii) Aloud.
iii) Switch parts.
iv) Switch parts again.

IN REHEARSAL

low re

New Concept: cues in non-melodic music

TIP: During each rehearsal, give the singers an opportunity to move about physically, even if it is just to sing while standing for a few minutes. A physical break will help their concentration:

> *"Stretch your right arm, left arm; stretch one leg, then the other; stretch your face (i.e. make grotesque faces to stretch the face muscles)."*

29

INTRODUCE

pick-up

EXPLAIN: A pick-up may have more than one note.

The first measure has only one beat. The note in Part 1 is a pick-up; it leads into the first full measure. The word(s) on the pick-up is not as important as the word on the first beat of the bar. The pick-up should be sung lightly.

REVIEW: Check the score for imitation:

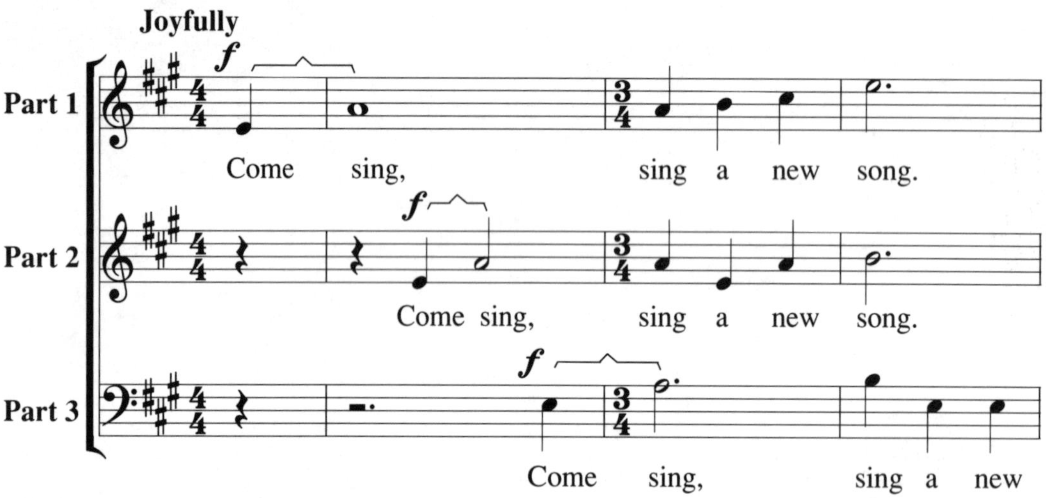

SING Exercise 29

READ the TIP under the music in the Vocal Edition. It is easier to sight-sing if all the singers sing the words precisely. They can concentrate on the music without a clutter of sound to distract them.

REPEAT Exercise 29:

i) One singer as a solo: Part 1.
Rest of the singers: Parts 2 and 3 (quietly).
ii) One singer as a solo: Part 3.
Rest of the singers: Parts 1 and 2 (quietly).

IN REHEARSAL

New Term: pick-up

New Concept: vowel on the beat

TIP: Whenever the singers have difficulty with the music, give them a few moments to determine the problem and choose a suitable strategy.

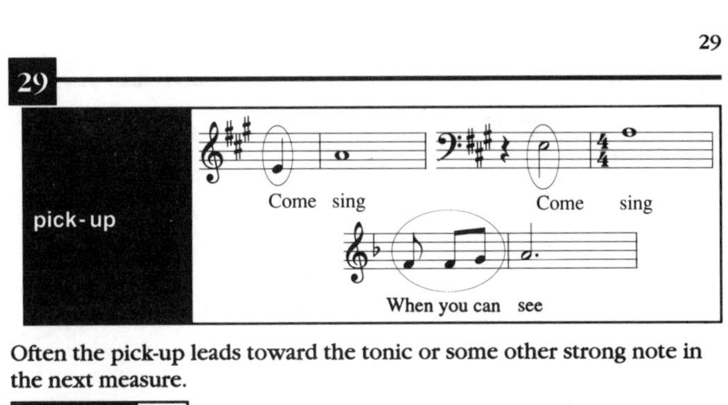

30

INTRODUCE

SPEAK the practice example in the singer's edition to "dah."

REPEAT making each pulse audible:

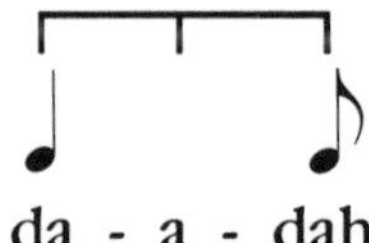

REPEAT with an inaudible pulse. Remind them to continue to feel the pulse even when they are not emphasizing it.

PREVIEW TIP: Check for imitation:

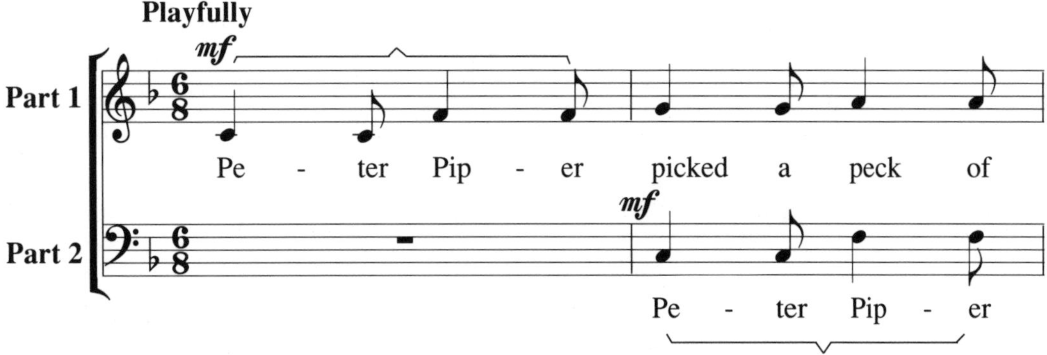

SING Exercise 30:

Singers seated in the middle: Part 1.
Singers on the sides: Part 2.

READ the TIP under the music in the Vocal Edition.

REPEAT Exercise 30:

i) Using the vertical lines.
ii) Switch parts.

IN REHEARSAL

New Term: pulse

TIP: Check the lighting in your rehearsal area as the seasons change. Good lighting is essential for good sight-singing.

31

NOTE: i) Each ♩ ♪ may include more than one pitch.
ii) "Sean" is pronounced: "Shahn."

INTRODUCE

The pick-up at the beginning of Exercise 31 comes on an off-beat. The conductor must give either:

i) A very definite single beat (♩) in preparation;
or
ii) Two beats (♩. ♩) in preparation.

TIP: Have the singers memorize the high D in Part 1 and the B♭ in Part 2 as frequent pitches.

SING Exercise 31:

Silently.

REPEAT Exercise 31:

i) Aloud.
ii) Switch parts. Add more details (i.e. dynamics, phrasing, etc.).

If the singers have difficulty singing an accurate eighth note pick-up, the conductor may speak the pulse during the preparatory beats:

| Da da da Da da "Twas | in the early

REPEAT without speaking the pulses.

IN REHEARSAL

New Concept: pick-up on an off-beat

TIP: For warmups in parts, occasionally divide the singers by alternate rows.

32

REVIEW: 𝅗𝅥. in simple time.

INTRODUCE

𝅗𝅥. in compound time

SING Exercise 32:

Singers with birthdays in a month beginning with "J" or "O": Part 3.
Singers with birthdays in a month beginning with "M" or "A": Part 2.
Rest of singers: Part 1.

If the singers lose the feeling of the beat during the longer notes, ask them to mark the beat with vertical lines.

REPEAT Exercise 32:

i) Make each vowel sound as pure as possible.
ii) Switch parts.
iii) Switch parts again.

IN REHEARSAL | high re

New Concept: dotted half note in compound time

TIP: If the singers become lost during longer notes in compound time, ask them to mark the beat with vertical lines.

33

Exercise 34

Abraham Lincoln

Slowly

mf

Part 1 No man is good e - nough

Part 2 No man is good e - nough

Part 3 No man is good e - nough

INTRODUCE

REVIEW: Major and minor triads.

PREVIEW TIP: Check the modulation (C minor to C major).

SING Exercise 33

REPEAT Exercise 33:

i) Have the singers imagine the sound of a C major triad in measure 5.
ii) Switch parts. Parts 1 and 3 sing aloud with Part 2 singing silently.
iii) All parts sing aloud.
iv) Switch parts.

IN REHEARSAL

TIP: After the warmup, rehearse a familiar piece or two. Then sight-sing new music while the singers are warmed up but still fresh. If the entire rehearsal consists of new repertoire, start with an easy piece or one in a style to which the singers are accustomed.

34

REMINDER: i) Mark the page turn.
ii) Check posture.

SING Exercise 34:

Make each vowel sound pure.

REMINDERS:

i) Watch the conductor's downbeat carefully as it corresponds with each barline. Be conscious of a strong beat right before and after the rhythmic texture changes.

ii) Sing the last note for two whole beats. The "nt" should come on the cut-off right on the beginning of the third beat:

REPEAT Exercise 34:

i) Switch parts. Parts 1 and 2 sing aloud with Part 3 singing silently.

ii) All parts sing aloud.

READ the TIP under the music in the Vocal Edition. Repeated pitches are difficult to keep in tune; they tend to go either flat or sharp.

REPEAT Exercise 34:

Switch parts again. Concentrate on the tuning.

IN REHEARSAL

New Concepts: tuning repeated pitches, cut-off

TIP: Sopranos and tenors tend to go sharp on repeated pitches; altos and basses tend to go flat. Ask the singers to listen carefully and keep the energy alive in their voices.

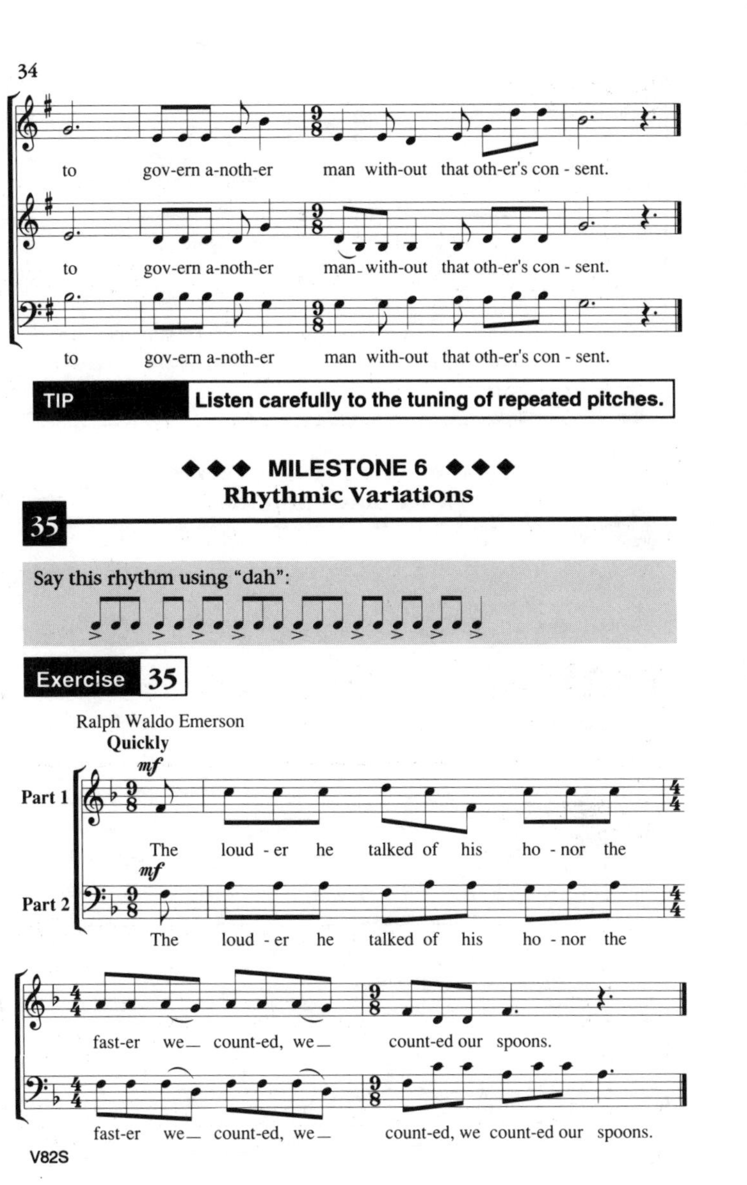

◆ ◆ ◆ Milestone 6 ◆ ◆ ◆
RHYTHMIC VARIATIONS

35

SPEAK the practice example in the Vocal Edition.

Tell the singers how many preparatory beats you will be conducting before their entry on the off-beat. The eighth note pulse will be constant throughout the exercise.

SING Exercise 35:

Standing. Check posture; encourage each singer to monitor their own progress.

REPEAT Exercise 35:

i) Facing the back of the room. Be ready to whip the eyes down quickly to the next line.

ii) Singers who prefer red: Part 1.
Singers who prefer blue: Part 2.

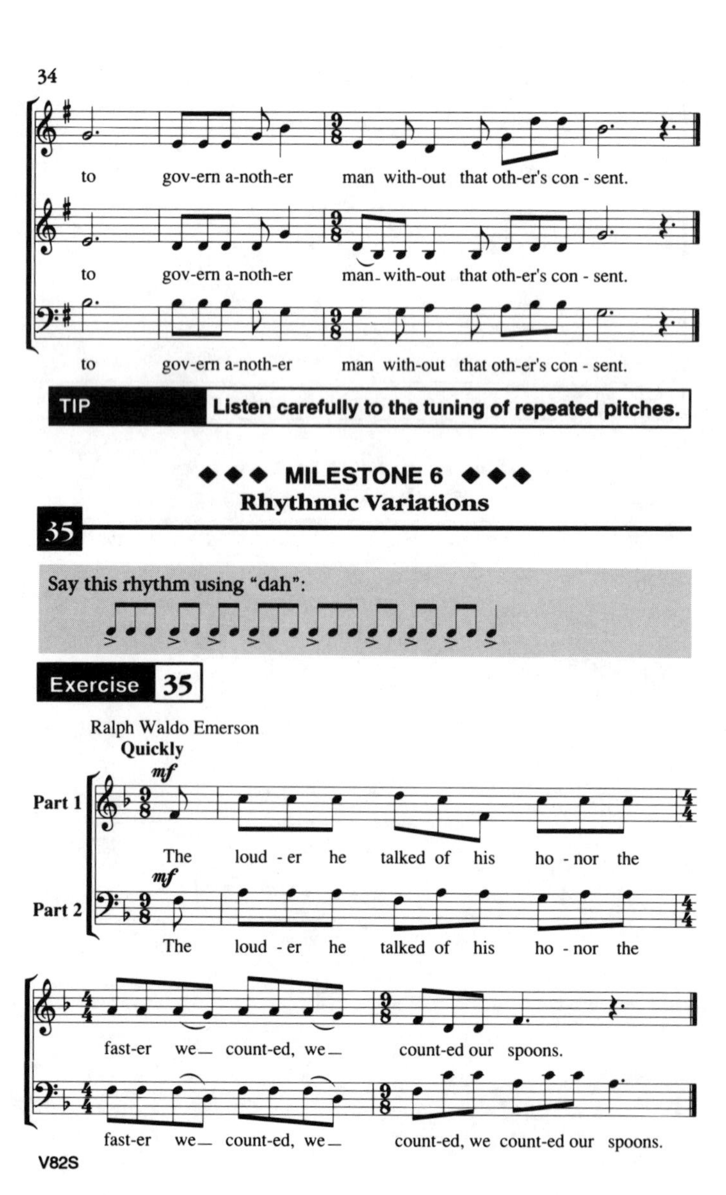

IN REHEARSAL

New Concept: changing from compound to simple time

TIP: It may be helpful for some singers to sing with a slight accent on each beat during changing meters:

When the rhythms are more accurate, remove the accent.

36

INTRODUCE

marking the pulse at a transition

SING Exercise 36:

Second and fourth rows: Part 1 silently.
First and third rows: Part 2 silently.

REPEAT Exercise 36:

After the singers have had a moment to silently work out any problems, sing aloud.

Have the singers mark a comma above the music as a breath mark in Part 1:

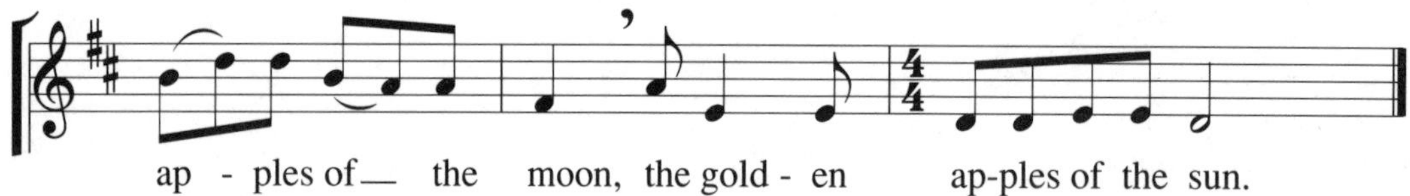

REPEAT Exercise 36:

i) Switch parts.
ii) Front row sitting, second row standing, etc.

IN REHEARSAL

New Concepts: marking the pulse at a transition, marking a comma for breathing

TIPS:

i) When the time changes from simple to compound, ask the singers to be aware of the eighth note pulse. Mark the transitional measures.
ii) When there are no rests, mark the breathing places.

37

INTRODUCE

$\frac{7}{8}$

SPEAK the first type of $\frac{7}{8}$ several times to "dah." Emphasize the first eighth note in each group.

REPEAT with the second type of $\frac{7}{8}$.

35

36

When music changes from simple to compound time, mark the measures just before and after the change. Feel the pulse of the eighth notes:

Emphasize the first note in each beat.

Exercise 36

William Butler Yeats

Not too quickly

37

V82S

SING Exercise 37

REPEAT Exercise 37:

i) Face the back of the room.
ii) Switch parts.
iii) Switch parts again. Face one side of the room.

IN REHEARSAL

TIP: In asymmetrical time signatures (i.e. $\frac{7}{8}$, $\frac{5}{8}$), singers often hold the quarter notes for too long. **See page 182** in the Teacher's Edition for an activity for pulse.

38

INTRODUCE

homophonic, harmonic
polyphonic, contrapuntal
unison, monophonic
marking the score at texture changes

Have the singers mark the texture change in pencil in Exercise 38 (the third measure).

PREVIEW TIP: Check for cues.

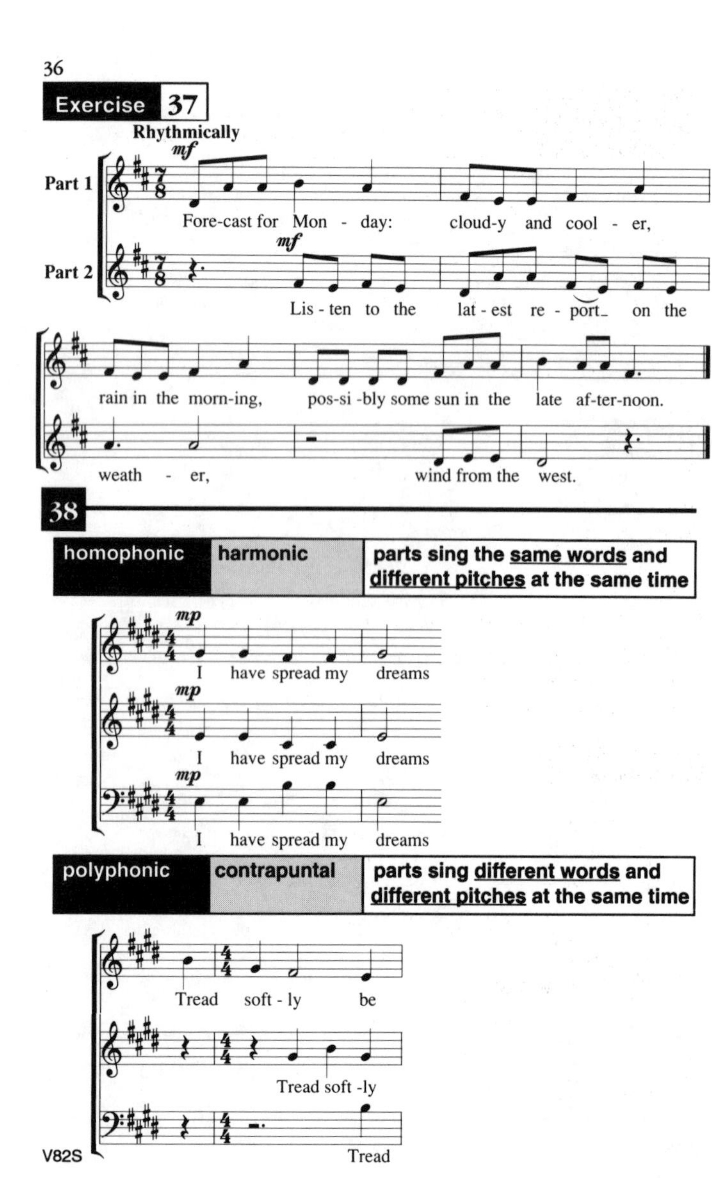

SING Exercise 38:

Singers with birthdays from January to April: Part 3.
Singers with birthdays from May to August: Part 2.
Singers with birthdays from September to December: Part 1.

REPEAT Exercise 38:

Give the singers a moment to work out any problems silently. Be ready for a quick page turn.

NOTE: Lesson 38 is continued on page 82.

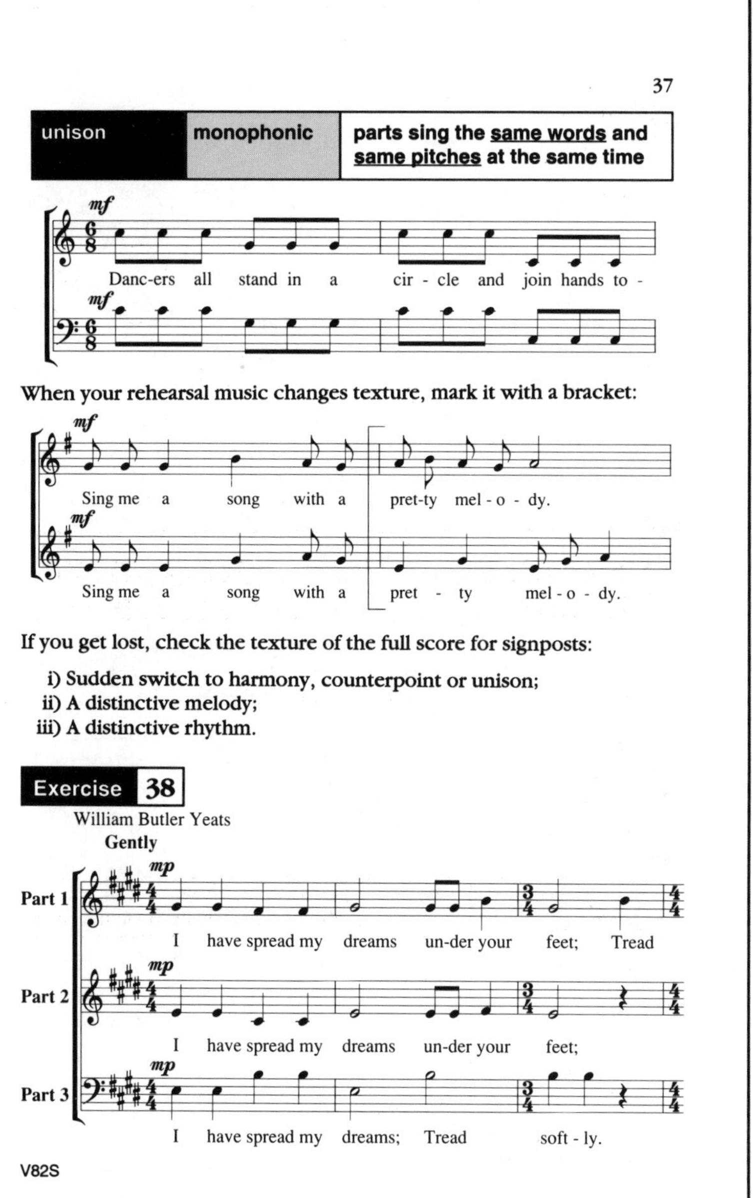

INTRODUCE

tempo and expression markings

REPEAT Exercise 38:

i) Parts 2 and 3 sing aloud with Part 1 singing silently.
ii) All parts sing aloud.
iii) Switch parts. Add more details (i.e. better diction, phrasing, etc.).
iv) Switch parts again.

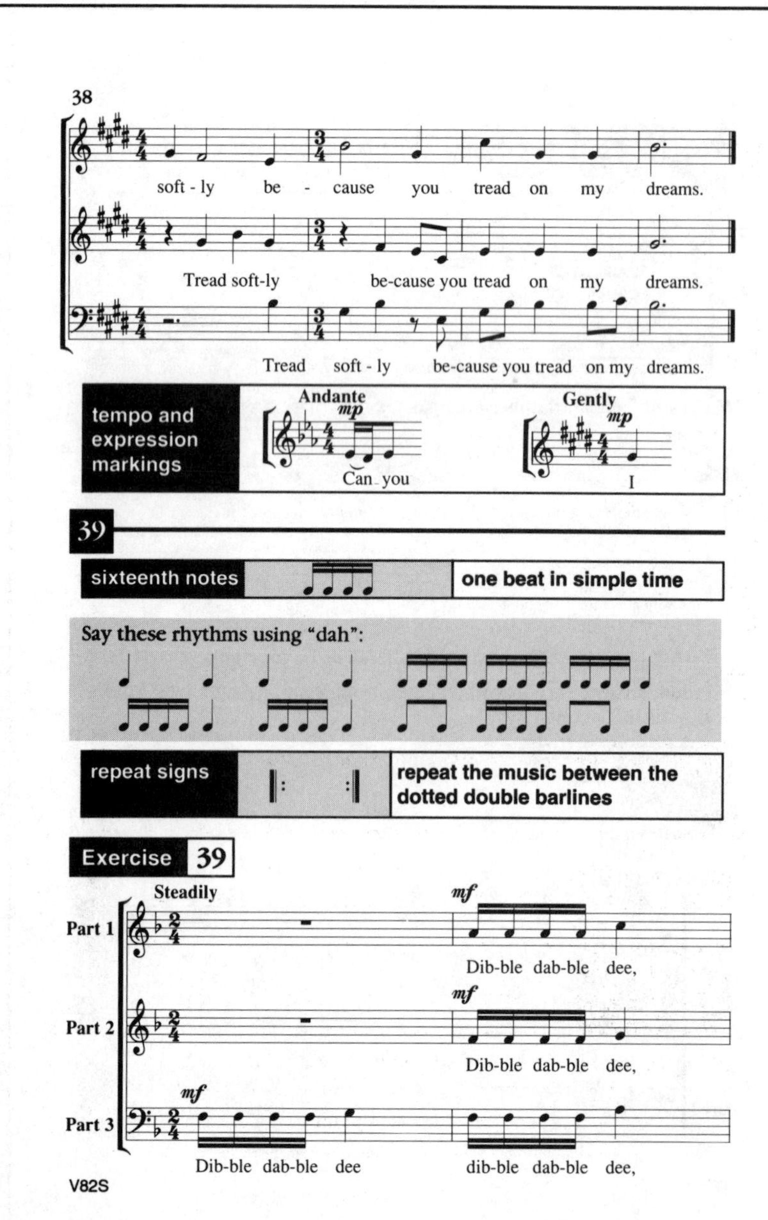

IN REHEARSAL

New Terms: homophonic/harmonic, polyphonic/contrapuntal, unison/monophonic, tempo and expression markings

New Concepts: marking texture changes, checking the texture for signposts

TIPS:

i) Encourage the singers to know what is happening in the full score rather than just following their own part.

ii) Introduce the terms for new tempo or expression markings as they appear in the repertoire. The singers will understand and remember their meanings better if they connect them with specific pieces of music rather than a list of terms.

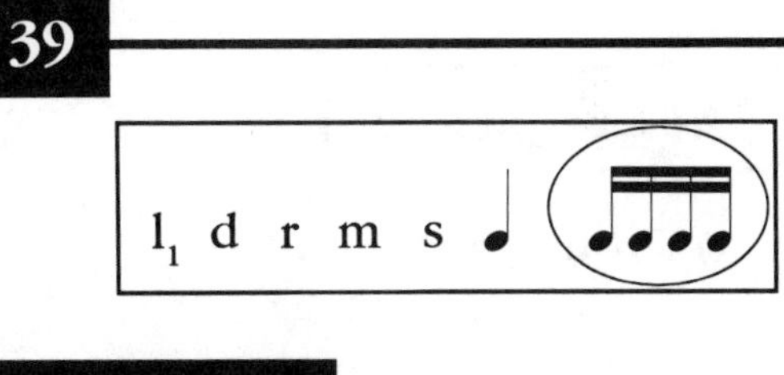

INTRODUCE

SPEAK the practice example. Ask the singers to emphasize the first sixteenth note in each group:

Have half of the singers say the first line while the rest say the second line. Switch parts.

INTRODUCE

repeat signs

SING Exercise 39:

Front singers: Part 1
Middle singers: Part 2.
Back singers: Part 3.

NOTE: Lesson 39 continued on Page 84.

TIP: If Part 2 singers have difficulty hearing the D in the third measure, ask them to sing an intermediary note silently:

REPEAT Exercise 39:

Three singers singing Parts 1, 2 and 3 as a trio.

EXPLAIN: ***f-p*** means ***f*** the first time; ***p*** on the repeat

REPEAT Exercise 39:

i) Front singers: Part 2.
   Middle singers: Part 3.
   Back singers: Part 1.
ii) Switch parts again.

IN REHEARSAL

New Terms: sixteenth notes, repeat signs

New Concept: intermediary pitches

TIP: To encourage independence, occasionally have the singers form two or three circles and rehearse a piece in this formation. This works particularly well for madrigal-style music.

40

NOTE: Each [sixteenth-note group] may include more than one pitch.

REVIEW: Major seconds.

INTRODUCE

ti
minor seconds (semi-tones)

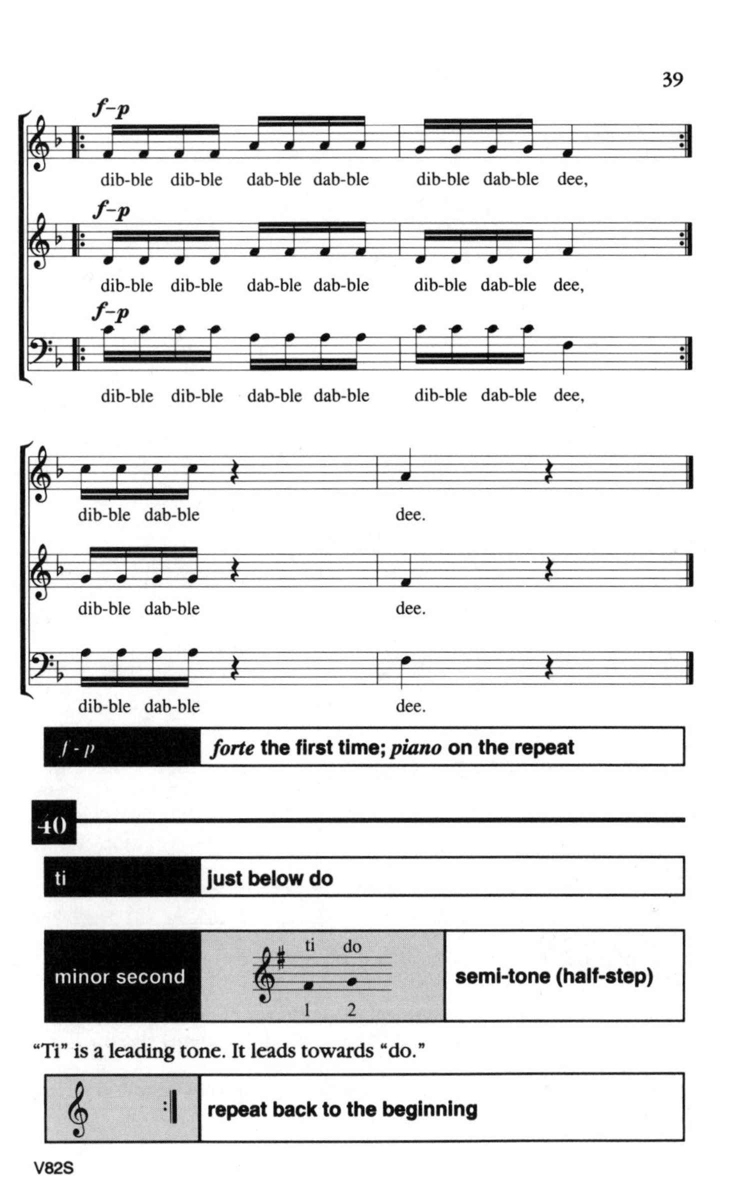

EXPLAIN: Minor intervals are always smaller than major intervals (i.e. a minor third is smaller than a major third).

See page 179 in the Teacher's Edition for an activity to memorize the interval of a semi-tone.

INTRODUCE

SING Exercise 40

REVIEW: Ask the singers to sing right in the center of each pitch. This is particularly important for "ti" because "do" and "ti" are just a semi-tone apart and must be clearly heard as separate pitches.

REPEAT Exercise 40:

i) Emphasize the first sixteenth note in each grouping of four sixteenths. The half notes in the last measure should get two full beats.
ii) Switch parts. Face one side of the room.

40

Exercise 40

Slowly

41

USING CUES **When there is a choice of cue, if possible it is better to choose a cue:**

i) From a reliable source (the accompaniment or another vocal part which you can hear clearly and which is usually right!);
ii) As close as possible in time to your entry;
iii) At the same pitch as your entry or an octave from your entry.

V82S

IN REHEARSAL | low ti

New Terms: ti, minor second, semi-tone, leading tone, repeat back to beginning

TIP: Have the singers circle the note when "ti" is in a prominent position. Ask them to check the tuning and notice how the "ti" leads up to the "do." Listen carefully to the tuning of all semi-tones.

41

INTRODUCE

choice of cues

NOTE: Two singers on the same vocal part may choose different cues depending on what other vocal part is closest to them or their own particular preference. It is important that singers learn a variety of strategies for cues. On some days, their cue may be absent (i.e. the reliable tenor is sick) and so they must choose an alternate cue.

Have the singers choose cues for Exercise 41.

INTRODUCE

SPEAK the practice example. Divide the choir into three parts; have each part speak a different line. Switch parts. Switch parts again.

SING Exercise 41:

Singers with birthdays in a month which is spelled with the letter "e": Part 1 silently.
Rest of the singers: Part 2 silently.

REPEAT Exercise 41:

i) Aloud. Remind the singers to begin the breath early in rhythm.
ii) Switch parts.

IN REHEARSAL

New Concept: choice of cues

TIP: Each singer should be responsible for marking the cues in their own score.

42

NOTE: Each may include more than one pitch.

42

Preview Checklist

1. Key signature, key signature changes.
2. Time signature.
3. Texture and cues.
4. Imitation.
5. Tempo and expression markings.
6. Posture.

During the preview, add your own markings to your music in pencil.

V82S

INTRODUCE

preview checklist

The preview checklist is a more sophisticated version of the sight-singing checklist found in Book 1 of **Successful Sight-Singing.**

INTRODUCE

two parts crossing on one staff

SING Exercise 42:

First and third rows sitting: Part 1.
Second and fourth rows standing: Part 2.

REMINDER: Sing every pitch in tune. Make sure the "ti" is high enough in tune.

REPEAT Exercise 42:

i) Sing the vowel sound on the beat.
ii) Switch parts. Sing the first measure aloud, second measure silently, etc.
iii) Sing entire exercise aloud.

IN REHEARSAL

ti

New Concept: preview checklist

TIP: Have the singers memorize the preview checklist and use it for each new piece. A preview takes time in rehearsal but the singers will sight-sing so much better that it actually saves rehearsal time. With practice, the singers can do the preview quite quickly.

43

INTRODUCE

SPEAK the practice example. Have half of the singers say the first line while the rest say the second line. Switch parts.

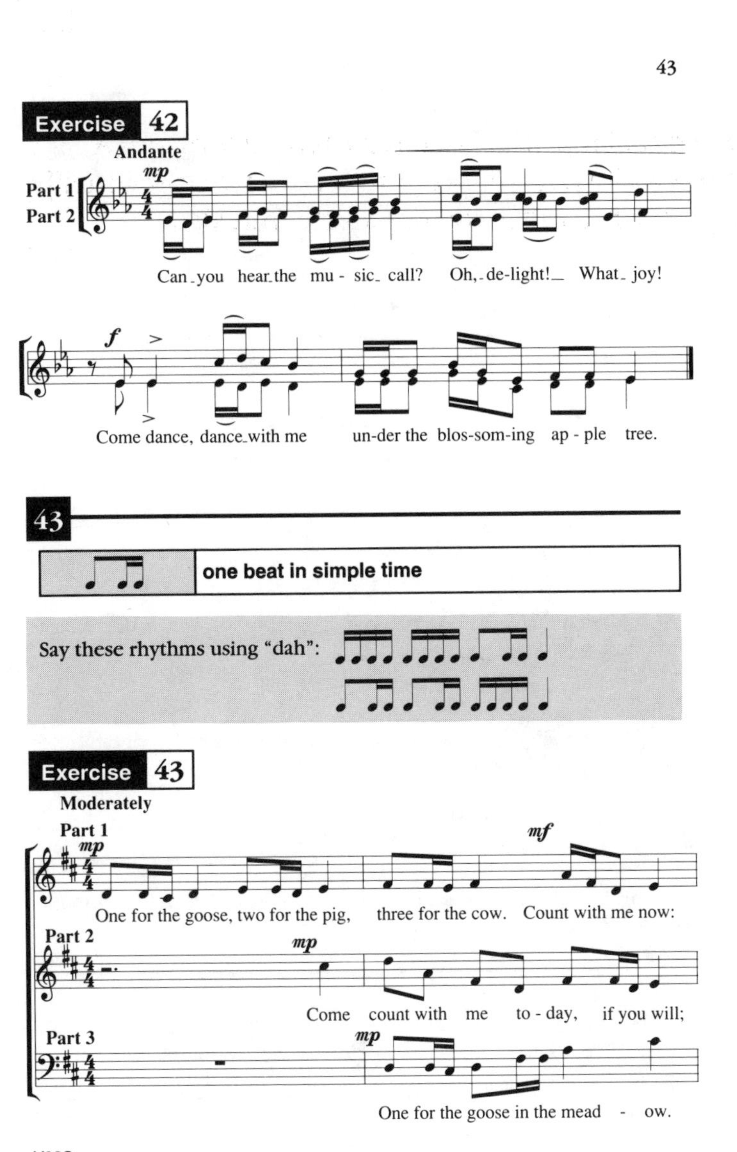

PREVIEW TIPS:

i) Use the preview checklist.

ii) Notice the change in texture at the beginning of the second system.

iii) Each singer should determine a strategy for each entry pitch:

- Part 1, measure 5: Think "home" or "tonic."
- Part 2, measure 1: Think "leading tone" leading up to the tonic.
- Part 3, measure 2: Think "home" or "tonic."

SING Exercise 43

INTRODUCE

sequence

Have the singers find a sequence in Exercise 43:

Have all the singers sing this sequence. A sequence is a type of imitation.

REPEAT Exercise 43:

i) Switch parts. Encourage each singer to monitor their own progress.
ii) Switch parts again.

NOTE: Whenever necessary, have the singers practice the page turn.

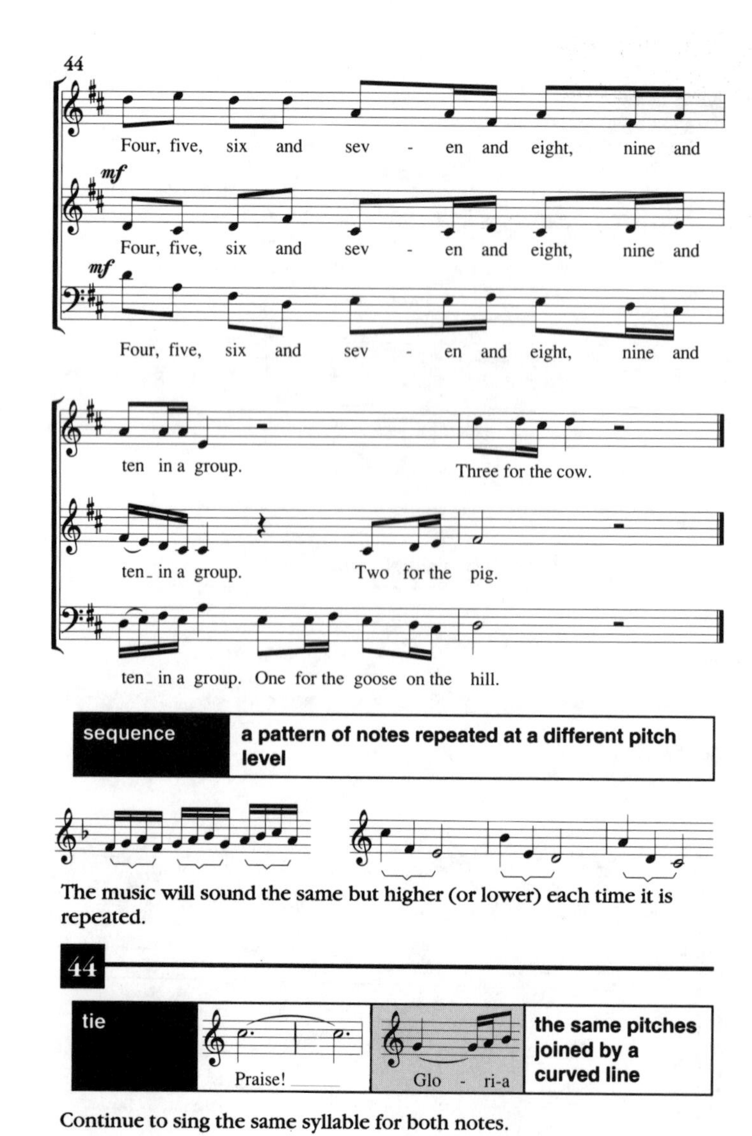

IN REHEARSAL

New Term: sequence

TIP: It saves rehearsal time if you begin with warmups. When the voice is properly warmed up, it is easier to sing correct pitches. When the ears are warmed up, it is easier to sing in tune, sing precisely together and hear whether you are singing your own part correctly. When the mind is warmed up, it is easier to follow the music and to sing musically and intelligently.

44

INTRODUCE

tie

Let the singers have time to preview the ties in Exercise 44 silently.

PREVIEW TIP: Check Exercise 44 for a sequence:

SING Exercise 44:

Silently. Check posture.

REPEAT Exercise 44:

i) Aloud, using only the vowels of each word in the lyrics:

ii) Using only the vowels. Concentrate on the purity of each vowel sound.
iii) Using the full lyrics. Continue to sing with pure vowels.
iv) Switch parts.

IN REHEARSAL

New Term: tie

TIP: Concentrate on the beat during any tied notes with long durations.

45

s_1 l_1 t_1 d m s l t 

INTRODUCE

major seventh
minor seventh

See page 179 in the Teacher's Edition for an activity to memorize the intervals of a major and minor seventh.

SING Exercise 45:

Musically.

TIP: If Parts 1 and 2 have difficulty with the fifths at the end of Exercise 45, ask them to add an intermediary pitch silently:

REPEAT Exercise 45:

i) Make each vowel sound pure.
ii) Switch parts. Have one singer sing Part 1 as a solo while the rest of the singers sing Parts 2 and 3 quietly.

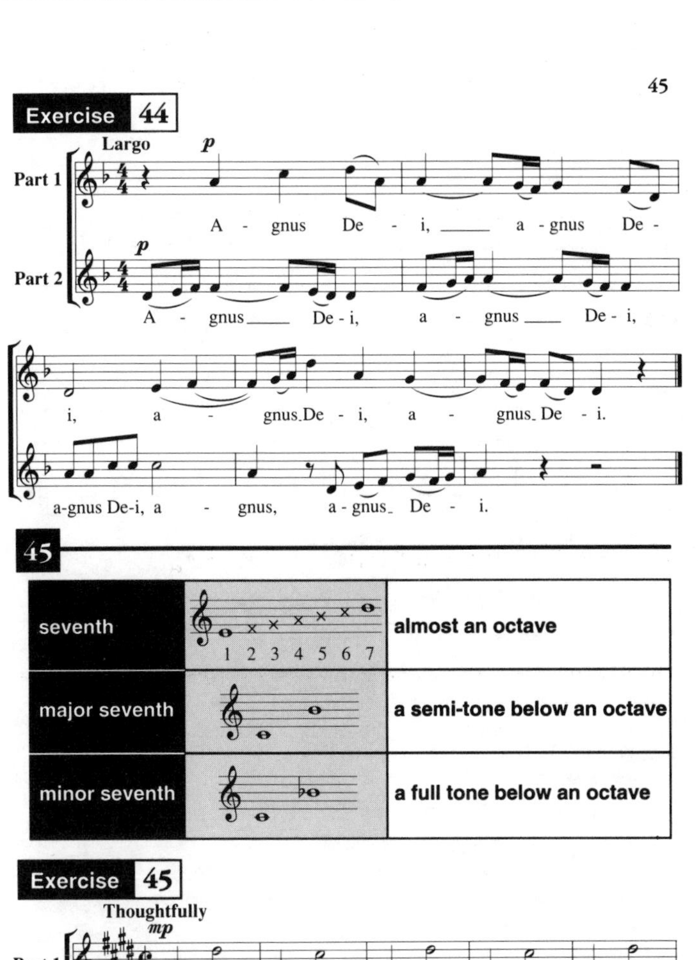

IN REHEARSAL

New Terms: major seventh, minor seventh

TIP: Frequently rehearse without piano accompaniment to build up the independence of the singers.

46

INTRODUCE

SPEAK the practice example. Divide the choir into three parts; have each part speak a different line. Switch parts. Switch parts again.

SING Exercise 46:

Standing.

REVIEW: Encourage the singers to let their eyes bounce continuously across the page. Their eyes should be ahead of their voices.

REPEAT Exercise 46:

i) Use pure vowel sounds.
ii) Switch parts.

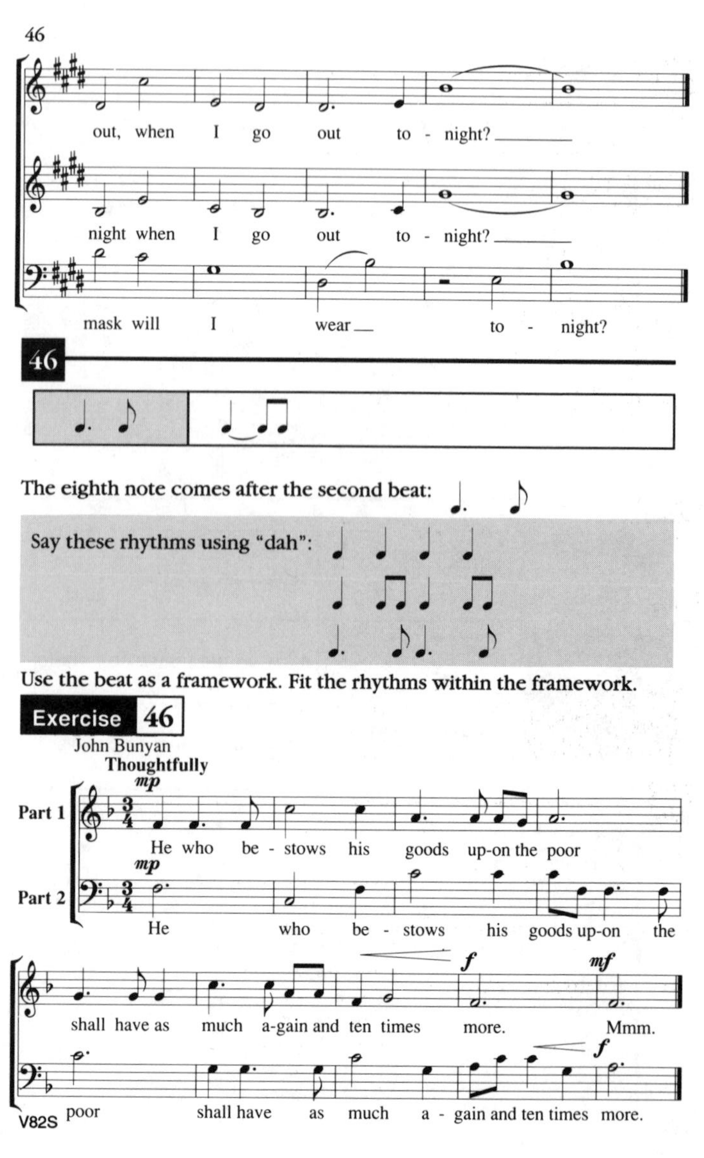

IN REHEARSAL

TIP: It may help to put a slight push on the second beat of a dotted quarter note in simple time.

47

NOTE: Each ♩. ♪ may include more than one pitch.

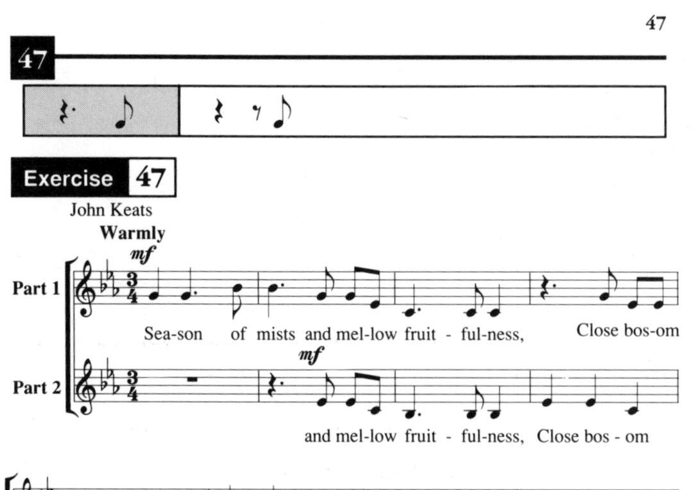

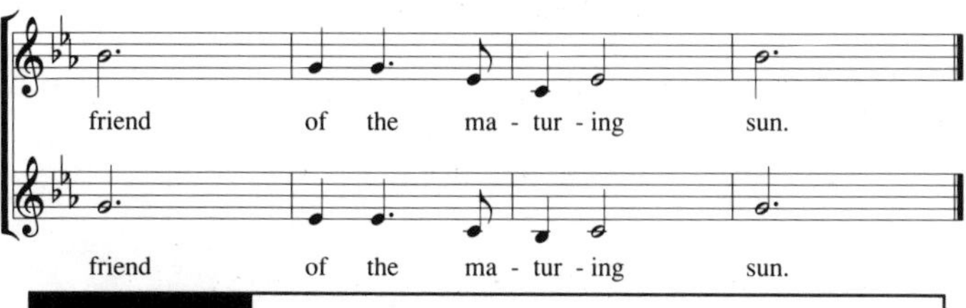

TIP	To keep in tune, sing each note right in the center of the pitch.

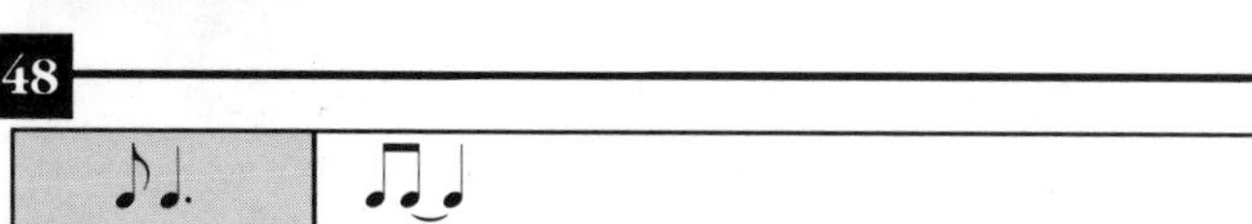

The second note comes before the second beat:

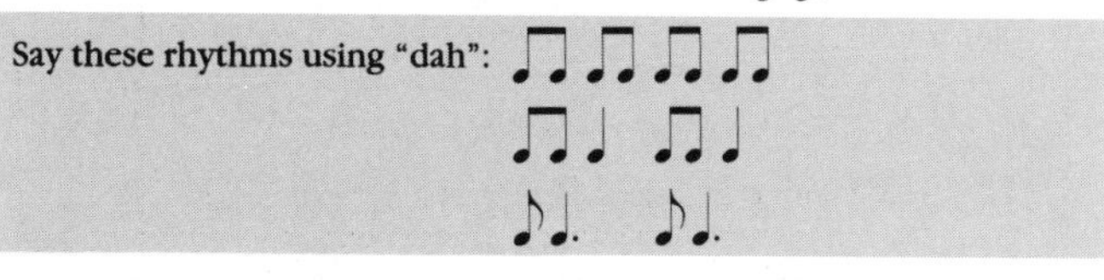

V82S

INTRODUCE

SING Exercise 47:

Silently.

TIP: If Part 2 singers have difficulty with the C in the fourth measure, have them remember the B♭ from the second measure; the C is just one step above it.

REPEAT Exercise 47:

Aloud.

TIP: If the singers are not precise with the rhythm of the tongue-twister in the fourth measure of Part 1, ask them to sing the consonants quickly and clearly.

NOTE: Lesson 47 is continued on page 98.

READ the TIP under the music in the Vocal Edition.

Have the singers think of the sound shaped as a circle. If they sing only the top half of the circle, it sounds sharp. The bottom half alone sounds flat. When they sing in the center of the pitch, the music will be in tune and it is easier to sing the correct intervals.

REPEAT Exercise 47:

i) Switch parts. Sing with each note in the center of the pitch.
ii) Front row sitting, second row standing, etc.

Ask the singers to spot where Parts 1 and 2 are singing a second apart:

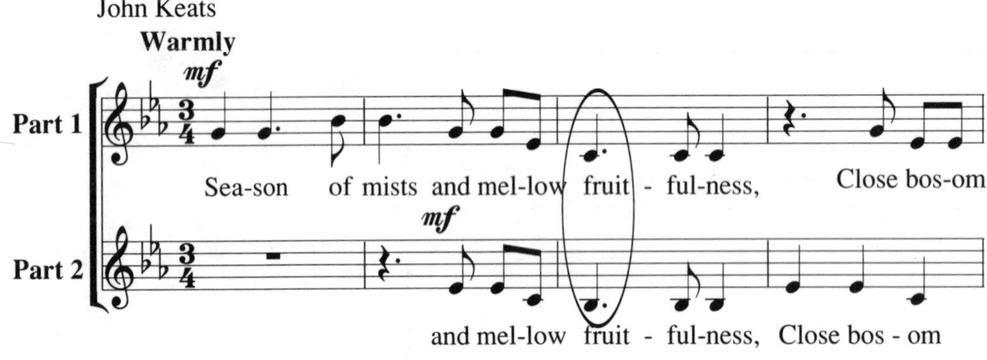

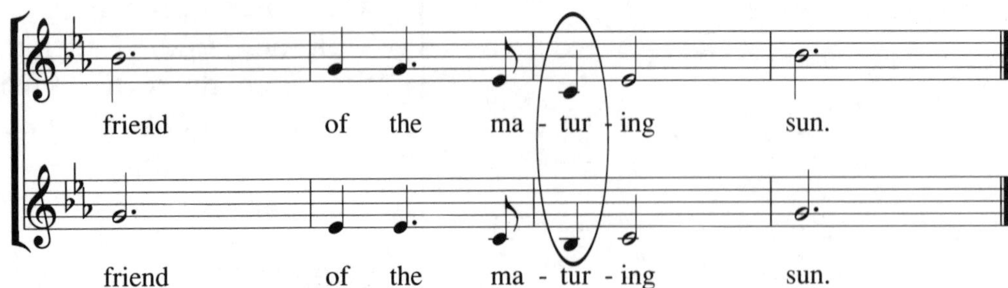

REPEAT Exercise 47:

Notice the sound of the harmony in seconds.

IN REHEARSAL

New Concepts: sound shaped as a circle, singing in center of pitch

TIP: Singers who drink plenty of water have more energy, are less vocally stressed and tend to sight-sing better. For small choirs, a set of glasses and a pitcher of water is a welcome addition. For large choirs, remind the singers to drink sufficient amounts of water before the rehearsal and during the break.

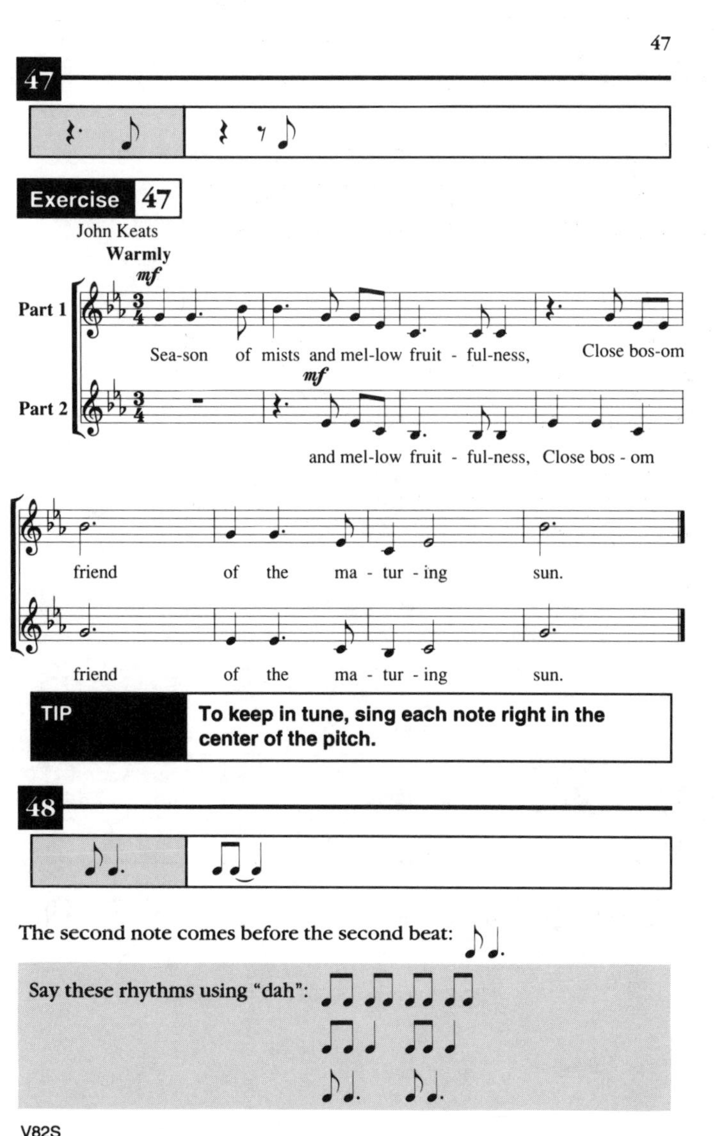

47

47

Exercise 47

John Keats

Warmly

mf

Part 1: Sea-son of mists and mel-low fruit - ful-ness, Close bos-om friend of the ma - tur - ing sun.

Part 2: *mf* and mel-low fruit - ful-ness, Close bos - om friend of the ma - tur - ing sun.

TIP	To keep in tune, sing each note right in the center of the pitch.

48

The second note comes before the second beat:

Say these rhythms using "dah":

48

INTRODUCE

SPEAK the practice example. Divide the choir into three parts; have each part speak a different line. Switch parts. Switch parts again.

SING Exercise 48:

Singers with birthdays from January to June: Part 1.
Singers with birthdays from July to December: Part 2.

READ the REMINDER under the music in the Vocal Edition.

REPEAT Exercise 48:

i) After the singers have time to silently correct any problems.
ii) Switch parts. Face one side of the room.

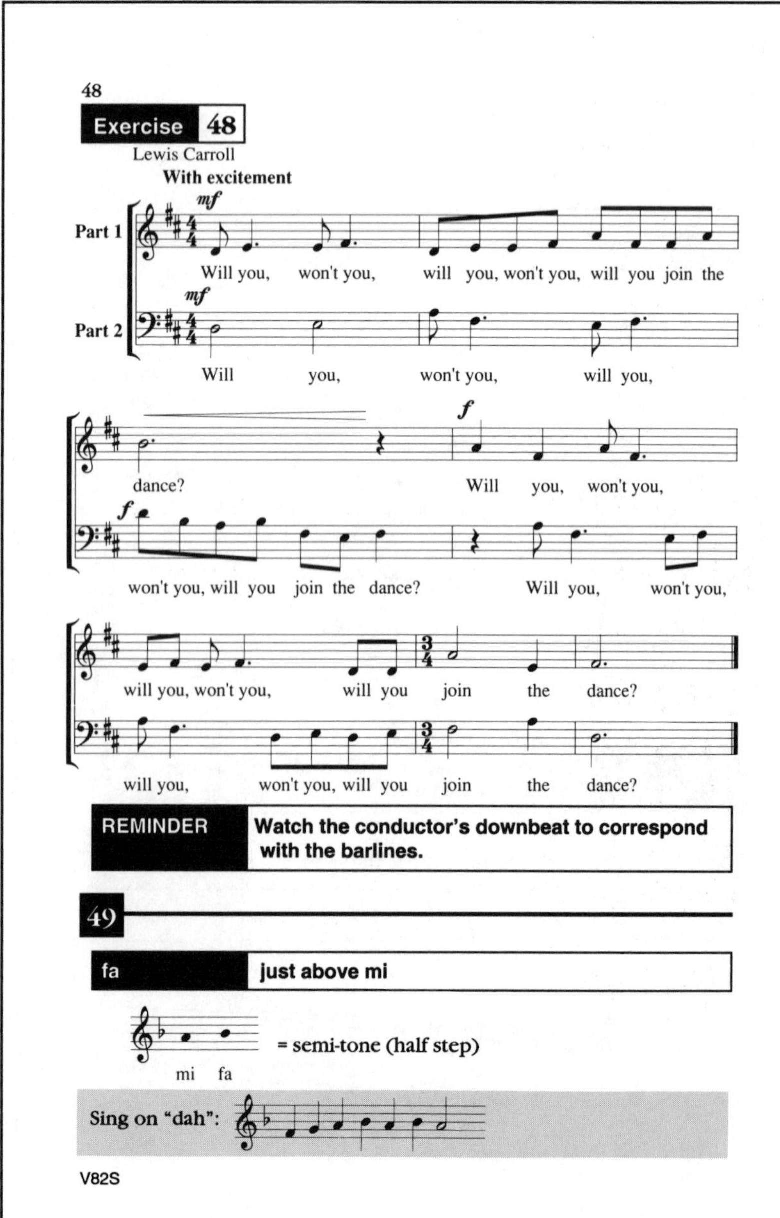

IN REHEARSAL

TIP: Adult and changing voices take much longer to warm up than unchanged voices. Just as athletes begin their day with a warmup, singers should begin their day with a vocal warmup. Humming is the fastest way to warm up a voice and may be done while the singer is engaged in other early morning activities. Singers sight-sing much better when their voices are warmed up.

49

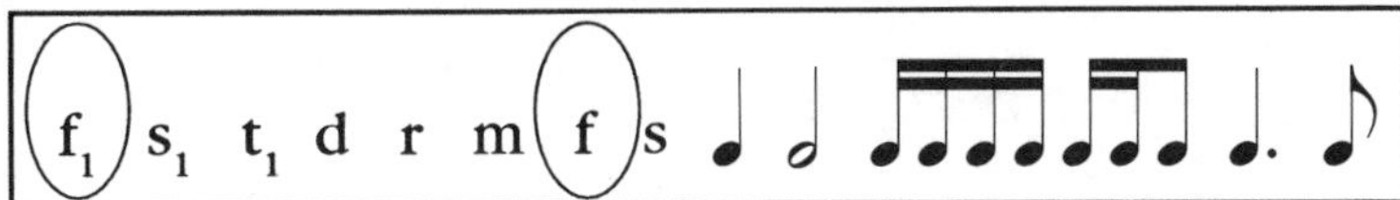

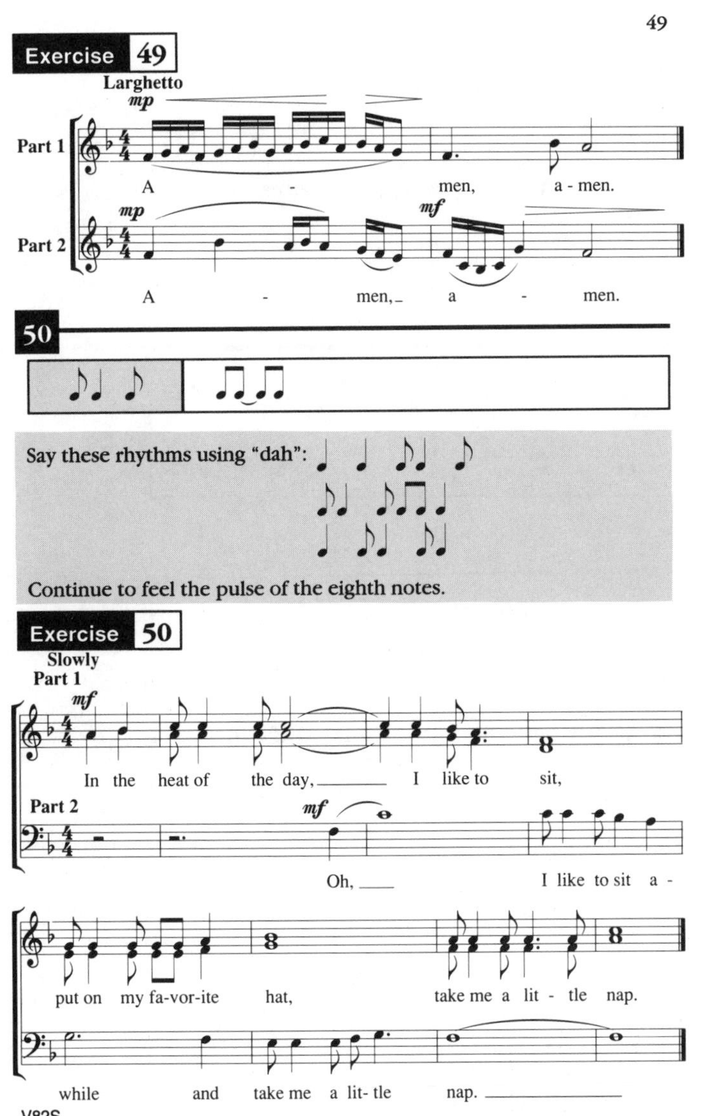

INTRODUCE

fa

SING the practice example before Exercise 49 in the Vocal Edition.

PREVIEW TIP: Look for a sequence:

SING Exercise 49

REPEAT Exercise 49:

i) Make each vowel sound pure.
ii) Switch parts. Sing the first beat aloud, second beat silently, etc.
iii) Sing the entire exercise aloud.

NOTE: "Amen" has been associated with the "fa" sound for centuries because the traditional chords for an Amen have been I (major triad based on "do") and IV (triad based on "fa").

IN REHEARSAL

fa, low fa

TIP: For warmups in two parts, have the singers seated in the middle sing one part while the singers at the sides sing the other part.

50

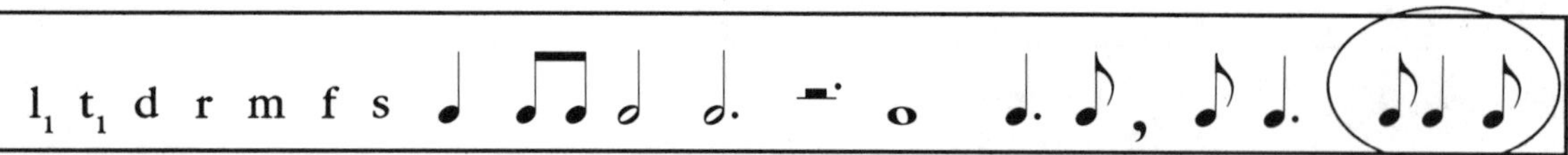

INTRODUCE

SPEAK the practice example. Divide the choir into three parts; have each part speak a different line. Switch parts. Switch parts again.

SING Exercise 50:

Standing.

REPEAT Exercise 50

i) Facing the back of the room.
ii) Switch parts. Back singers face front singers.
iii) Switch parts again.

IN REHEARSAL

TIP: Occasionally have the back singers face the front singers as they sing.

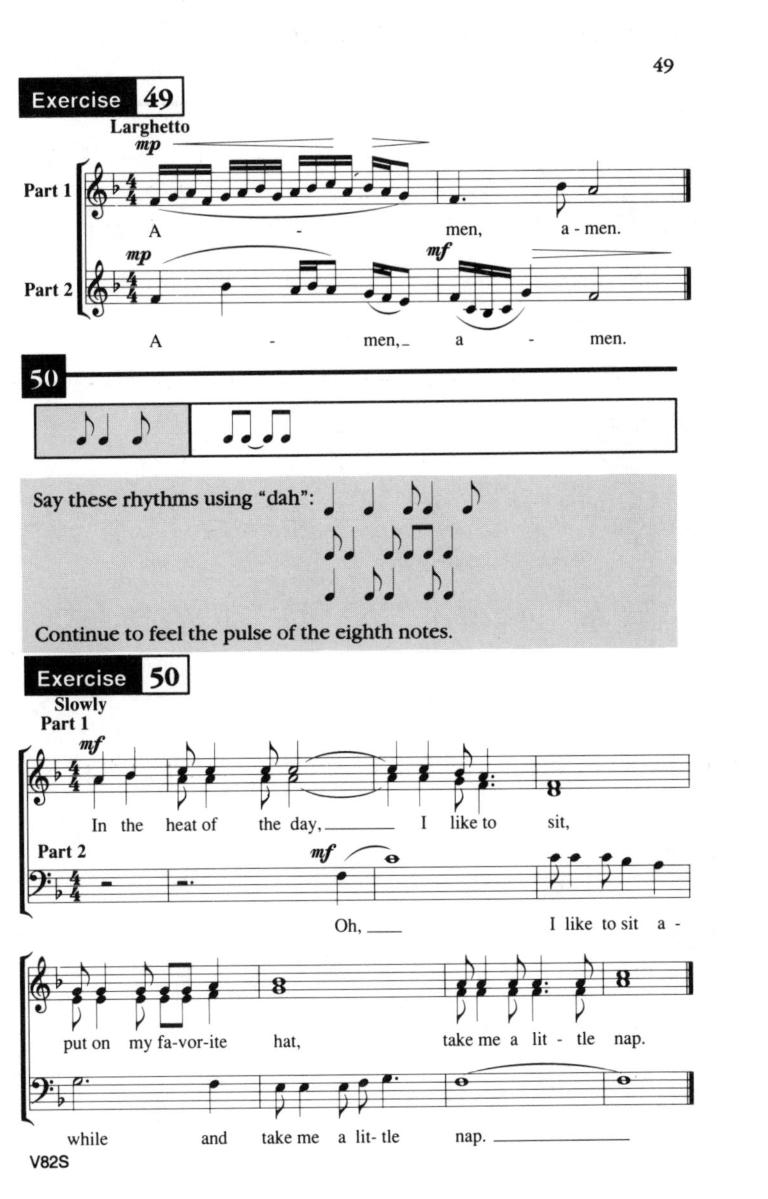

51

NOTE: Each ♪♩ ♪ may include more than one pitch.

INTRODUCE

first ending
second ending

REVIEW: Preview check-list. The singers should always do the preview as quickly as possible.

SING Exercise 51:

First row of singers: Part 1 silently.
Second row of singers: Part 2 aloud.
Third row of singers: Part 3 aloud.

REVIEW: Bounce the eyes continuously across the page slightly ahead of the music.

REPEAT Exercise 51:

All parts aloud.

TIP: For precision in the last two measures, mark the beats with a vertical line above the music.

REPEAT Exercise 51:

i) Switch parts.
ii) Switch parts again.

1) Start at the beginning of the music;
2) When you reach the repeat sign, go back to the beginning;
3) Start singing the first part again;
4) Omit the music in the first ending;
5) Go directly to the second ending;
6) Continue singing until the last measure.

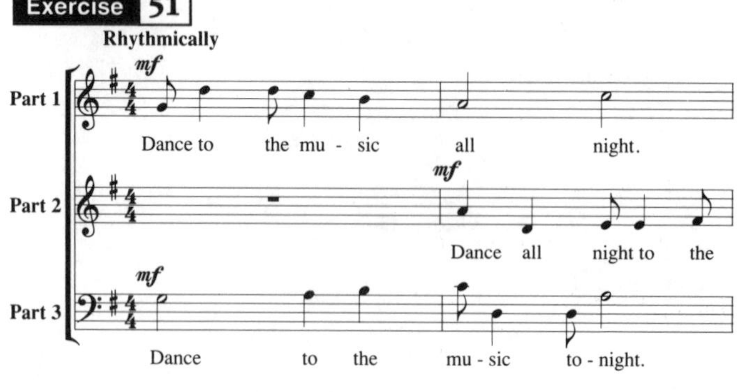

V82S

IN REHEARSAL

New Terms: first ending, second ending

TIP: Singers stay fresh (and sight-sing better) if the rehearsal is paced with a variety of music. Alternate different types of music:

fast/slow
loud/soft
serious/amusing
difficult/easy
rhythmic/melodic/harmonic
familiar/a bit familiar/new

52

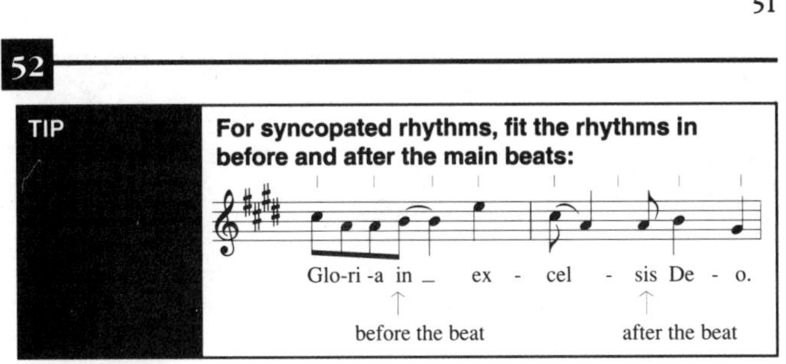

52

NOTE: Sing Exercise 52 with 3 parts together or each part separately.

READ the TIP in the Vocal Edition. Syncopated rhythms have the strong sound on the off-beat.

REMINDER: Mark the tonic at the beginning.

SING Exercise 52:

Silently.

REPEAT Exercise 52:

i) Aloud. In the last two measures emphasize the first eighth note in each grouping of three eighths.
ii) Singers who prefer green: Part 1.
Singers who prefer blue: Part 2.
Singers who prefer red: Part 3.
iii) Sing a part you have not already sung.

IN REHEARSAL

New Term: syncopated

TIP: For better precision with rhythmic music, play an imaginary game of catch with the singers. **See page 185** in the Teacher's Edition for the "rules."

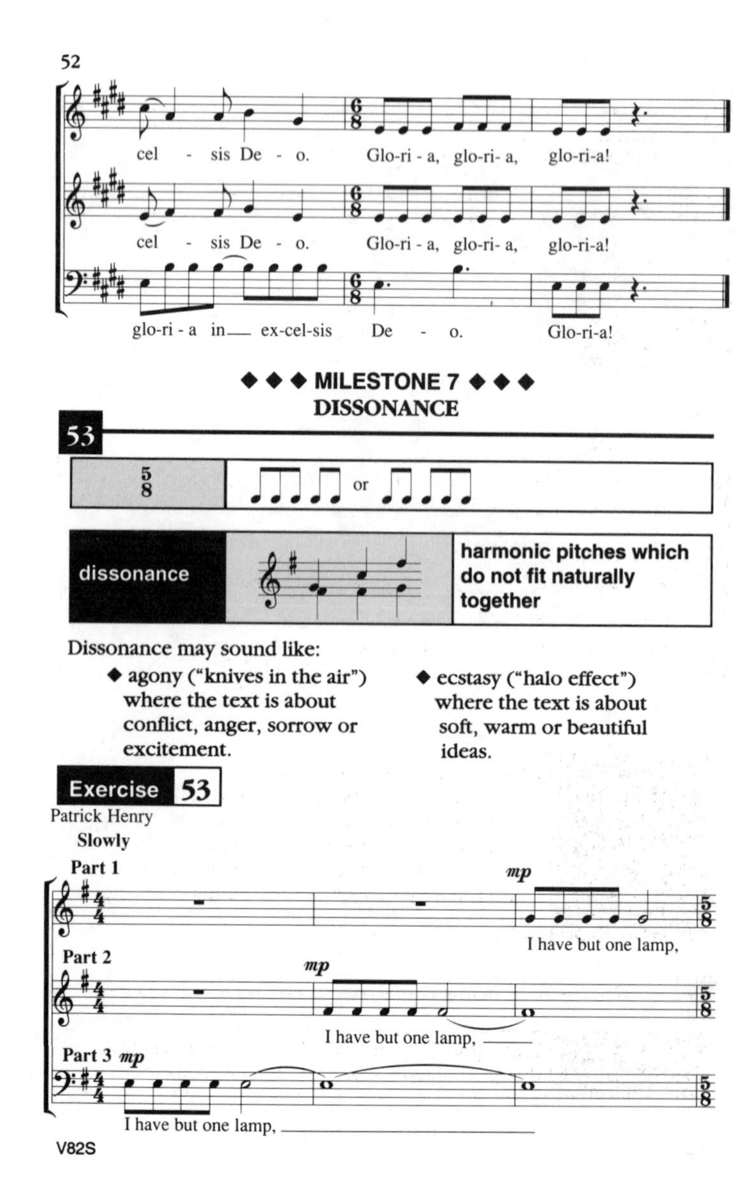

52

cel - sis De - o. Glo-ri - a, glo-ri- a, glo-ri-a!
cel - sis De - o. Glo-ri - a, glo-ri- a, glo-ri-a!
glo-ri - a in___ ex-cel-sis De - o. Glo-ri-a!

◆ ◆ ◆ **MILESTONE 7** ◆ ◆ ◆
DISSONANCE

53

5/8	or

dissonance		**harmonic pitches which do not fit naturally together**

Dissonance may sound like:

- agony ("knives in the air") where the text is about conflict, anger, sorrow or excitement.
- ecstasy ("halo effect") where the text is about soft, warm or beautiful ideas.

Exercise 53

Patrick Henry

Slowly

V82S

◆ ◆ ◆ Milestone 7 ◆ ◆ ◆
DISSONANCE

53

INTRODUCE

$\frac{5}{8}$

dissonance

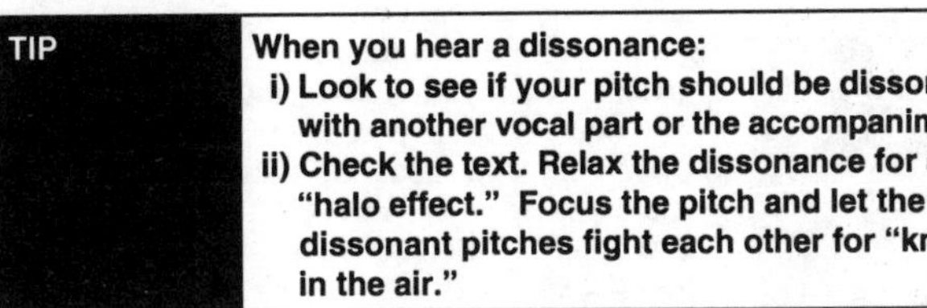

TIP

When you hear a dissonance:

i) Look to see if your pitch should be dissonant with another vocal part or the accompaniment.

ii) Check the text. Relax the dissonance for a "halo effect." Focus the pitch and let the dissonant pitches fight each other for "knives in the air."

54

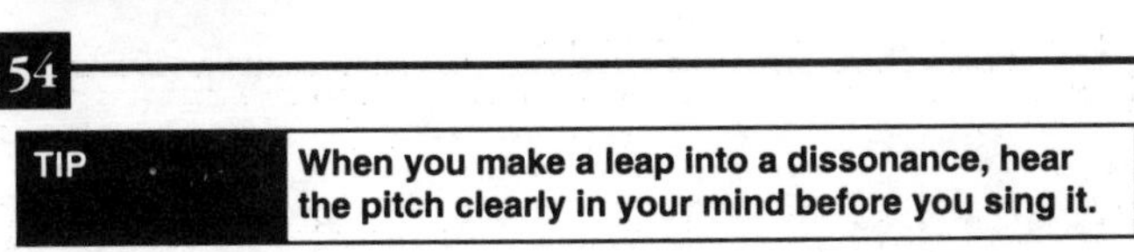

TIP

When you make a leap into a dissonance, hear the pitch clearly in your mind before you sing it.

V82S

See page 181 in the Teacher's Edition for an activity to illustrate "knives in the air" and "halo effect." Singers show less resistance to dissonance when they understand how and why dissonance is used.

SING Exercise 53:

Listen for the dissonance.

READ the TIP under the music in the Vocal Edition.

REPEAT Exercise 53:

i) Concentrate on the "halo effect."

ii) Switch parts. Concentrate on "knives in the air."

IN REHEARSAL

New Term: dissonance

New Concepts: "knives in the air," "halo effect"

TIP: As a warmup, form a 4-part tone cluster ("do[1] ti la so") by adding one pitch at a time.
REPEAT starting on a different pitch.
REPEAT using "do re mi fa" or four semi-tones.

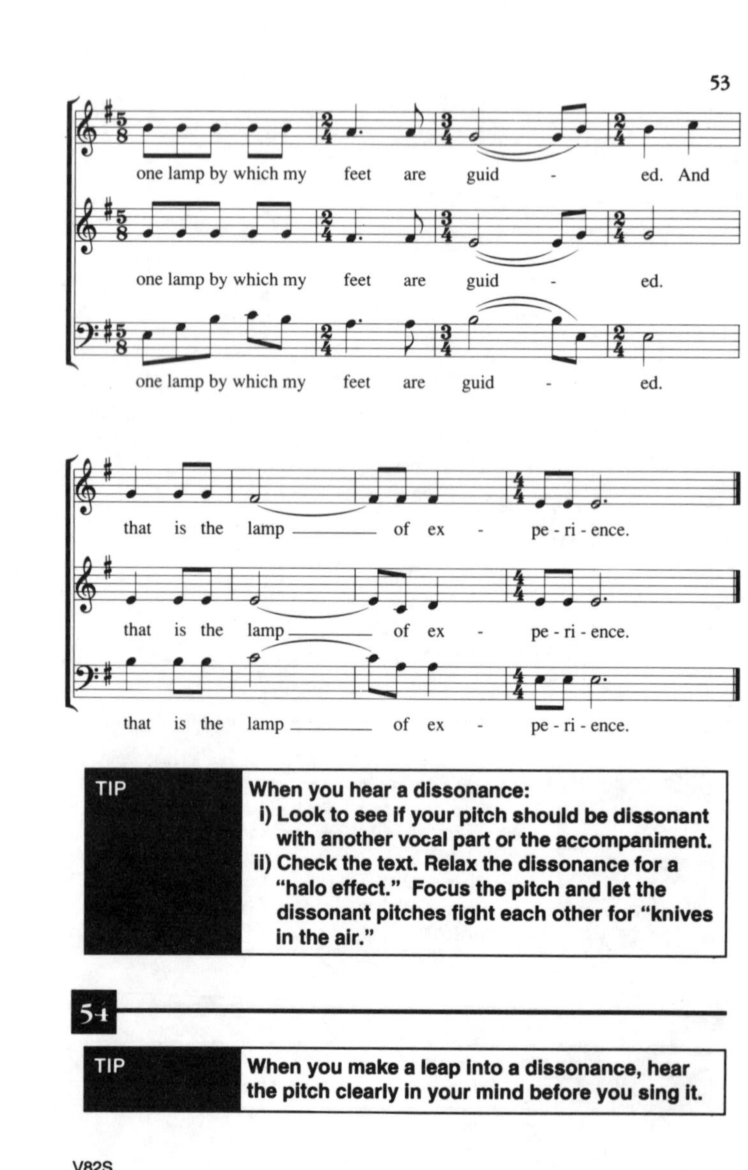

54

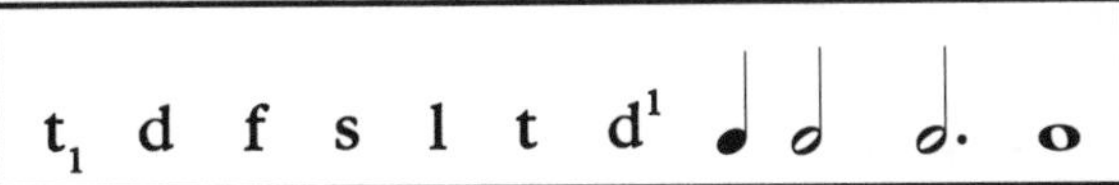

READ the TIP in the Vocal Edition. Find the dissonances in Exercise 54:

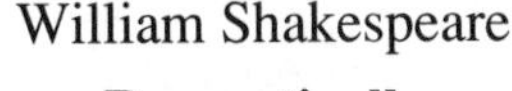

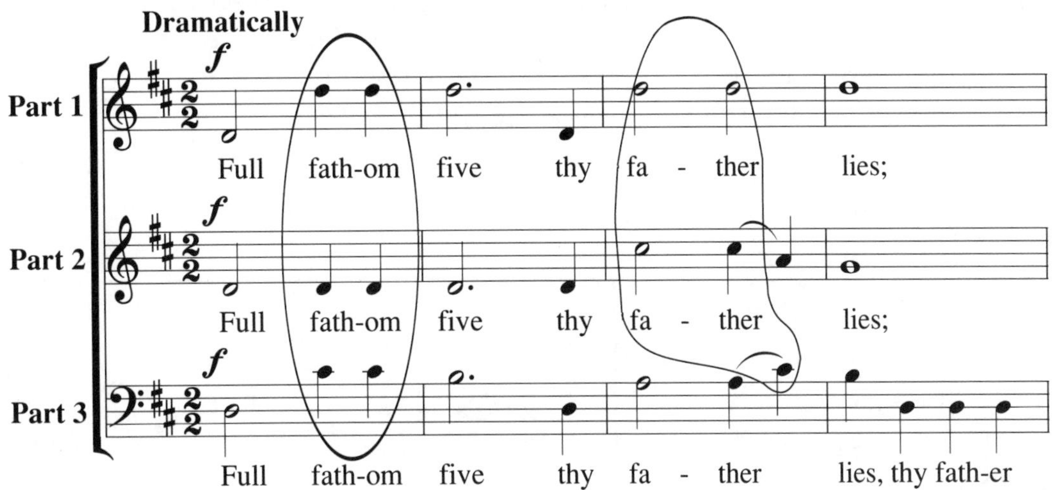

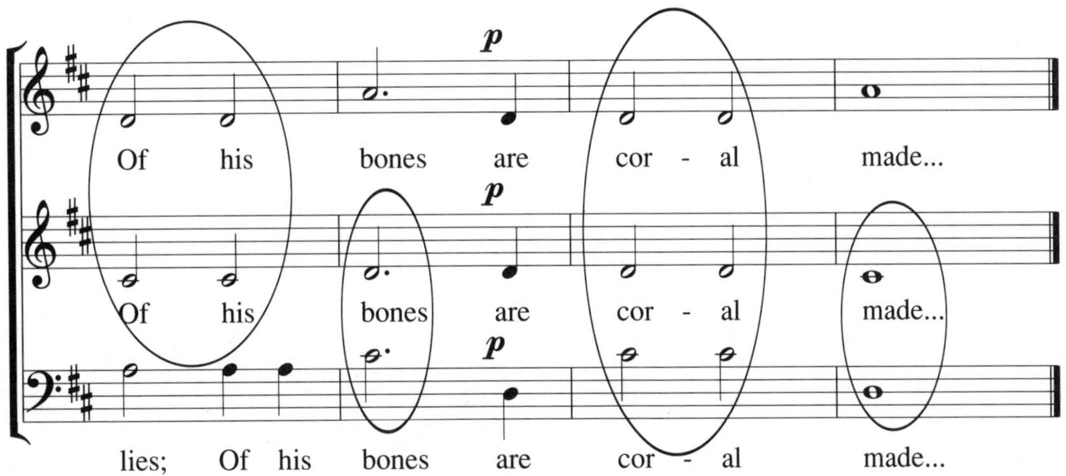

SING Exercise 54:

Silently. Check posture.

REPEAT Exercise 54:

i) Aloud.
ii) Sing each part separately. Use a firm voice to sing the pitches which will be dissonant with another part. Center the pitch quickly and keep it centered through the entire duration of that note.
iii) Sing in three parts. Scan the eyes over the full score as you sing.

IN REHEARSAL

New Concept: leaping into dissonance

TIP: If the singers are having difficulty with precision in a particular piece, sing the music to "doo." It will be obvious if the "d's" are not together.

REPEAT with more precision.
REPEAT with "loo;" go through the "l" quickly.
REPEAT with the words; place the vowel on the beat.

55

READ the TIP above the music in the Vocal Edition.

SING Exercise 55:

First row standing: Part 1.
Second row sitting: Part 2.
Third row standing: Part 3.

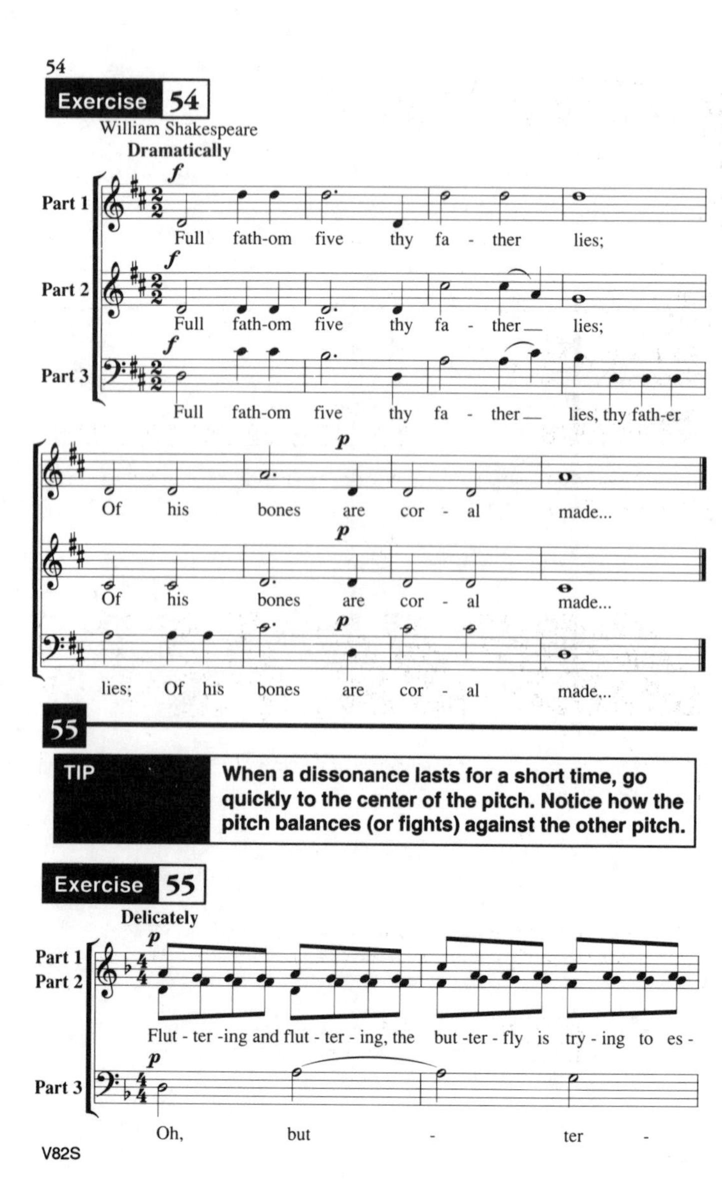

REPEAT Exercise 55:

i) Very slowly.
ii) More quickly with the dissonances just as clearly defined as they were at the slower tempo.
iii) Switch parts.

IN REHEARSAL

New Concept: dissonances of short duration

TIP: During warmups, have only first and third rows stand. **REPEAT** with only second and fourth rows standing.

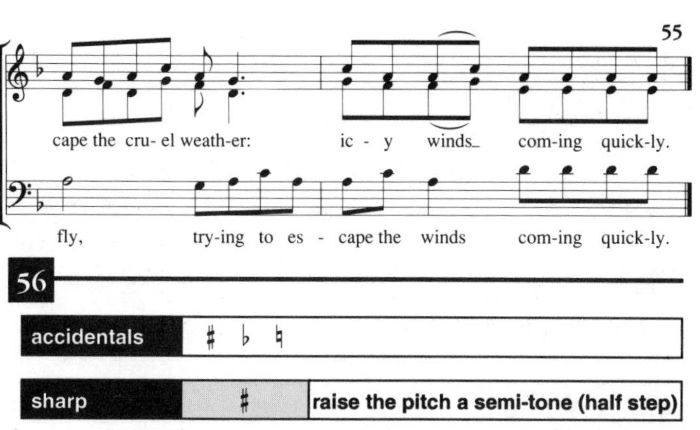

The black keys on a keyboard are one semi-tone higher or lower than the white keys right beside them.

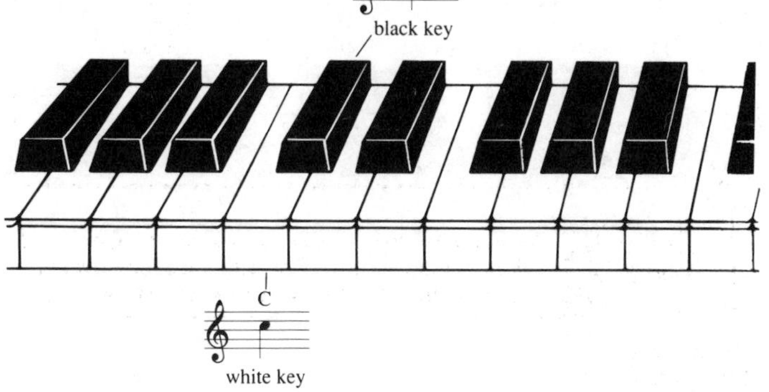

A sharp sign that appears after the key signature is valid to the end of the measure in which it appears. In the next measure, that pitch returns to normal:

V82S

56

INTRODUCE

accidentals
sharp
keyboard

Ask the singers to play a C major scale on the keyboard in the Vocal Edition. Use a pencil to play the scale if the keys are too narrow for the fingers. Sing the letter names:

EXPLAIN: If there is no black key between two white keys, the interval is a semi-tone.

REPEAT and sing the whole tones and semi-tones:

REPEAT with a G major scale using the letter names; F♯ will be a black key.

REPEAT and sing the whole tones and semi-tones.

Play these pitches on the keyboard and sing the letter names:

B A♯ B	D C♯ D
A G♯ A	E D♯ E

Notice how close the A♯ sounds to the B for a semi-tone.

SING Exercise 56:

Musically.

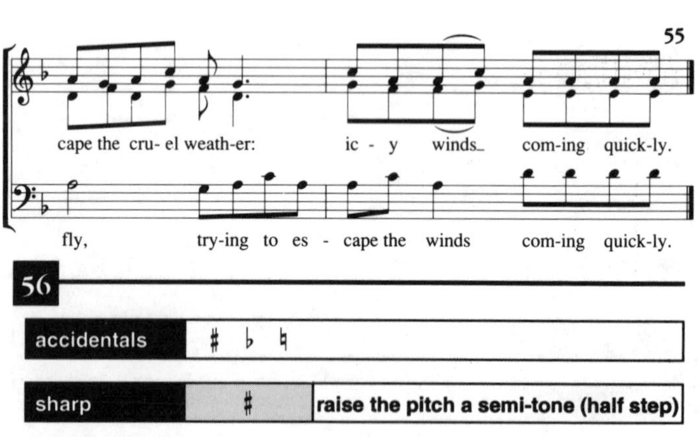

The black keys on a keyboard are one semi-tone higher or lower than the white keys right beside them.

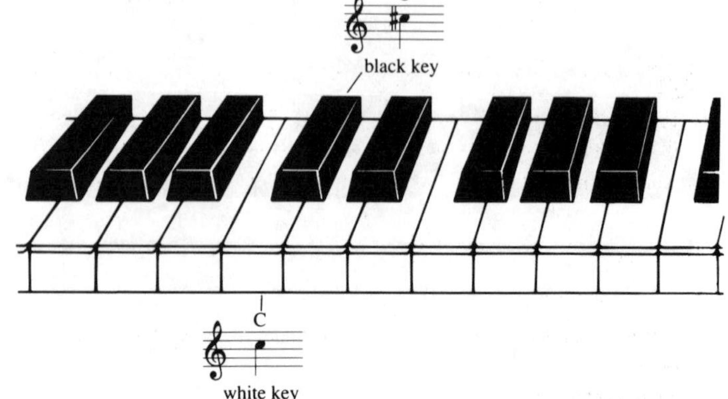

A sharp sign that appears after the key signature is valid to the end of the measure in which it appears. In the next measure, that pitch returns to normal:

V82S

REPEAT Exercise 56:

i) Switch parts. Make sure that each sharp note (including F♯) is close to the pitch above it. It should have the feeling of leading to the higher pitch.

ii) Face a partner who is singing the other part. Encourage each singer to monitor their own progress.

IN REHEARSAL

♯

New Terms: accidental, major scale

New Concepts: semi-tones and whole tones on a keyboard, sharp sign valid to end of measure

TIP: Point out any sevenths in the music. Ask the singers if the sevenths are major or minor.

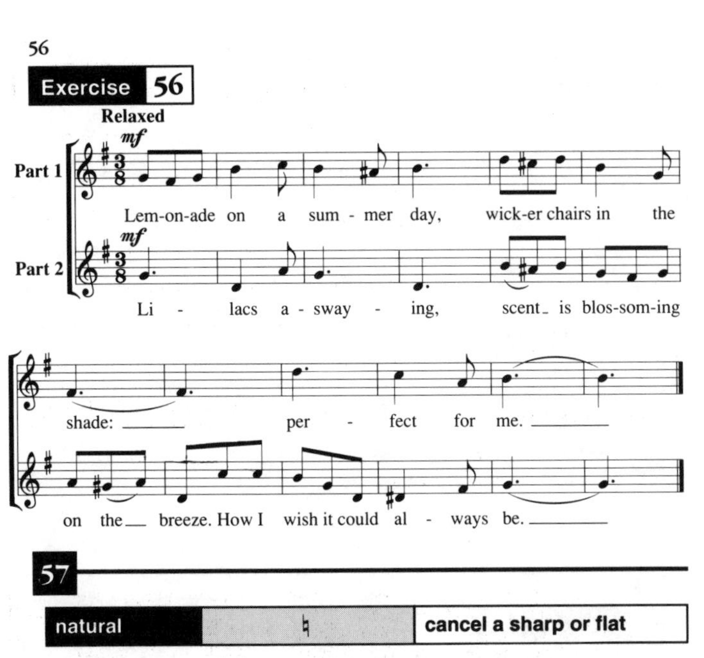

If a note is normally sharp, a natural will **lower** the pitch a semi-tone.

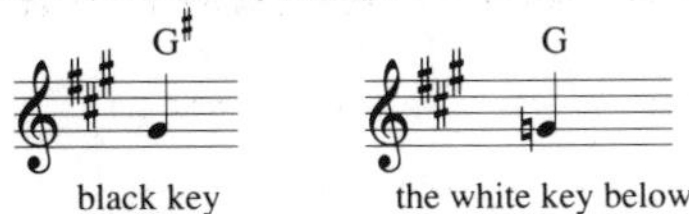

A natural sign that appears after the key signature is valid to the end of the measure.

57

INTRODUCE

natural (after a sharp)

SING Exercise 57:

Standing.

The music switches back and forth from modal to major. Make sure that the G is low enough for a definite modal sound and the C♯ is high enough for a definite major sound. Notice the G♯ in the sixth measure.

REPEAT Exercise 57:

i) Part 1 aloud, Part 2 silently.
ii) Part 2 aloud, Part 1 silently.
iii) Both parts aloud.
iv) Switch parts.

IN REHEARSAL ♮

TIP: It is not necessary for the singers to analyze every temporary shift of key or mode. Sometimes it is enough that they simply sing the accidentals as marked and recognize a change in the sound.

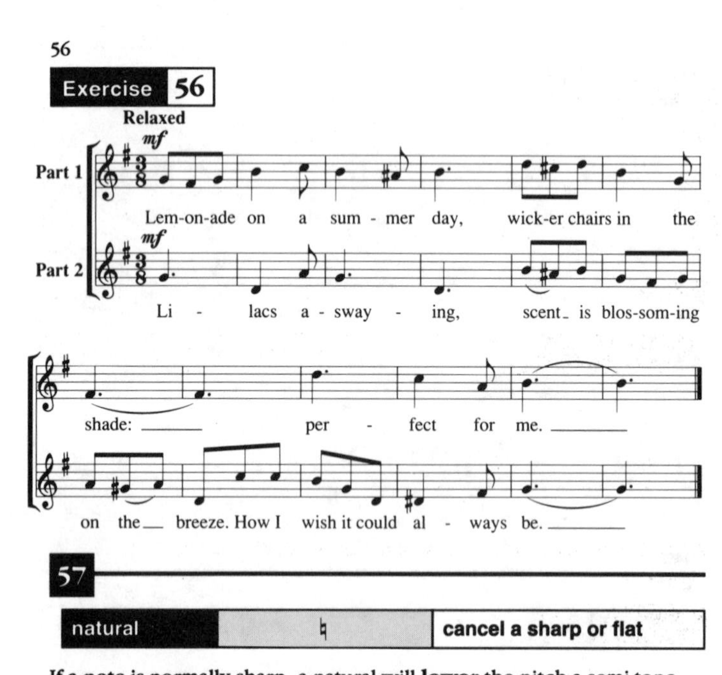

natural	♮	cancel a sharp or flat

If a note is normally sharp, a natural will **lower** the pitch a semi-tone.

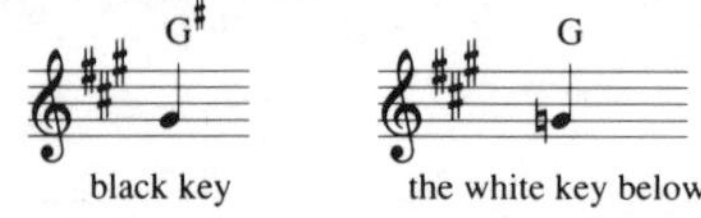

A natural sign that appears after the key signature is valid to the end of the measure.

58

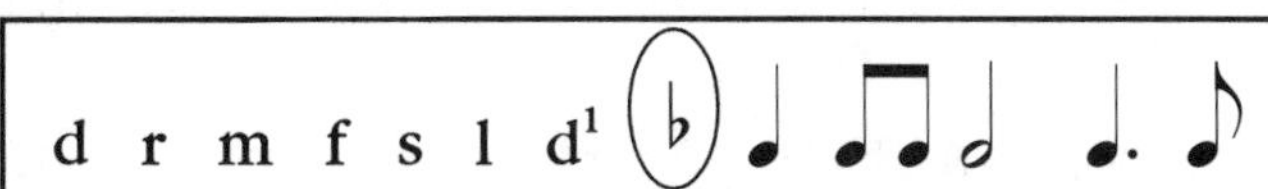

INTRODUCE

flat

Have the singers find D♭ on the keyboard in Lesson 56. D♭ is the same pitch as C♯. Have the singers give another name for:

A♭ (G♯) B♭ (A♯) E♭ (D♯) G♭ (F♯)

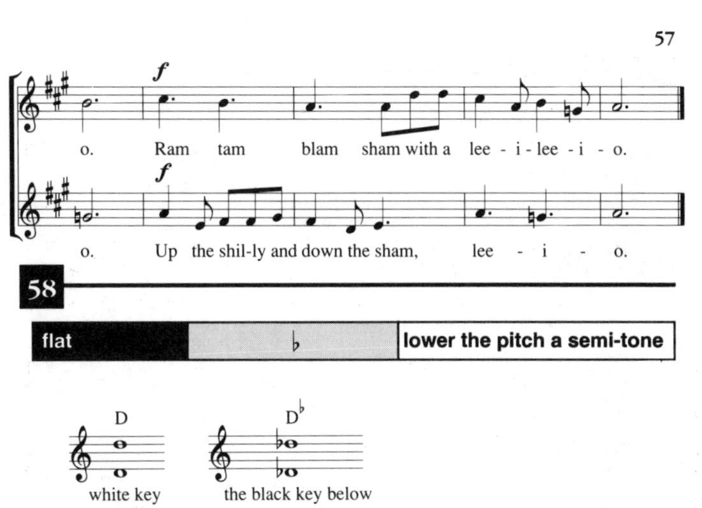

REVIEW: Breathing early in rhythm.

SING Exercise 58:

Singers who prefer brown: Part 1.
Singers who prefer black: Part 2.

NOTE: When an accidental is used consistently with a pitch, the music is probably modal, minor or in some unusual scale. Exercise 58 is in a Mixolydian mode.

REPEAT Exercise 58:

i) If necessary, the singers may mark the beat with vertical lines:

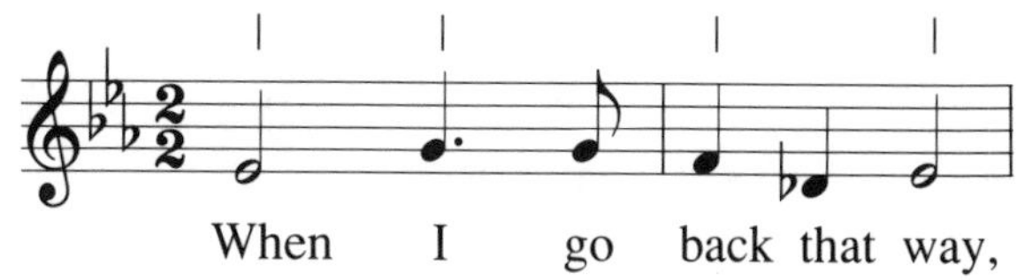

ii) Switch parts.

IN REHEARSAL ♭

TIP: To build up concentration skills, take a few moments in the middle of rehearsal to have the singers imitate the movements of the conductor as he or she does a series of slow movements with arms (and legs if they can be seen by all the singers). Use movements that switch from two to three dimensions to get the mind to think in different ways:

> Move one fist high above the head and slowly to the right. Stop. Move that fist slowly to the left. Stop. Move the fist slowly to the right. Stop and open up the hand with each finger separate. Continue with other movements.

59

INTRODUCE

natural sign (after a flat)

SING Exercise 59:

Be careful not to stretch out the quarter notes for more than two eighth note pulses.

REPEAT Exercise 59:

i) Parts facing each other.
ii) Switch parts.

INTRODUCE

chromatic scale

A chromatic scale may use sharps or flats.

IN REHEARSAL

New Term: chromatic scale

New Concept: natural sign after a flat

TIP: Use a clear downbeat. If singers get lost, remind them to check for the downbeats and barlines.

60

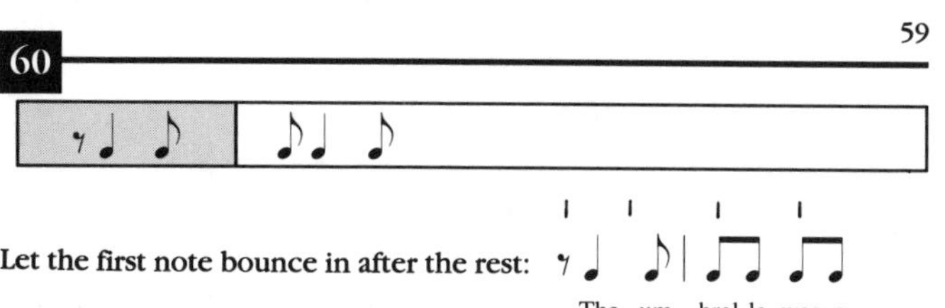

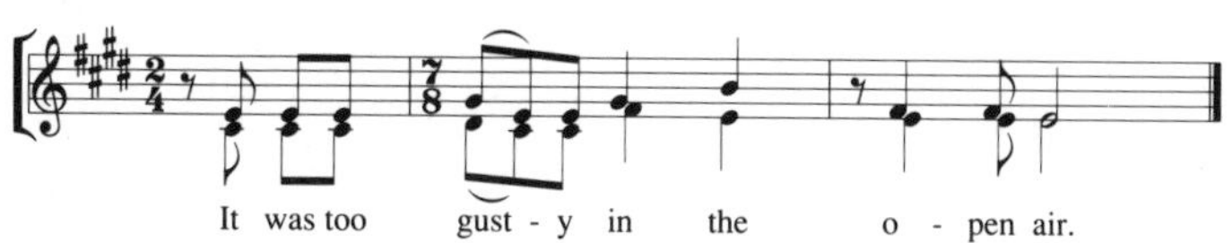

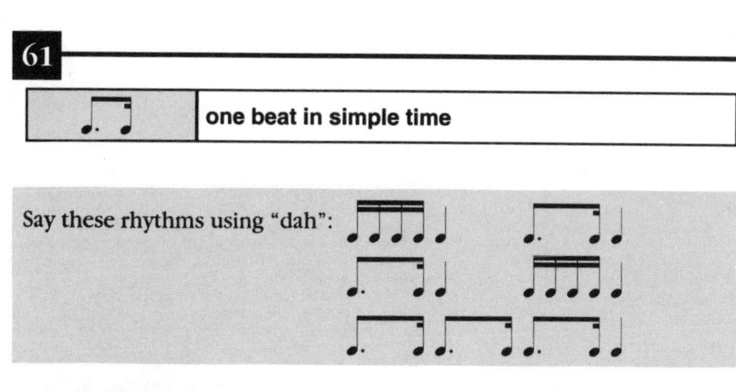

REMINDER Preview the music before you begin.

V82S

REVIEW:

INTRODUCE

SING Exercise 60:

Right side: Part 1 standing.
Left side: Part 2 standing.

REPEAT Exercise 60:

i) Sing the rhythms precisely together. Sing the pitches exactly in tune.
ii) Switch parts.
iii) Front row standing, second row sitting, etc.

IN REHEARSAL

TIP: For accompanied music, play the piano part along with the choir the first time through. Do not play the choral parts. The piano accompaniment will help to give the singers the overall picture of the music; it is easier to sight-sing when you hear your own part in context with the overall picture and the singers will get to the heart of the music more quickly.

61

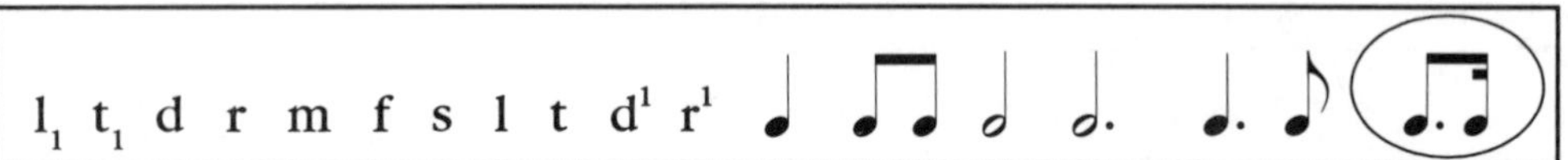

Ask the singers to play a B minor scale on the keyboard on page 55 in the Vocal Edition. Sing the letter names using G♯ A♯ going up and A♮ G♮ going down:

REPEAT naming the whole tones and semi-tones:

EXPLAIN: Sometimes minor scales use accidentals on the sixth or seventh pitches of the scale. Sometimes a minor scale has no accidentals.

SPEAK the practice example. Encourage the singers to feel the sixteenth pulses in each rhythm. Divide the choir into three parts; have each part speak a different line. Switch parts. Switch parts again.

READ the REMINDER in the Vocal Edition.

Ask the singers to determine strategies for finding difficult pitches.

Part 1, third measure:
Sing along silently with Part 2 and sing up a third from the B in the second measure.

Part 2, second measure:
i) Sing along silently with Part 1 until the A. Remember the A until the entry of Part 2;
ii) Sing along silently with Part 1 and then think up a third from the F♯ in the second measure.

SING Exercise 61:

Facing the side of the room.

TIP: If the singers have difficulty with the interval of a fourth, review fourths with them.

READ the REMINDER below the music in the Vocal Edition.

REPEAT Exercise 61:

i) With crisp diction.
ii) Switch parts.

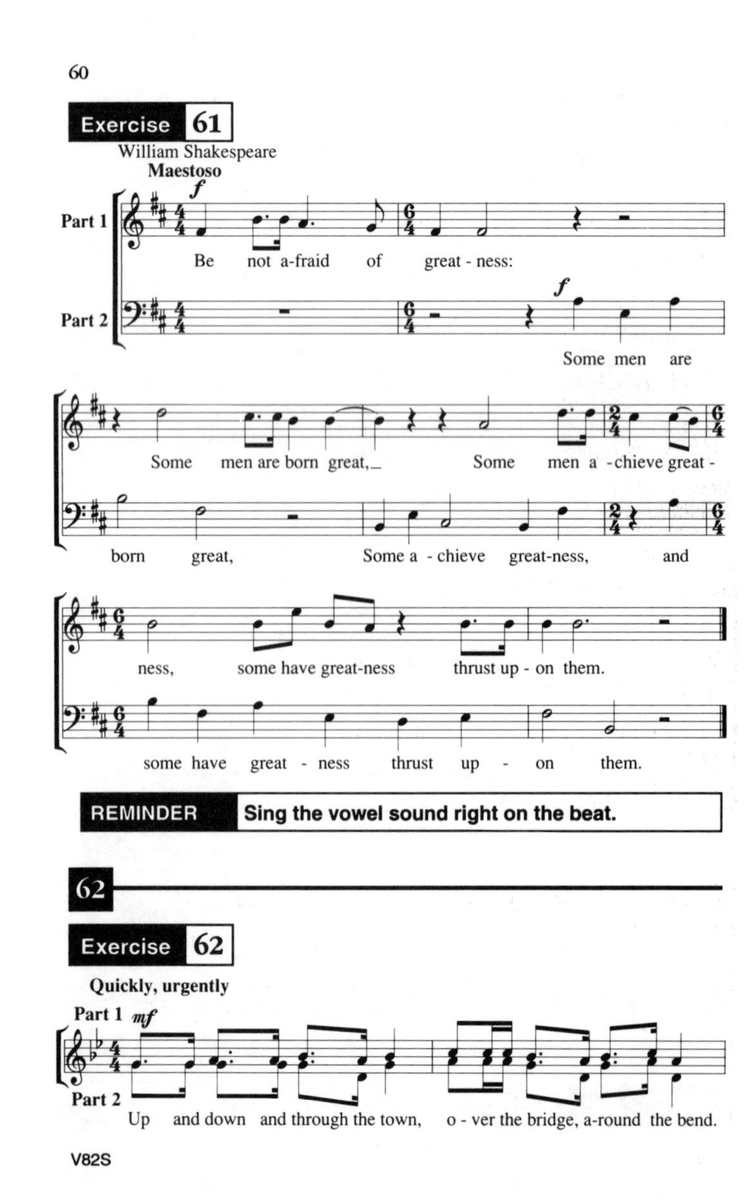

IN REHEARSAL

New Term: minor scale

TIP: Watch the individual singers as they sight-sing. Poor posture means they are not doing their best and may indicate that they are having technical difficulties with the music. Encourage them to sing with a confident posture. Use your eyes (as well as your ears) to spot singers who may need individual attention.

62

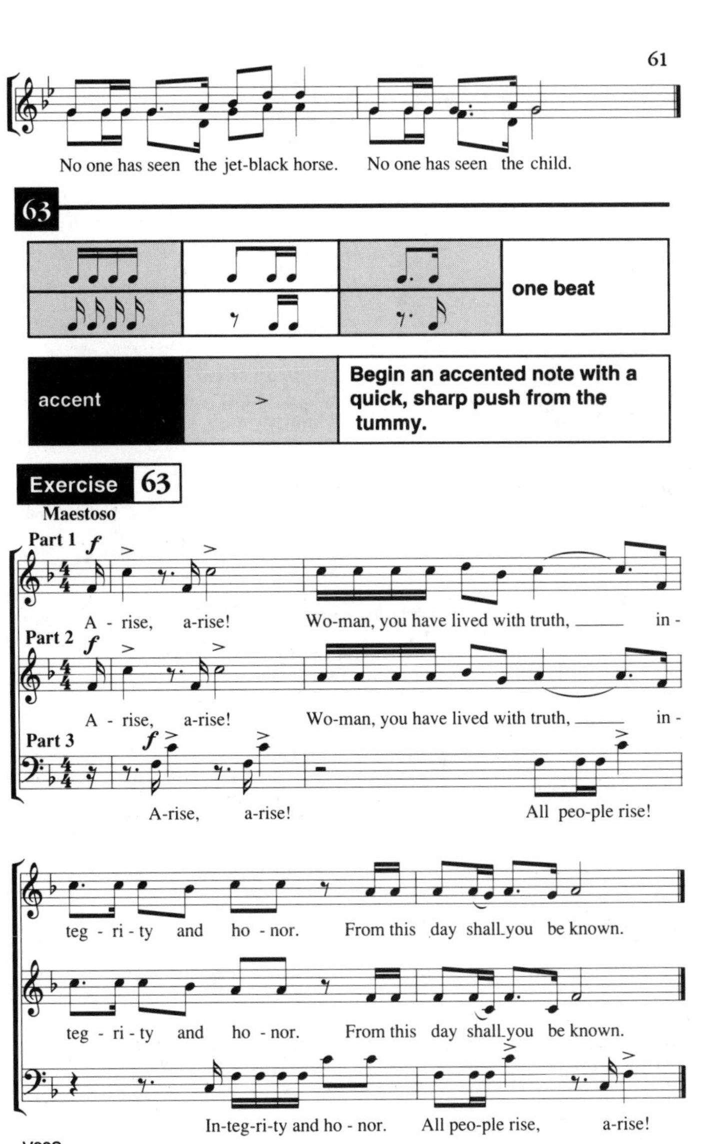

NOTE: Each ♩. ♪ may include more than one pitch.

SING Exercise 62:

Silently.

REPEAT Exercise 62:

i) Aloud.
ii) Switch parts.

IN REHEARSAL

TIP: Let your eyes make contact with each singer sometime during the rehearsal. This helps to give the singers the courage to think of themselves as individuals (rather than just part of an ensemble) so that they will become more independent in their sight-singing.

63

INTRODUCE

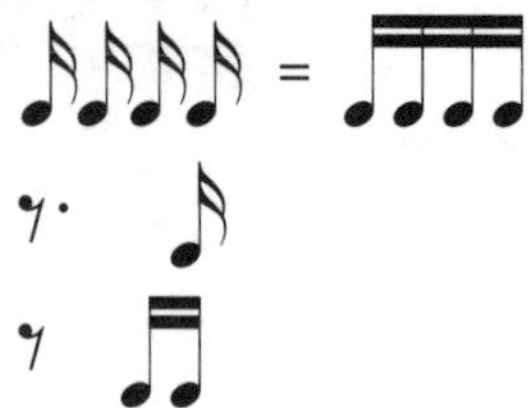

EXPLAIN: A sixteenth note has two flags; the sixteenth rest, in the first measure of part three, has two flags.

INTRODUCE

accent

The throat tends to be more relaxed for an accent if the singer is concentrating on the tummy.

SING Exercise 63:

Standing.

REPEAT Exercise 63:

Switch parts. Check posture.

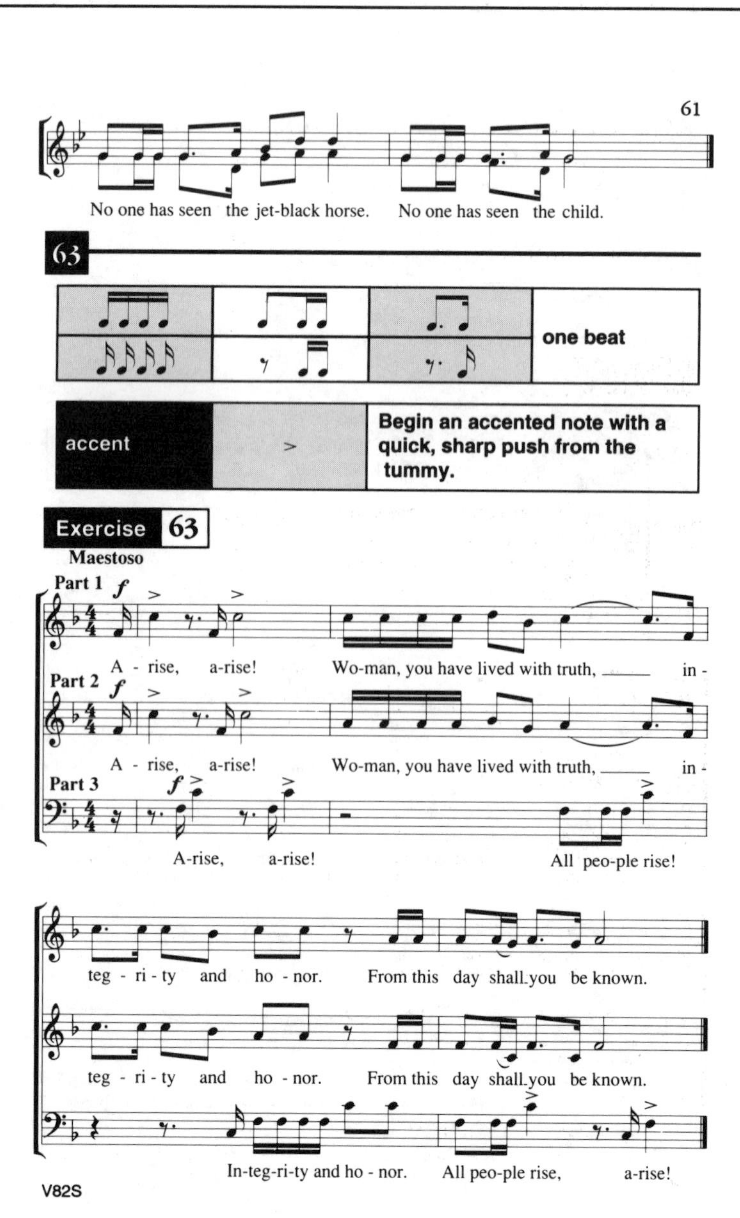

IN REHEARSAL

New Term: accent

TIP: To improve concentration skills, have the singers focus on the conductor's pencil while they sing a familiar piece. The conductor moves the pencil to different locations (i.e. right, left, on top of the head, bouncing on one arm) and then moves to different locations in the rehearsal room as they sing. As the conductor moves about the room, he or she should change direction frequently.

64

INTRODUCE

SPEAK the practice example. Encourage the singers to feel the sixteenth pulses in each rhythm. Put the emphasis on the beat:

Divide the choir into three parts; have each part speak a different line. Switch parts. Switch parts again.

NOTE: Exercise 64 starts on "ti," the leading tone.

SING Exercise 64:

Singers with birthdays from January to April: Part 1.
Singers with birthdays from May to August: Part 2.
Singers with birthdays from September to December: Part 3.

REVIEW: Dissonance.

REPEAT Exercise 64:

i) Emphasize the first sixteenth note in each grouping.
ii) Have a singer choose a tempo and conduct.
iii) Switch parts. Use a different conductor.
iv) Switch parts again.

IN REHEARSAL

TIP: Each time you repeat a passage in the music, give the singers something different to concentrate on so that the singers will be thinking about the music itself instead of just "singing along." The better they understand music intellectually and emotionally, the more their sight-singing will improve.

65

65

Exercise 65

66

triplet		one beat
fermata		hold

2/4 sounds like 6/8

Say these rhythms using "dah":

NOTE: Each (rhythm) may include more than one pitch.

SING Exercise 65:

Male singers: Part 3.
Female singers who prefer lemon flavor: Part 1.
Female singers who prefer orange flavor: Part 2.

REPEAT Exercise 65:

i) Facing the back of the room.
ii) Choose a different part.

IN REHEARSAL

TIP: During warmups in parts, divide the singers according to their preference for different flavors (i.e. lemon, orange, cherry).

66

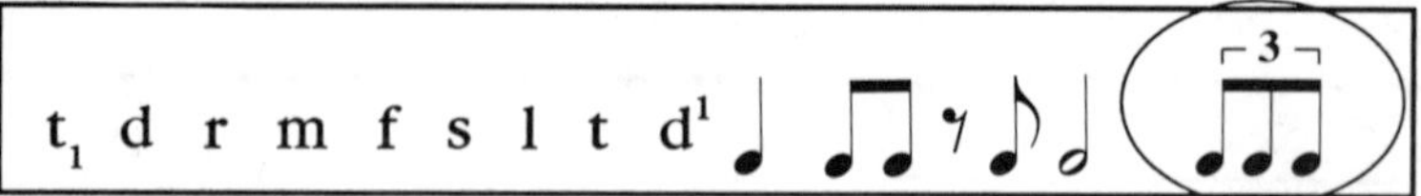

INTRODUCE

triplet

SPEAK the practice example. Have half of the singers say the first line while the rest say the second line. Switch parts.

INTRODUCE

fermata

63

65

Exercise 65

William Butler Yeats

Simply *mf*

Part 1: When I play on my fid-dle in _ Doo-ney, _ folk _ dance like a wave of the sea. They _ dance.

Part 2: When I play ___ on my fid-dle, folk dance _ like a wave of the sea. They _ dance.

Part 3: When I play on my fid-dle in Doo-ney, _ folk _ dance like a wave _____ of the sea. They dance like a wave.

66

triplet	3	one beat

2/4 sounds like 6/8

Say these rhythms using "dah":

fermata	𝄐	hold

V82S

SING Exercise 66:

First row of singers: Part 3 silently.
Second row of singers: Part 2 silently.
Third row of singers: Part 1 silently.

REVIEW: Pitch framework.

REPEAT Exercise 66:

Aloud (after the singers have had a moment to work out any problems silently).
Smooth out the triplets and be ready for the fermata.

NOTE: Lesson 66 is continued on page 128.

REVIEW: Check Exercise 66 for dissonances:

REPEAT Exercise 66:

i) Switch parts. Center the dissonant pitches quickly.
ii) Switch parts.

IN REHEARSAL

TIP: Occasionally use several unexpected fermatas in a warmup or rehearsal piece.

67

INTRODUCE

cue for entry on the tonic

PREVIEW TIP: Check for imitation:

SING Exercise 67:

Singers who prefer brown: Part 1.
Singers who prefer black: Part 2.

REPEAT Exercise 67:

i) Switch parts.
ii) Front row standing, second row sitting, etc.

IN REHEARSAL

TIP: It is easier to sight-sing music at a fast tempo if you sing lightly because then the voice is more flexible for changing rhythms and pitches.

65

67

one beat

USING CUES If your entry is on the tonic, simply think "home."

Exercise 67

A. W. E. O'Shaughnessy

V82S

68

SING Exercise 68:

Silently.

REPEAT Exercise 68:

Aloud. Notice the F♯ in the fourth measure of Part 2.

REPEAT Exercise 68:

Switch parts. Remind the singers to watch the conductor's downbeat for the barlines.

IN REHEARSAL

TIP: When beginning a new piece, occasionally ask the singers to memorize a phrase or two before they are familiar with the music. Sing without looking at the music. Then have them check the details of the music again to see how well they have done.

This activity trains the eyes to look intensively at all the details.

69

67

69

MODULATION **Before starting a new piece, find all the key signature changes and mark each tonic in pencil. In measure 3, think of the B as "so" in the new key.**

Exercise 69

V82S

NOTE: Sing Exercise 69 with 3 parts together or each part separately.

INTRODUCE

modulation from major to major

Have the singers mark the tonic at the beginning of each section:

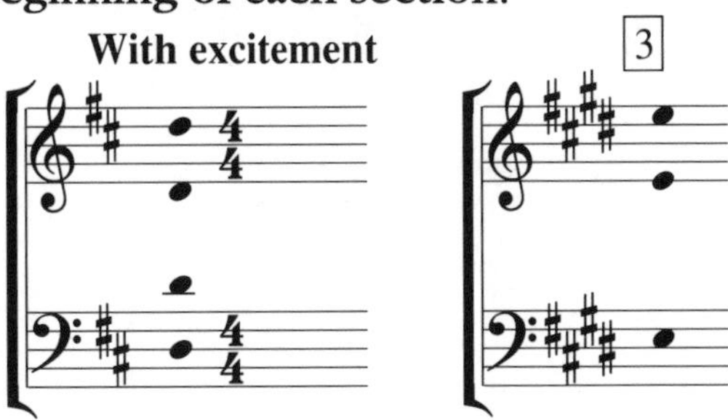

TIP: Part 2 singers can think "mi" in the new key for their entry in the fourth measure.

SING Exercise 69:

Singers who prefer lemon flavor: Part 2.
Singers who prefer orange flavor: Part 1.
Singers who prefer cherry flavor: Part 3.

REPEAT Exercise 69:

i) Add more details (i.e. dynamics, better diction, etc.); encourage each singer to monitor their own progress.
ii) Switch parts.
iii) Switch parts again.

IN REHEARSAL

New Concept: modulation from major to major

TIP: Singers should keep their pencil ready in one hand throughout the rehearsal so that they can mark their scores as they sing. It is amazing how quickly they learn how to manipulate the page turns while holding a pencil.

70

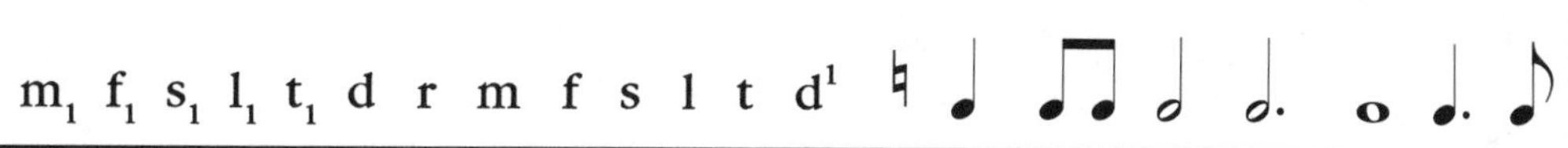

REVIEW: Octaves.

PREVIEW TIPS: i) Mark the tonic at the beginning of each section:

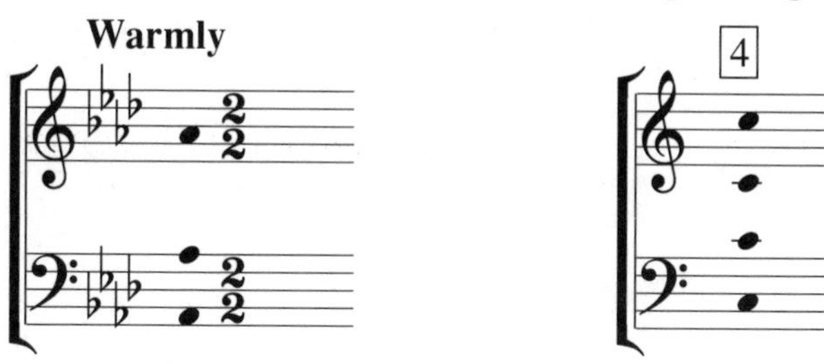

ii) Ask the singers to think of a strategy for the modulation (think "home" while singing the C in the fourth measure).

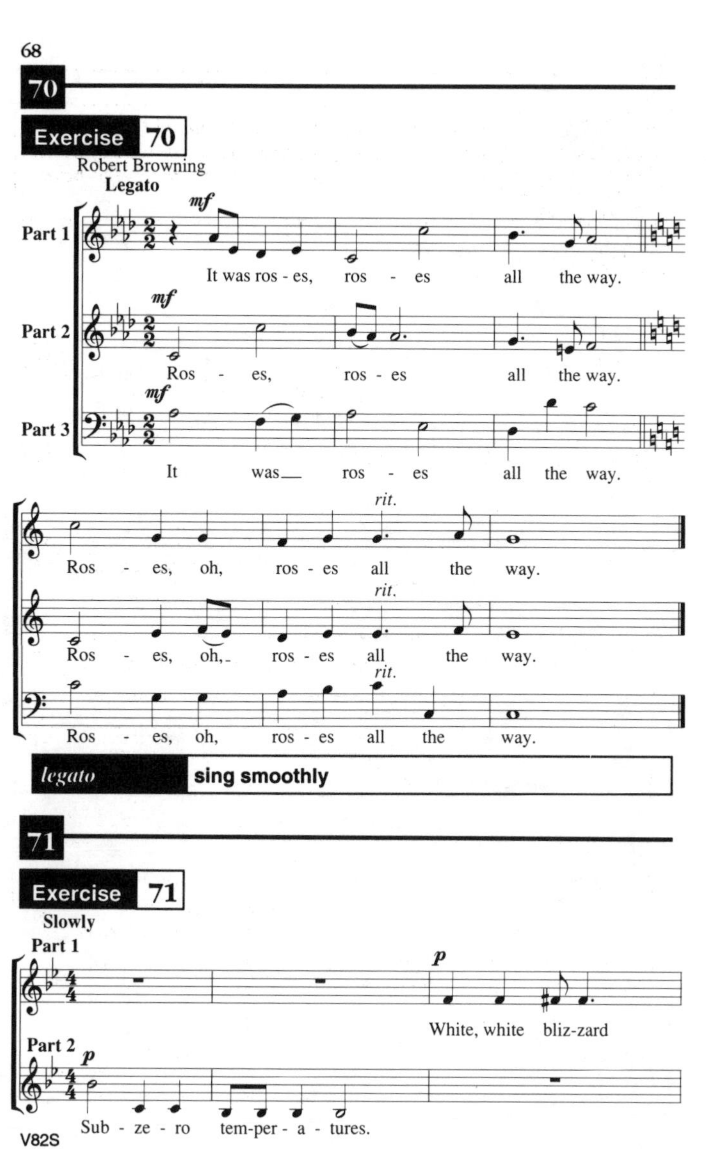

SING Exercise 70:

Standing.

INTRODUCE

legato

REMINDER: Keep your eyes moving a measure ahead of the sound.

REPEAT Exercise 70:

i) Face the back of the room.
ii) Switch parts.

IN REHEARSAL

New Term: ***legato***

TIP: Encourage the singers to look ahead with their eyes.

71

SING Exercise 71:

First and third rows of singers: Part 1.
Second and fourth rows of singers: Part 2.

If the singers have difficulty with the seventh in the first measure, ask them to add an intermediary pitch:

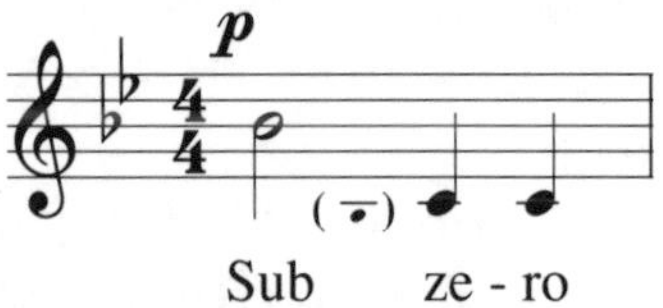

REPEAT Exercise 71:

i) Add more details (i.e. dynamics, phrasing, etc.).
ii) Switch parts.

IN REHEARSAL

TIP: Occasionally alternate measures aloud and silent to improve precision and independence of singers or to help memorize the music.

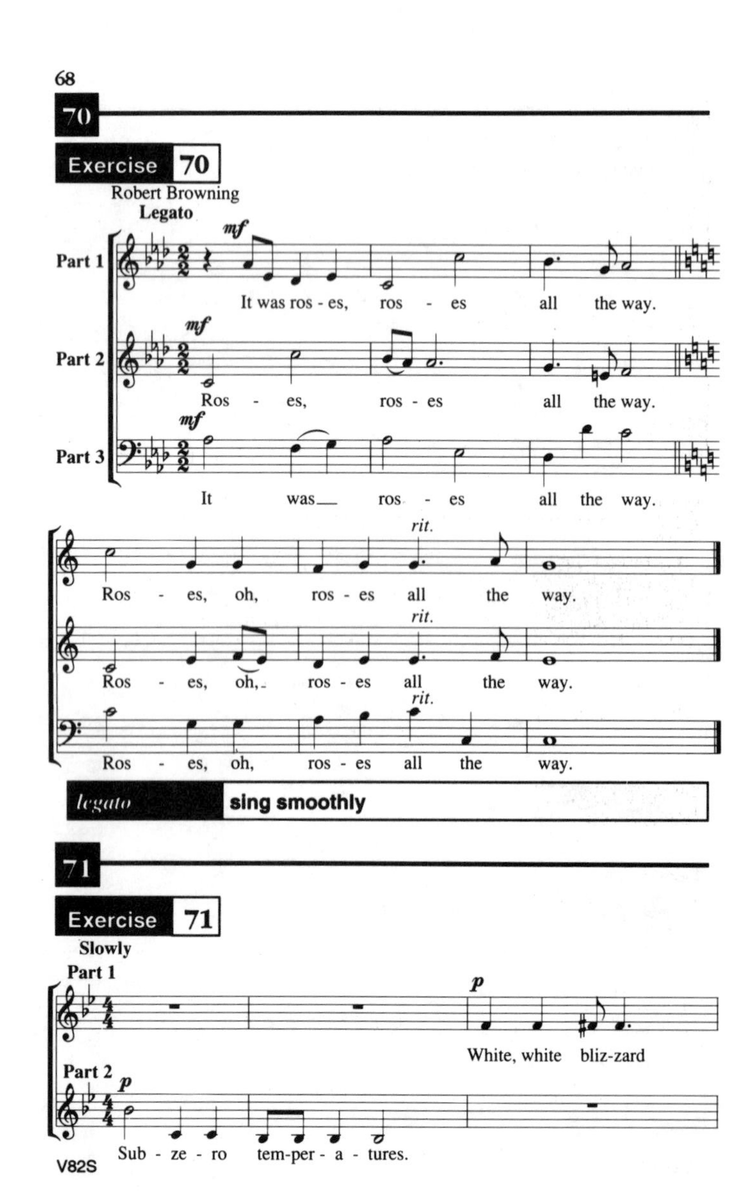

72

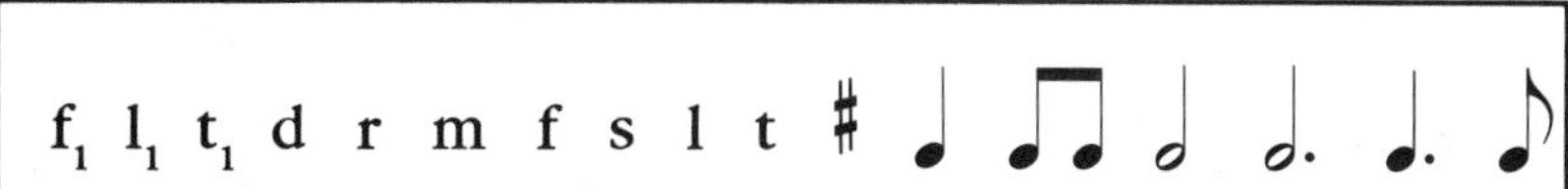

INTRODUCE

ninth

SING the practice example above the music in the Vocal Edition.

PREVIEW TIP: Mark the tonic at the beginning of each section:

SING Exercise 72:

Singers who prefer blue: Part 1.
Singers who prefer green: Part 2.

TIP: If Part 2 singers have difficulty with the pitch for the eighth measure, they may listen to the pitch of Part 1 in the preceding measure while continuing to sing their own part:

REPEAT Exercise 72:

i) Make each vowel sound pure.
ii) Switch parts.

IN REHEARSAL

New Term: ninth

TIP: Occasionally use silent singing to have the singers imagine the best quality tone or more musical expression. "Imaging" can make dramatic changes in a short time.

73

INTRODUCE

modulation from minor to minor

Have the singers mark the tonic at the beginning of each section:

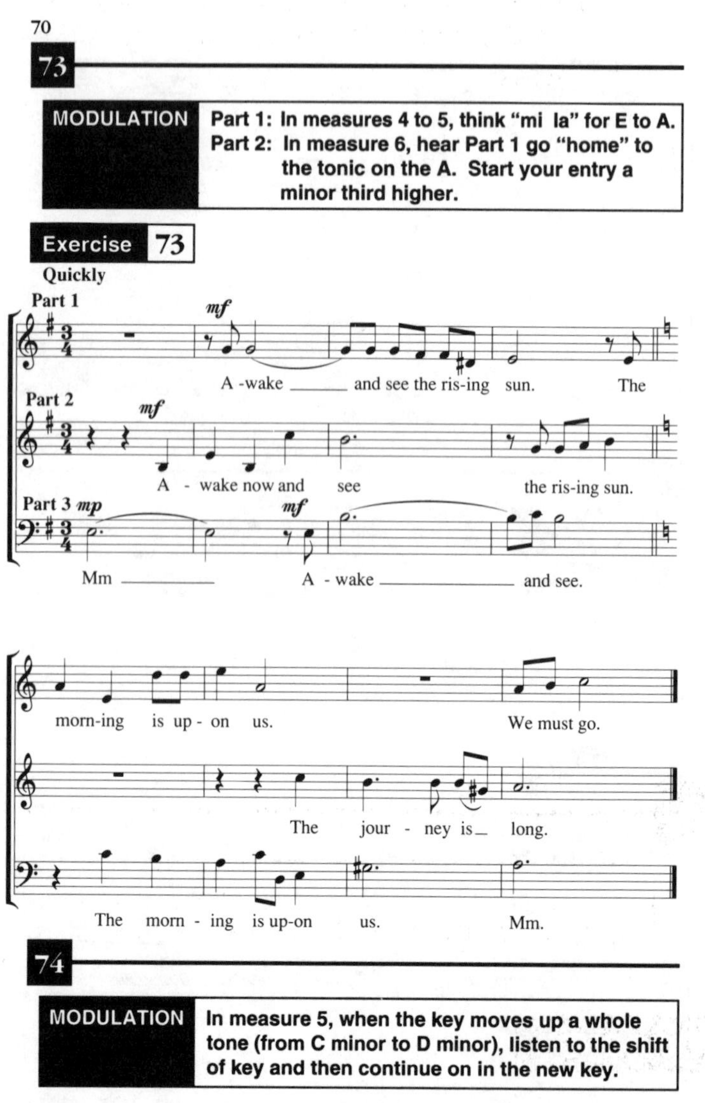

SING Exercise 73

REPEAT Exercise 73:

i) Standing.
ii) Singers with birthdays in a month beginning with "J" or "O": Part 3.
Singers with birthdays in a month beginning with "M" or "A": Part 2.
Rest of singers: Part 1.

IN REHEARSAL

New Concept: modulation from minor to minor

TIP: If the singers do not always have a pencil:
i) Ask them to keep a sharpened pencil in their choir folders; or
ii) Pass around a box of sharpened pencils at the beginning of each rehearsal. At the end of the rehearsal they can leave the pencils in the box as they leave.

74

INTRODUCE

modulation with a shift in key

REMINDER: Mark the tonic at the beginning of each section:

SING Exercise 74:

Silently.

NOTE: Part 2 has an E natural in the fifth measure.

REPEAT Exercise 74

i) Aloud. Check posture.
ii) Face the back of the room.
Switch parts.

IN REHEARSAL

New Concept: modulation with a shift in key

TIP: If the singing is mechanical-sounding, ask the singers to put a slight emphasis on the important words or on the first eighth note of each group of eighth notes.

75

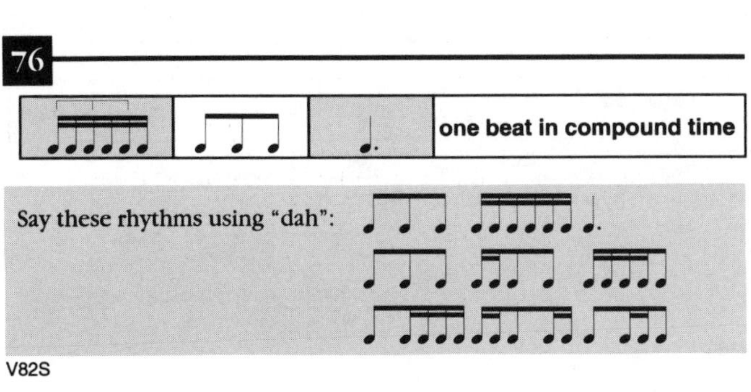

SING Exercise 75:

Facing a partner who is singing a different part.

If necessary, ask the singers to mark the beat with vertical lines.

REPEAT Exercise 75:

i) Switch partners.
ii) Switch parts.

IN REHEARSAL

TIP: During a warmup ask the singers to face a partner who is singing a different part.

76

INTRODUCE

SPEAK the practice example. Divide the choir into three parts; have each part speak a different line. Switch parts. Switch parts again.

READ the REMINDER above the music in the Vocal Edition.

TIP: Tell the singers whether you will be conducting two preparatory beats or six pulses before beginning Exercise 76.

SING Exercise 76:

Singers in the middle: Part 2.
Singers on the two sides: Part 1.

REVIEW: Breathing early in rhythm.

REPEAT Exercise 76:

i) Sing the vowel sound on the beat. Do not stretch out the "l."
ii) Switch parts. Bounce each sixteenth note for clarity of pitch.

IN REHEARSAL

TIP: Sometime during each rehearsal, ask a singer to sing a phrase solo.

77

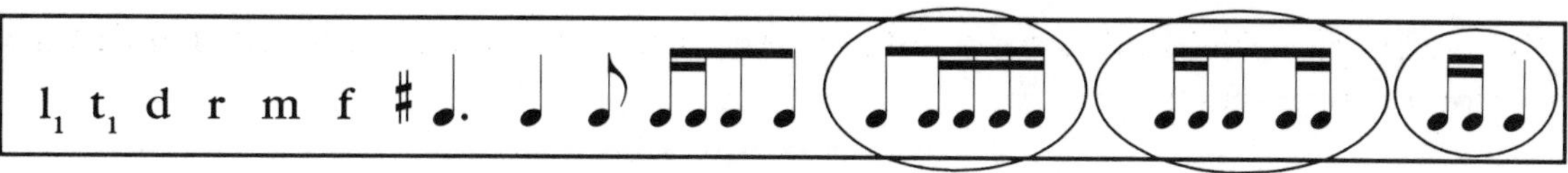

73

REMINDER Check your posture.

Exercise 76

Brightly

Part 1 *mf* Let — the – trum-pet re - sound. Oh, — let the trum-pet re - sound.

Part 2 *mf* Let — the – trum-pet re - sound. Let – the loud cym - bals crash. Oh, – let – the – trum-pet re - sound.

77

V82S

TIP: Because of the slow tempo, Exercise 77 should be conducted with 6 beats to the measure, rather than two.

SING Exercise 77

REPEAT Exercise 77:

i) Facing one side of the room.
ii) Switch parts. Singers on right side stand; singers on left side sit.

IN REHEARSAL

TIP: Sometimes the conductor will decide to conduct $\frac{4}{4}$ music with two beats to the bar, rather than four. Inform the singers about the change in conducting pattern and ask them to change the time signature to cut time.

78

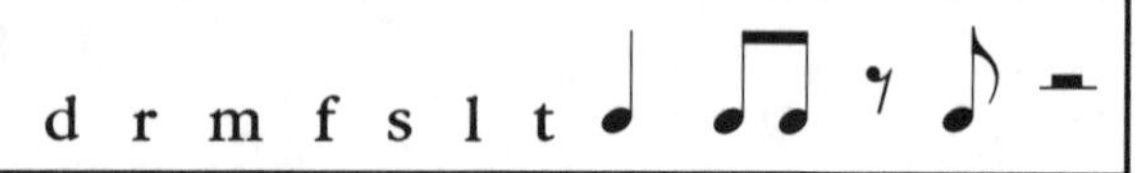

INTRODUCE

major and minor thirds

SING the practice example in the Vocal Edition at a slow tempo.

REPEAT at a faster tempo.

See page 179 in the Teacher's Edition for an activity to memorize the intervals of a major and minor third.

NOTE: Although the singers have learned the sound of a third, now they need to memorize major and minor thirds so well that they will be able to remember them when they appear in unusual context in the music.

For most tonal music, the singer need not be concerned whether a third is major or minor; the singer will usually sing the right interval to fit with the sound of the major or minor key of the music. However, when the music is chromatic or atonal, it is important to know the difference between major and minor thirds.

INTRODUCE

staccato

SING Exercise 78:

Singers with birthdays in a month beginning with "J" or "O": Part 3.
Singers with birthdays in a month beginning with "M" or "A": Part 2.
Rest of singers: Part 1.

REVIEW: Ask the singers to find which intervals are semi-tones in Exercise 78 (F♯ to G).

REMINDER: Have the singers watch the conductor's downbeat for the barlines. Sing every pitch in tune.

REPEAT Exercise 78:

i) Sing the first measure aloud, second measure silently, etc.
ii) Sing entire exercise aloud.

IN REHEARSAL

New Terms: major third, minor third

TIP: For warmups in parts, divide singers according to their birthdays (see previous page).

79

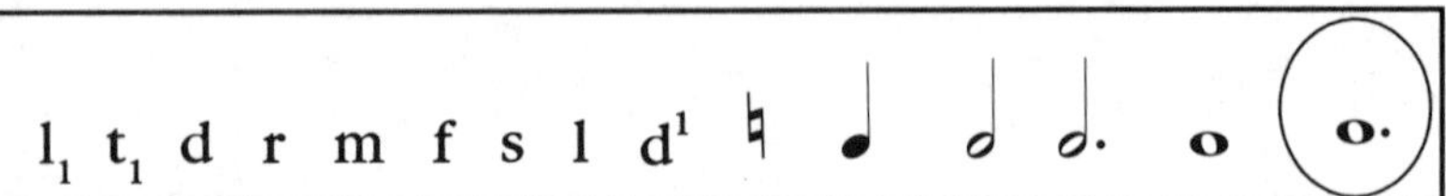

INTRODUCE

whole note gets the beat

Cut time is often used in early music. The eyes should do two bounces in each measure:

REVIEW: i) Cut time when 𝅗𝅥 = one beat.
ii) Major and minor thirds.

PREVIEW TIPS: i) Check the modulation (D minor to A minor).
ii) Check for imitation:

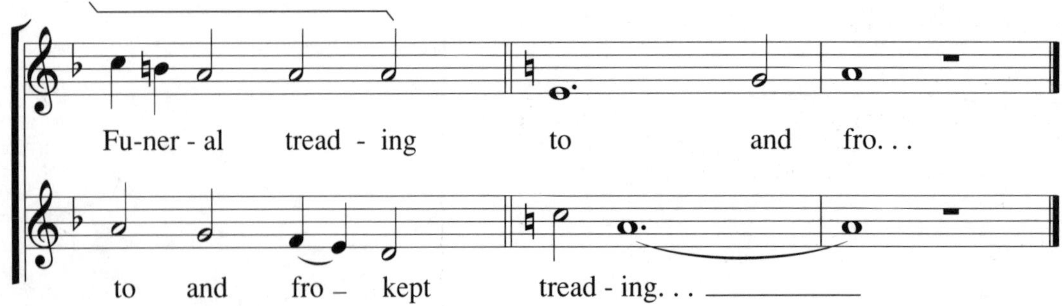

SING Exercise 79:

Singers with birthdays from January to April: Part 1.
Singers with birthdays from May to August: Part 2.
Singers with birthdays from September to December: Part 3.

REPEAT Exercise 79:

i) Facing the side of the room.
ii) Each singer choose a new part to sing.

IN REHEARSAL

New Concept: whole note gets the beat

TIP: In music where the whole note gets one beat, the singers may wish to mark their scores with vertical lines.

80

INTRODUCE

alternating time signatures

SING Exercise 80:

Silently.

REMINDER: Encourage the singers to let their eyes bounce continuously across the page slightly ahead of the music.

REPEAT Exercise 80:

i) Aloud. Notice how the pitch shifts back and forth from F♯ to F♮.
ii) Have two singers sing it as a duet.
iii) Everyone stand and sing. Switch parts.

IN REHEARSAL

New Concept: alternating time signatures

TIP: If the music is sectional, sight-sing part of the piece; then rehearse that section for a few moments. Then sight-sing a new section of the piece.

81

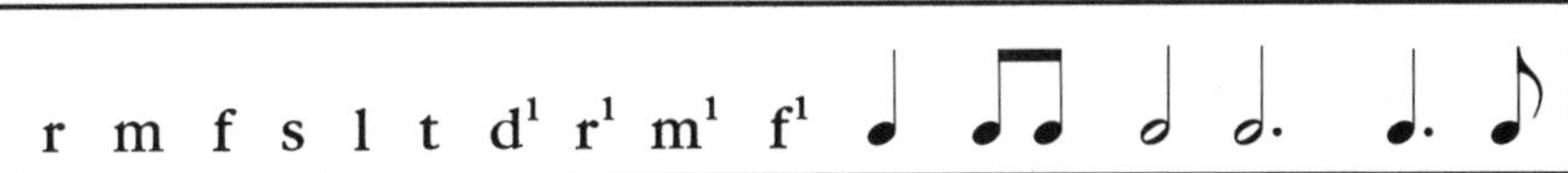

77

ii) At measure 3, the tactus changes to 𝅗𝅥. ; here each measure has only one tactus (or strong beat). The conductor will conduct a steady tactus throughout Exercise 81:

D.C. al Fine	go back to the beginning and start singing it again; stop at "*Fine*"
Fine	the end

Exercise 81

Lightly

mf

Part 1: Spring is a time for love, Fa la la la la la la la la. Ev - 'ry hawk be - comes a dove, Fa la la la la la.

Part 2: Spring is a time for love, Fa la la la la la la la la. Ev - 'ry hawk a dove, Fa la la la la la.

Fine

D. C. al Fine

V82S

INTRODUCE

tactus

For the $\frac{3}{4}$ measures, the conductor will use one beat per bar. This beat will be at the same speed as each of the beats in cut time. The music in $\frac{3}{4}$ will seem fast because there will be three quarter notes for each beat instead of two. This gives a dance-like feeling typical of early music.

INTRODUCE

D.C. al Fine
Fine

SING Exercise 81

TIP: Mark the beat for the transition:

REPEAT Exercise 81:

i) Concentrating on the tuning.
ii) Facing a partner who is singing a different part (imagine you are madrigal singers).
iii) Switch parts.

IN REHEARSAL

New Terms: tactus, ***D.C. al Fine, Fine***

TIP: Whenever the singer has a problem while sight-singing, they should quickly mark the top corner of that page and continue singing without a break:

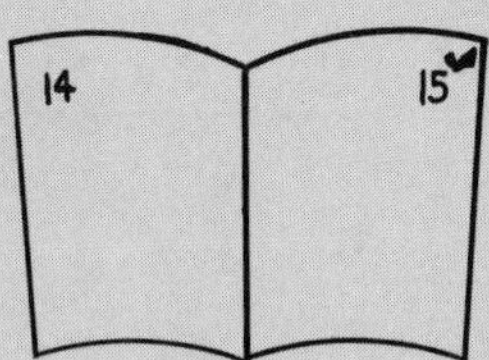

When the singer has time, they can find the problem page easily and determine a strategy to correct the problem.

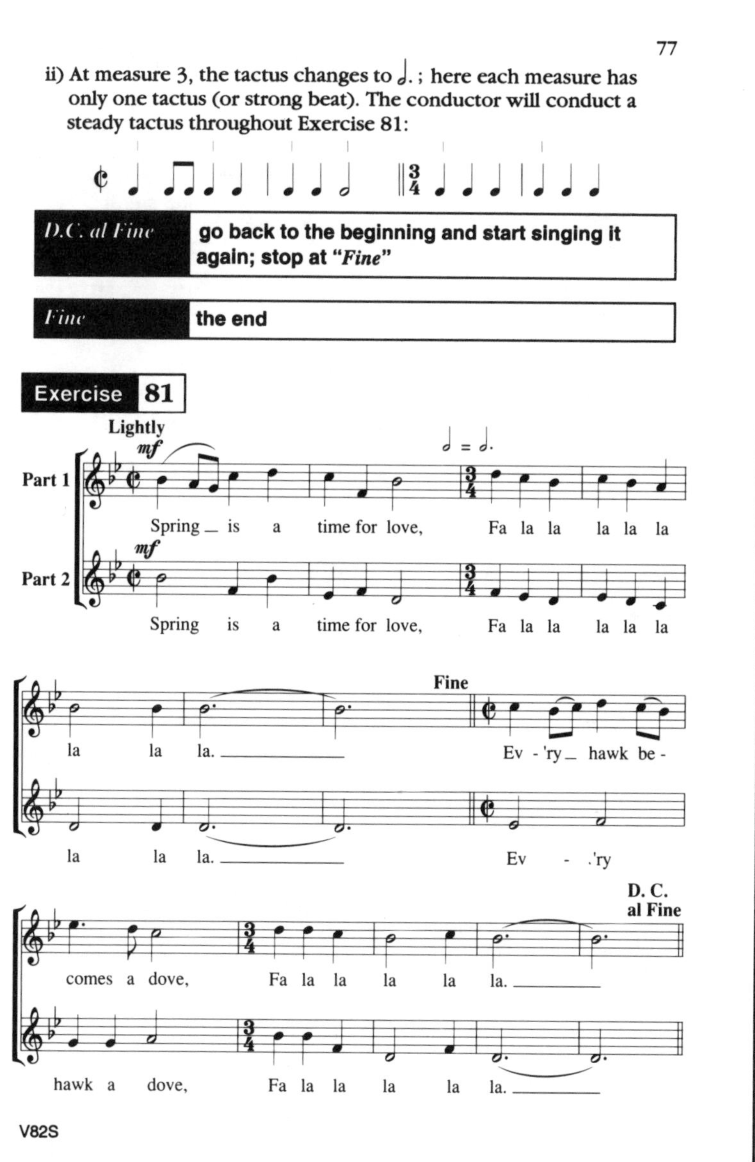

77

ii) At measure 3, the tactus changes to 𝅗𝅥. ; here each measure has only one tactus (or strong beat). The conductor will conduct a steady tactus throughout Exercise 81:

D.C. al Fine	**go back to the beginning and start singing it again; stop at "*Fine*"**
Fine	**the end**

Exercise 81

V82S

◆ ◆ ◆ Milestone 8 ◆ ◆ ◆
ADVANCED INTERVAL TRAINING

82

INTRODUCE

tritone

Sometimes the tritone is called "the devil's interval" because it sounds so harsh.

See page 179 in the Teacher's Edition for an activity to memorize the interval of a tritone.

INTRODUCE

(double whole note)

PREVIEW TIP: Check the tactus.

SING Exercise 82:

Part 1 facing Part 2.

REPEAT Exercise 82:

i) Scanning the eyes over the full score.
ii) Switch parts. Make each vowel sound pure.

78

◆ ◆ ◆ MILESTONE 8 ◆ ◆ ◆
Advanced Interval Training

82

tritone		augmented fourth or diminished fifth	between a fourth and a fifth
			four beats in 4/2

Exercise 82

V82S

IN REHEARSAL

New Terms: tritone, augmented fourth, diminished fifth, double whole note

TIP: Review the pitch framework. As the singers memorize more intervals, they can find (or confirm) unusual pitches by comparing them with the framework (i.e. in Exercise 82, F♮ is a semi-tone above E).

83

INTRODUCE

courtesy accidentals

When it is not necessary to mark accidentals, sometimes the publisher may put them in anyway to help the singer. The courtesy accidentals have brackets around them.

PREVIEW TIP: Ask the singers to use the keyboard on page 55 of the Vocal Edition to find:

i) C♯ ii) D♭ iii) A♭ iv) G♯

Check the fourth measure of Part 3. What is the other letter name for the A♭ (G♯)? A♭ to B is really a minor third but looks like a second. It may help if the singers think of G♯ to B and mark it in their scores as an enharmonic change:

REVIEW: Major and minor seconds.

SING Exercise 83:

Each part separately at a slow tempo.

TIP: In Exercise 83, semi-tones are much more common than whole tones. Circle the whole tones in each part.

REPEAT Exercise 83:

i) All parts together (sopranos on Part 1, altos on Part 2, baritones on Part 3).
ii) Switch parts. Encourage each singer to monitor their own progress.
iii) Switch parts.

IN REHEARSAL

New Term: courtesy accidental

TIP: Notice any enharmonic changes where it would be easier for the singers to rename a pitch (i.e. A♭ to G♯). Mark the score.

84

REVIEW: Fourths.

See page 179 in the Teacher's Edition for an activity to memorize the interval of a fourth.

PREVIEW TIP: Check the cues.

READ the REMINDER in the Vocal Edition.

SING Exercise 84:

Singers who prefer cherry flavor: Part 1.
Singers who prefer lemon flavor: Part 2.
Singers who prefer orange flavor: Part 3.

READ the TIP after the music in the Vocal Edition.

REPEAT Exercise 84:

i) Scanning the eyes over the full score. On a new entry, it is usually easier to sing an easy interval from a pitch in another part than to sing a tritone from the last pitch in your own part (i.e. Parts 2 and 3, fourth measure).
ii) Switch parts and stand.
iii) Switch parts and face the back of the room.

IN REHEARSAL

TIP: The conductor should always look supportive when the choir is sight-singing a new piece.

85

INTRODUCE

It is important to feel a strong beat and fit the rhythm within the framework of the beat.

SPEAK the practice example. Divide the choir into three parts; have each part speak a different line. Switch parts. Switch parts again.

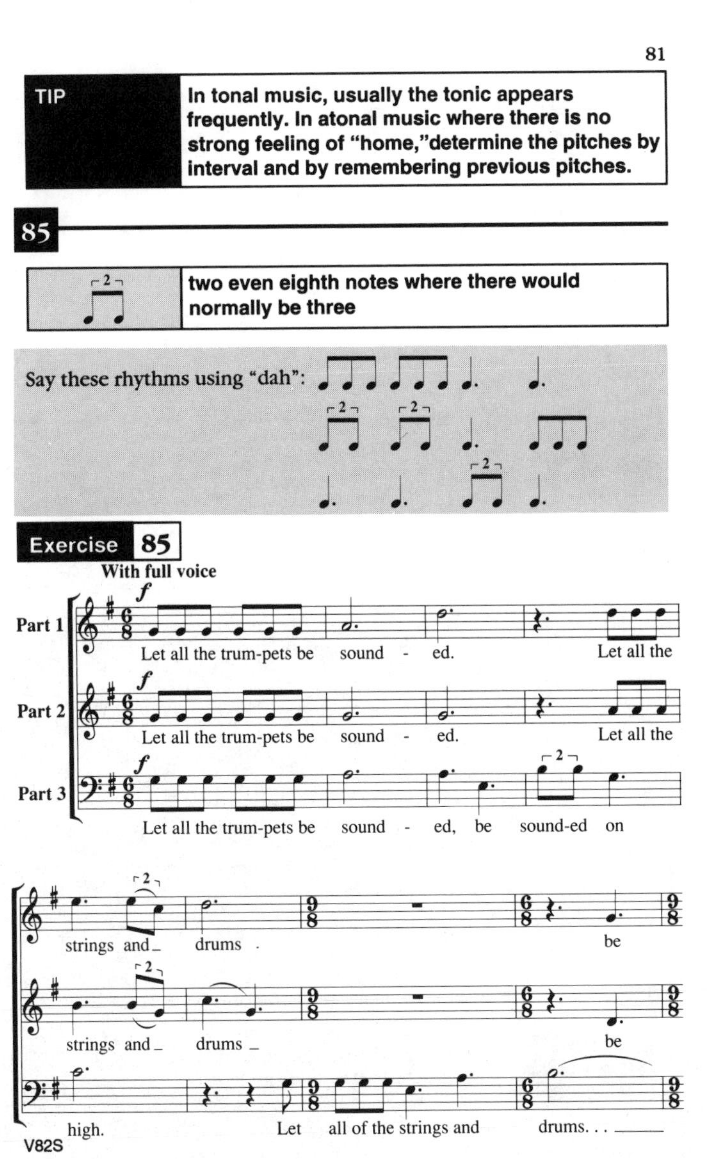

81

TIP In tonal music, usually the tonic appears frequently. In atonal music where there is no strong feeling of "home,"determine the pitches by interval and by remembering previous pitches.

85

two even eighth notes where there would normally be three

Say these rhythms using "dah":

Exercise 85

With full voice

Part 1: Let all the trum-pets be sound - ed. Let all the strings and_ drums . be

Part 2: Let all the trum-pets be sound - ed. Let all the strings and_ drums_ be

Part 3: Let all the trum-pets be sound - ed, be sound-ed on high. Let all of the strings and drums. . . ___

V82S

SING Exercise 85:

First row sitting: Part 1.
Second row standing: Part 2.
Third row sitting: Part 3.

REPEAT Exercise 85:

i) Scanning the eyes over the full score.
ii) Switch parts. Emphasize the first note in each grouping:

iii) Switch parts again.

IN REHEARSAL

TIP: In most situations it is best to seat your choir in this way:

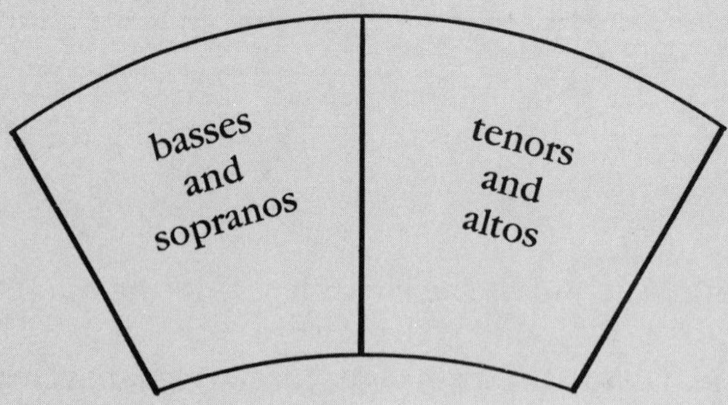

Because this setup helps the singers to tune better, it makes it easier for them to sight-sing. **See page 193** in the Teacher's Edition for a detailed explanation.

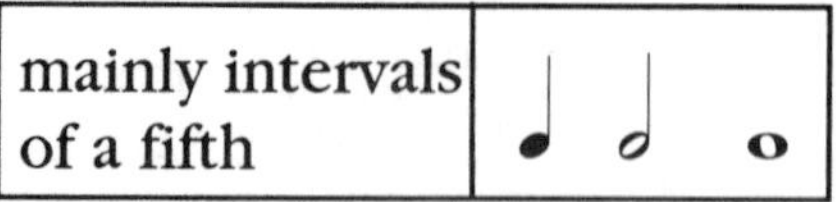

REVIEW: Fifths.

See page 179 in the Teacher's Edition for an activity to memorize the interval of a fifth.

SING Exercise 86:

Singers with birthdays in a month which is spelled with the letter "e": Part 1.
Rest of singers: Part 2.

REPEAT Exercise 86:

i) Facing the back of the room.
ii) Switch parts.

86

Exercise 86

Adagio

Part 1: Si - lent wa - ters flow - ing, si - lent...

Part 2: Si - lent wa - ters flow - ing, si - lent...

87

MODULATION At measure 5 all parts move up a minor third to modulate to the new key.

IN REHEARSAL

TIP: If a singer continually sings a pitch incorrectly, there is probably something that is confusing their ear (i.e. a similar melodic line from another piece, etc.). Ask them to circle the pitch and mark it with an arrow to show that the pitch should be higher (or lower):

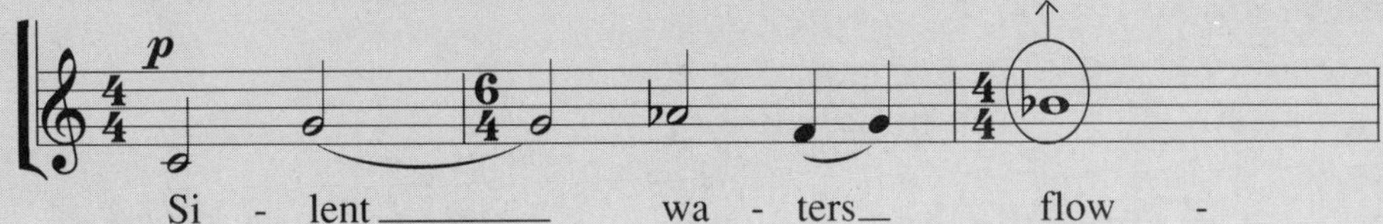

If an entire vocal part continues to sing a pitch incorrectly, it may be that another vocal part is confusing their ears. Have the incorrect vocal part sing their line by themselves several times to make the correction.

REPEAT with one other vocal part added (choose a vocal part that fits well harmonically with the first part).

REPEAT adding another vocal part, etc. In this way the singers can hear how their pitches fit in with the rest of the choir.

87

REMINDER: Mark the tonic at the beginning of each section:

INTRODUCE

modulation from minor to unrelated major

SING Exercise 87:

Moving up a minor third to modulate.

REPEAT Exercise 87:

Using this alternative strategy for the modulation:

Parts 1 and 3: Remember the first pitch (G♯ or C♯) in the first measure. The fifth measure starts a semi-tone lower (G or C) because the sharps have been removed from the key signature.

Part 2: Remember the first pitch in the first measure. The fifth measure starts with the same pitch.

Each singer should determine which strategy is better for them.

REPEAT Exercise 87:

i) Switch parts.
ii) Switch parts again with a different tempo.

IN REHEARSAL

New Concept: modulation from minor to unrelated major

TIP: Occasionally change the position of an entire vocal section (i.e. move sopranos from conductor's left to right) so that the singers listen for their cues from the other ear. Antiphonal and double choir music helps to improve the singers' ear-training.

88

REVIEW: Fifth.

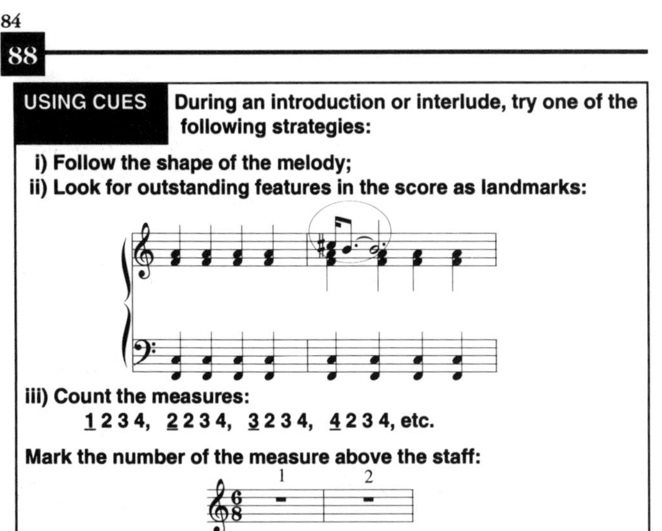
84

88

USING CUES During an introduction or interlude, try one of the following strategies:

i) Follow the shape of the melody;
ii) Look for outstanding features in the score as landmarks:

iii) Count the measures:
1 2 3 4, 2 2 3 4, 3 2 3 4, 4 2 3 4, etc.

Mark the number of the measure above the staff:

INTRODUCE

piano introduction or interlude

PREVIEW TIP: The accompaniment uses C (the dominant) frequently. The entry pitch is on the tonic (F). Think "home."

NOTE: For repeated pitches during humming, articulate each note with a slight push.

SING Exercise 88:

Silently.

READ the TIP on page 86 of the Vocal Edition.

REMINDER: Encourage the singers to let their eyes bounce continuously across the page slightly ahead of the music.

REPEAT Exercise 88:

i) Aloud.
ii) Switch parts.
iii) Switch parts again.

IN REHEARSAL

New Concepts: strategies for a piano introduction or interlude, marking your part in the system

TIP: If the singers have difficulty finding their part, give them an opportunity to mark their part with an arrow.

89

NOTE: This exercise starts with a dominant rather than a tonic chord.

INTRODUCE

86

TIP **If you have difficulty finding your part, mark it with an arrow.**

89

3	**three even quarter notes where there would normally be two**

Think 𝅗𝅥 = one beat:

Exercise 89

Rhythmically

V82S

TIP: Have the singers feel the eighth note pulse for the 7/8 and 6/8 measures. Then switch to a quarter note beat in 3/4. Then feel a half note beat in 4/4:

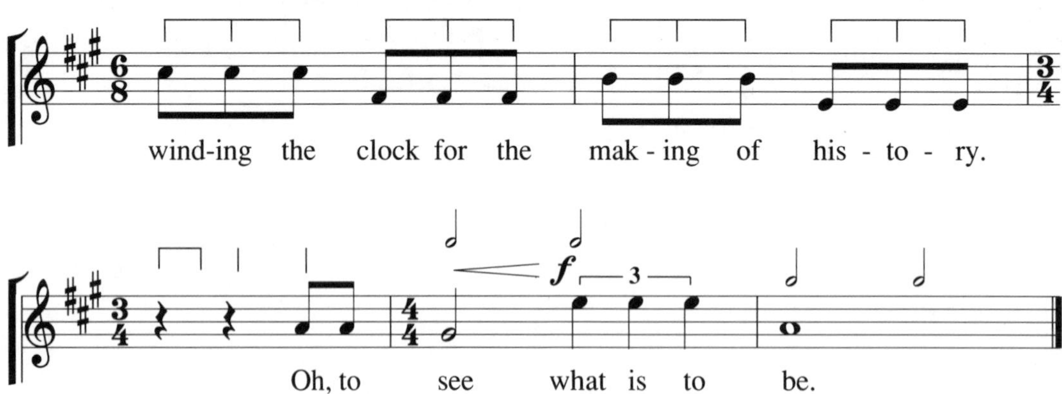

SING Exercise 89:

Right side standing: Part 1.
Left side sitting: Part 2.

REPEAT Exercise 89:

i) Silently; both parts standing.
ii) Aloud.
iii) Switch parts.

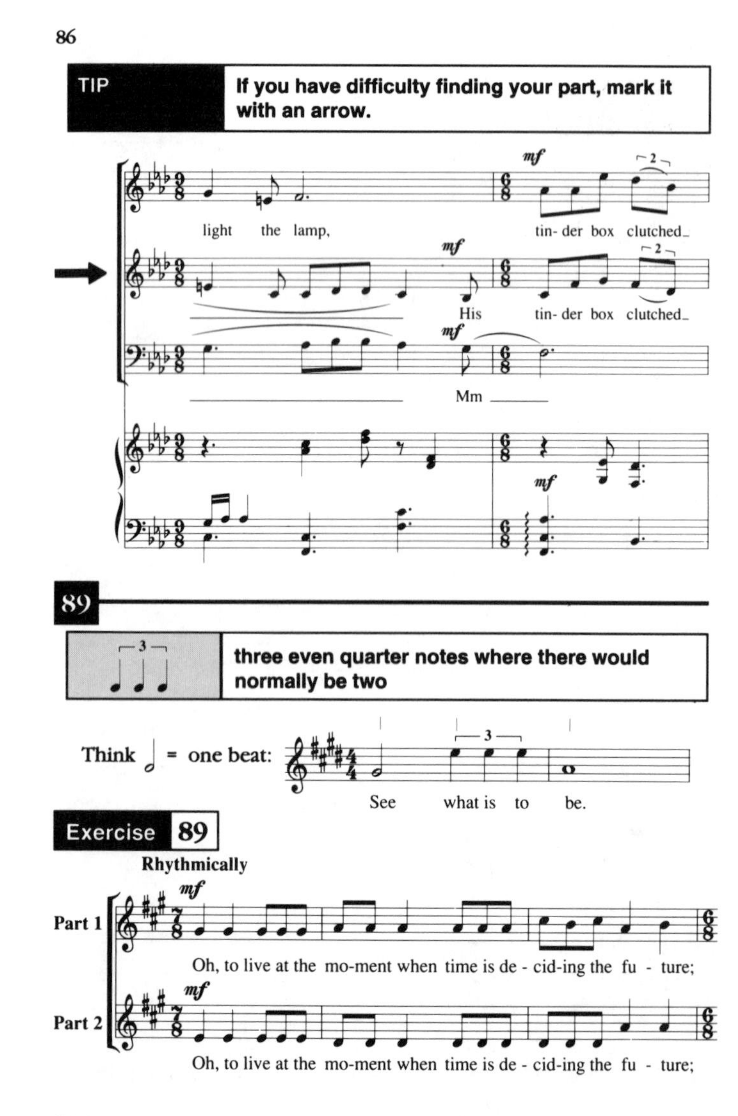

IN REHEARSAL

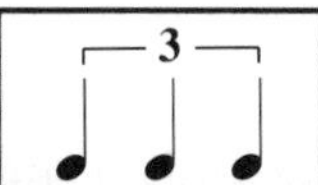

TIP: Whenever the choir regularly has rhythmic difficulty with a particular measure or section of the music, ask them to mark in vertical lines as an aid.

90

PREVIEW TIPS:

i) When the modulation happens gradually, determine the pitches by interval and by remembering previous pitches.

ii) In the fourth measure, Part 3 can think of the B as "ti" leading to the new tonic C.

SING Exercise 90:

Facing one side of the room.

TIP: Check the sixth measure of Part 2. Is there another letter name for the D♭ (C♯)? E to D♭ is really a minor third but looks like a second. It may help if the singers think of E to C♯ and mark it in their scores:

REPEAT Exercise 90:

i) Switch parts.
ii) Switch parts again.

IN REHEARSAL

New Concept: gradual modulation

TIP: On some days singers may be sluggish. During the rehearsal, use the hand rubbing activity to energize the bodies and get the concentration focused. **See page 189** in the Teacher's Edition for details.

91

t_1 d r m f s l t d^1 r^1 m^1 ♩ 𝅗𝅥 𝅗𝅥.

INTRODUCE

major sixth

See page 179 in the Teacher's Edition for an activity to memorize the interval of a major sixth.

PREVIEW TIP: Check for sequences:

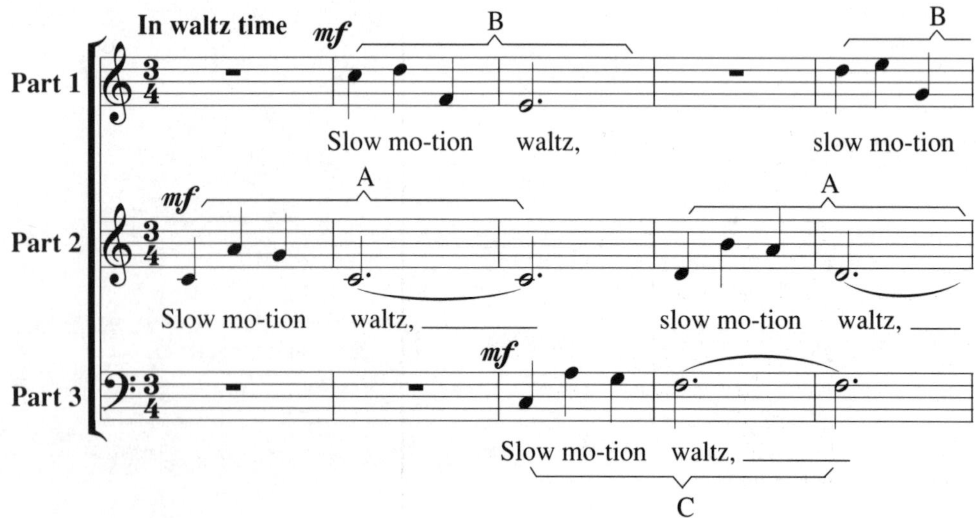

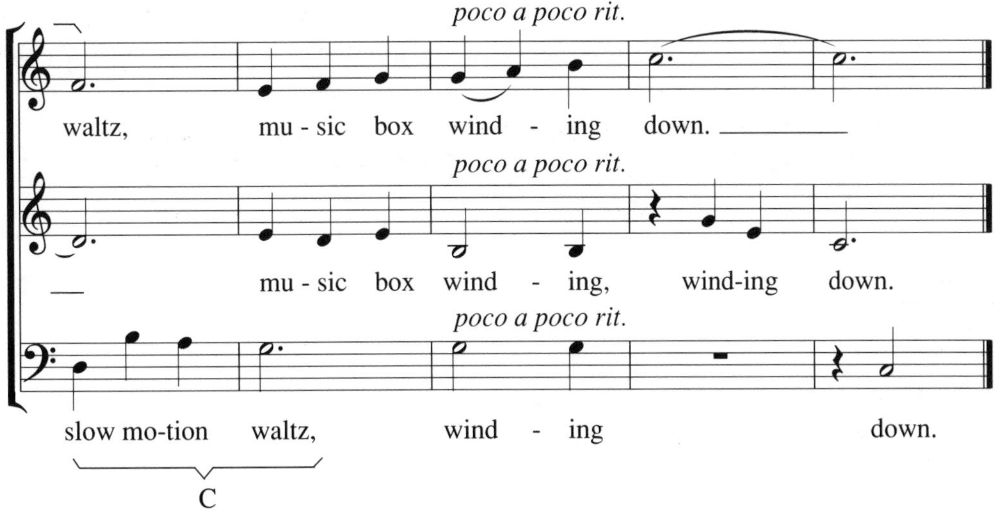

SING Exercise 91:

Singers who prefer cherry flavor: Part 3 silently.
Singers who prefer orange flavor: Part 2 silently.
Singers who prefer lemon flavor: Part 1 silently.

REPEAT Exercise 91:

i) Aloud. Scan the eyes over the full score.
ii) Switch parts. Sing the vowel sound on the beat.

IN REHEARSAL

New Term: major sixth

TIP: During warmups in parts, divide the singers by preference of color.

92

d r m s l t d' r' m' f' ♩ ♫ 𝅗𝅥 𝅝

REVIEW: Major sixth.

SING Exercise 92:

Singers who prefer yellow: Part 1.
Singers who prefer green: Part 2.
Singers who prefer pink: Part 3.

INTRODUCE

metronome marking

REPEAT Exercise 92:

i) At 𝅗𝅥 = 60.
ii) At 𝅗𝅥 = 80; switch parts.
iii) At 𝅗𝅥 = 44; switch parts.

IN REHEARSAL

New Term: metronome marking

TIP: Occasionally use a metronome to set the tempo before you begin a piece. Tell the singers what number setting you are using on the metronome.

93

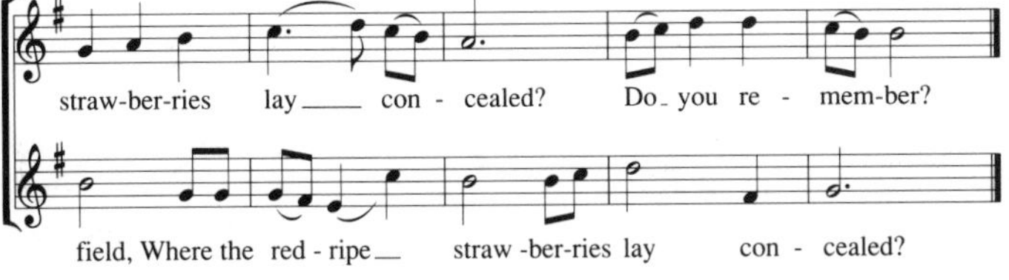

94

INTRODUCE

minor sixth

See page 179 in the Teacher's Edition for an activity to memorize the interval of a minor sixth.

SING Exercise 93:

Facing the back of the room.

REPEAT Exerise 93:

i) Silently while seated. Check posture.
ii) Aloud.
iii) Switch parts. Check the metronome for ♩ = 144.

IN REHEARSAL

New Term: minor sixth

TIP: Occasionally ask a quartet to sing a small section of the rehearsal music while the rest of the singers listen for phrasing, tuning or balance.

REPEAT this section with the entire choir singing, each singer listening carefully to implement what they have learned while listening to the quartet.

94

s_1 l_1 t_1 d r m f s l d^1 ♩ 𝅗𝅥 𝅝 𝅜

REVIEW: i) Double whole notes.
ii) Cut time.
iii) Minor sixths.

REMINDER: Always preview the music before you begin.

SING Exercise 94:

First row of singers: Part 1.
Second row of singers: Part 2.
Third row of singers: Part 3.

REPEAT Exercise 94:

i) Right side facing the left side. Check the metronome for 𝅗𝅥 = 69.
ii) Switch parts. Encourage each singer to monitor their own progress.
iii) Switch parts again.

IN REHEARSAL

TIP: Whenever the singers have difficulty with a page turn, have them practice the measures before and after the page turn.

95

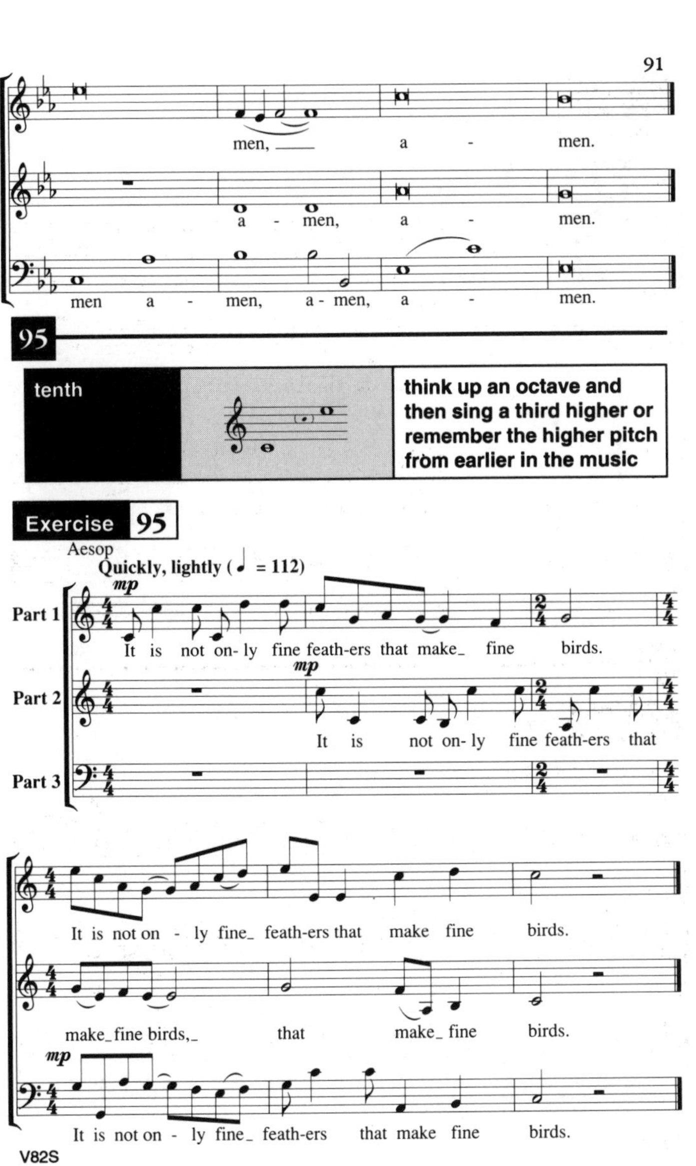

REVIEW: i) ♪♩♪
ii) Ninths.

INTRODUCE

tenth

SING Exercise 95:

Sopranos and tenors: Part 1 silently.
Altos: Part 2 silently.
Baritones: Part 3 silently.

REPEAT Exercise 95:

i) Aloud.
ii) Parts 2 and 3 switch.

IN REHEARSAL

New Term: tenth

TIP: To sing an interval that sounds different in the context of the music (i.e. a fifth which does not sound like a fifth when the rest of the choir is singing along), use:

i) An intermediary pitch; or
ii) The pitch framework.

96

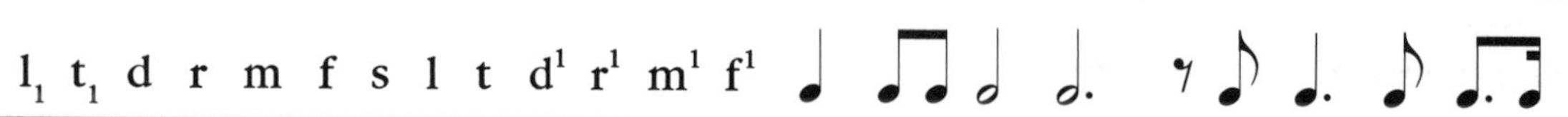

INTRODUCE

eleventh

SING Exercise 96:

Sopranos and tenors: Part 1 silently.
Altos: Part 2 silently.
Baritones: Part 3 silently.

NOTE: Exercise 96 switches from A minor to C minor to C major without a key signature change.

READ the TIP under the music in the Vocal Edition. Fit the pitches above and below the main pitches rather than using intervals alone.

REPEAT Exercise 96:

i) Aloud.
ii) Add more details (i.e. dynamics, phrasing, etc.).
iii) Parts 2 and 3 switch.

IN REHEARSAL

New Term: eleventh

TIP: If an inexperienced sight-singer joins the group, assign them as an apprentice to sit beside an experienced sight-singer who can quietly give them survival strategies to get them started. When inexperienced sight-singers are surrounded by competent sight-singers, they can learn the skills and habits at an accelerated pace.

97

mainly fifths and tritones	♩ ♫ 𝄾 ♪ 𝅗𝅥 𝅗𝅥. ♩. ♪

REVIEW: Tritone.

PREVIEW TIP: Identify the tritones in Exercise 97:

NOTE: In the second measure of Part 1, the first two B's are natural.

SING Exercise 97:

Silently.

REPEAT Exercise 97:

i) Aloud. Concentrate on the tuning.
ii) Switch parts.
iii) Switch parts again.
iv) Have three singers sing as a trio.

IN REHEARSAL

TIP: Singers are more relaxed and more productive right after a good laugh. Welcome humor in your rehearsal.

98

SING Exercise 98:

In 7-part round.

TIP: Do not be late after the quarter rest: 

REPEAT Exercise 98:

i) In 7-part round. As a challenge, have each vocal part sing the sections in the following order. Each section is two measures long.

1. 3. 5. 7. 2. 4. 6. 8.

ii) In 7-part round in this order:

2. 4. 6. 8. 1. 3. 5. 7.

STRATEGIES FOR PROBLEM AREAS

Problem	Strategy
Pitches	- check posture (head position) - use the pitch framework - memorize frequent pitches - sing in the middle of pitch - practice silent singing - memorize any problem intervals
Dissonance	- center the pitch immediately - think the pitch before you leap

V82S

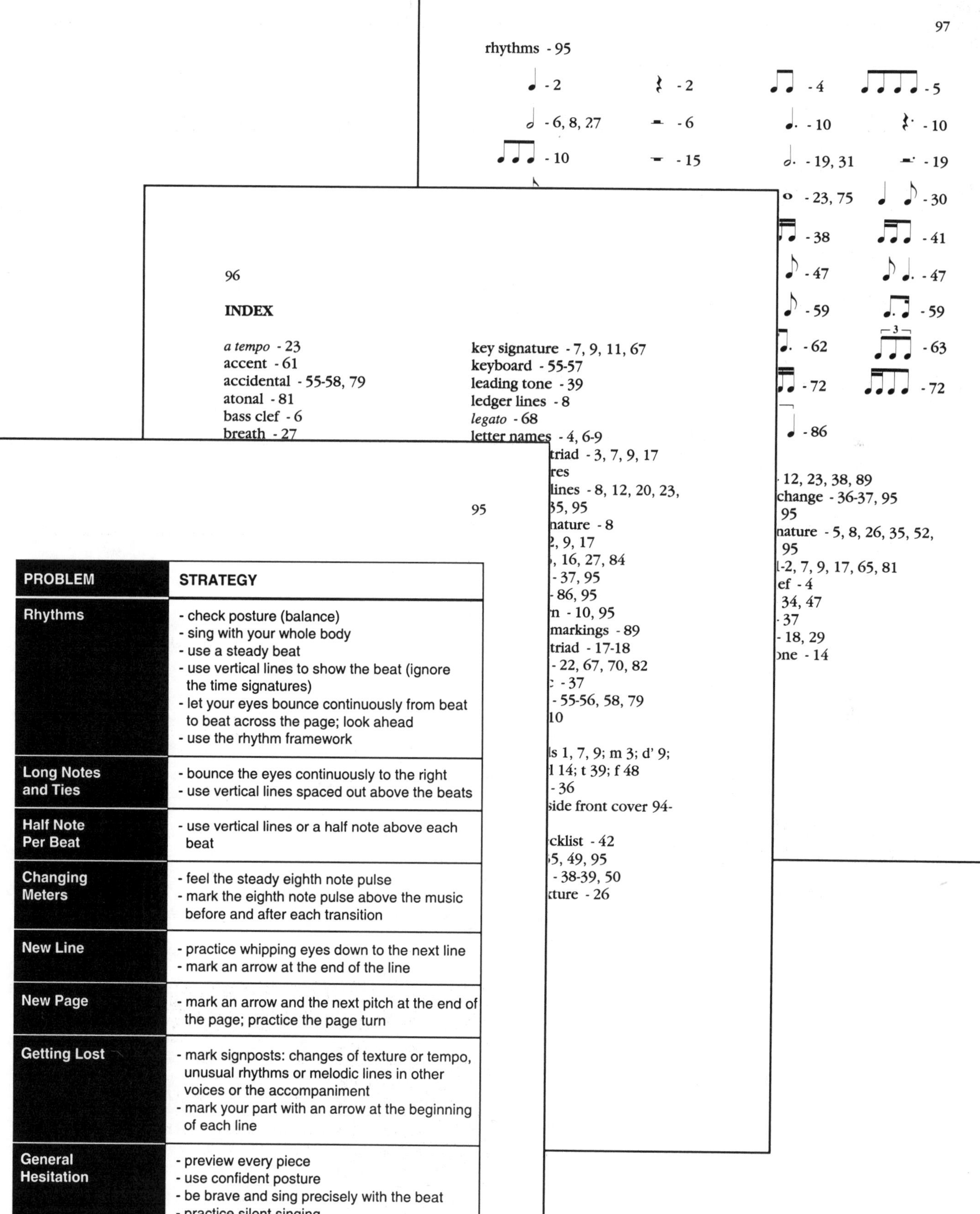

97

rhythms - 95

♩ - 2 | 𝄽 - 2 | ♫ - 4 | - 5
𝅗𝅥 - 6, 8, 27 | - 6 | ♩. - 10 | - 10
- 10 | - 15 | 𝅗𝅥. - 19, 31 | - 19
𝅝 - 23, 75 | - 30
- 38 | - 41
- 47 | - 47
- 59 | - 59
- 62 | - 63
- 72 | - 72
- 86

· 12, 23, 38, 89
change - 36-37, 95
95
nature - 5, 8, 26, 35, 52,
95
l-2, 7, 9, 17, 65, 81
ef - 4
34, 47
· 37
- 18, 29
one - 14

96

INDEX

95

PROBLEM	STRATEGY
Rhythms	- check posture (balance) - sing with your whole body - use a steady beat - use vertical lines to show the beat (ignore the time signatures) - let your eyes bounce continuously from beat to beat across the page; look ahead - use the rhythm framework
Long Notes and Ties	- bounce the eyes continuously to the right - use vertical lines spaced out above the beats
Half Note Per Beat	- use vertical lines or a half note above each beat
Changing Meters	- feel the steady eighth note pulse - mark the eighth note pulse above the music before and after each transition
New Line	- practice whipping eyes down to the next line - mark an arrow at the end of the line
New Page	- mark an arrow and the next pitch at the end of the page; practice the page turn
Getting Lost	- mark signposts: changes of texture or tempo, unusual rhythms or melodic lines in other voices or the accompaniment - mark your part with an arrow at the beginning of each line
General Hesitation	- preview every piece - use confident posture - be brave and sing precisely with the beat - practice silent singing

V82S

Individual singers may refer to these pages for reference or review.

Teaching Activities

I. PITCH

Tonic and Dominant

The tonic and dominant are used more frequently than any other pitches. As soon as the singers can consistently sing the tonic and dominant correctly in a piece of music, they have acquired one of the major skills in sight-singing. The singers can then use tonic and dominant as a framework for all the other pitches:

tonic dominant tonic

Each pitch fits in higher or lower than the pitches in the framework. Experienced sight-singers continue to use this framework for difficult passages of music for the rest of their lives.

Activities for Tonic and Dominant

i) Quick "blindfold" drill:

Ask the singers to close their eyes. Sing or play a short fragment of a melody. Ask the singers to think "tonic" and then, on cue, sing the tonic.

REPEAT with several different fragments in different keys.

ii) Before beginning a new sight-singing exercise or concert piece:

1) Have the singers mark the tonic in pencil:

2) Sing "do so do" (minor keys: "tonic dominant tonic").

iii) When you stop the choir in the middle of a piece to work out a problem:

1) Ask the singers to think "tonic";
2) Then, on cue, have them sing the tonic. Emphasize the feeling of "home."
3) Ask them where the tonic is on the staff so that they connect the position of the note with the sound of the pitch.
4) Continue on with the rehearsal.

REPEAT several times with different pieces in each rehearsal.

After a few weeks, they will be able to hear and see the tonic quickly and easily in any piece. The singers should check that they are on the correct pitch every time they see the tonic.

When they are confident with the tonic, use this activity with the dominant.

iv) Before beginning each familiar piece, have the singers check for the tonic they have already marked on the staff. Then sing the major or minor triad. Memorize the sight and sound of tonic in each piece.

NOTE: When the singers become more competent at sight-singing, give only the tonic pitch before you begin a new piece.

v) See Book 1 of **Successful Sight-Singing** for other activities for tonic and dominant.

Frequent Pitches

Memorize any pitches which are frequently used in a piece. If the highest pitches in the soprano and tenor parts are repeated in several places, these pitches are fairly easy to memorize and may be useful to the singer.

Intervals

Singers need to memorize each interval so well that they will be able to remember it when it appears in unusual context in the music.

For most tonal music, the singer does not need to be concerned whether a third is major or minor; the singer will usually sing the right interval to fit with the sound of the major or minor key of the music. However, when the music is chromatic or atonal, it is important to know the difference between major and minor thirds.

The concept of tones and semi-tones is easily demonstrated with the use of a keyboard (see Lessons 56 and 61). A visual picture of the close proximity of semi-tones helps many singers. Pianists may unconsciously pretend to "finger the keys" as they sight-sing difficult passages; they may find it helpful to relate the tactile sense to the intervals.

Activities for Interval Training

i) Quick drill for a specific interval:

1) Sing or play a pitch.
2) Have the singers sing it silently a semi-tone (major third, fifth, etc.) higher or lower. Concentrate on one interval for each session.
3) Have them sing the pitch aloud on the conductor's cue.

REPEAT with several other pitches given at random.

Continue to drill this interval for a few moments during each session until the singers are confident. Then continue on with a new interval.

ii) Quick drills for octaves:

- Have the tenors and basses sing one part of an exercise aloud while the sopranos and altos sing the same part silently an octave above. If there are no tenors or basses, play the bass part on the piano.

  REPEAT with both parts aloud.

- Have the sopranos and altos sing one part of an exercise while the tenors and basses sing the same part silently an octave below.

  REPEAT with both parts aloud.

- See Book 1 of **Successful Sight-Singing** for more activities with octaves.

iii) To sing an interval that sounds different in the context of the music (i.e. a fifth which does not sound like a fifth when the rest of the choir is singing along), use:

- The pitch framework; the pitch may be just above or below the tonic or dominant:

- The function of the pitch.

  Think "leading tone."

- An intermediary pitch:

Sing the C silently; the fifth may be easier to hear if you use the full triad.

iv) Notice any enharmonic changes where it would be easier for the singers to rename a pitch (i.e. A♭ to G♯). Mark the score:

A♭ to B is a third but does not look like a third. G♯ to B does look like a third and may be easier to read.

v) If a singer continually sings a pitch incorrectly, something could be confusing their ear (i.e. the memory of a similar melodic line from another piece, etc.). Have them circle the incorrect pitch and mark it with an arrow to show that the pitch should be higher (or lower) than they are hearing it:

vi) If an entire vocal part continues to sing a pitch incorrectly, another vocal part may be confusing their ears. Have the singers in difficulty sing their line by themselves several times correctly.

REPEAT with one other vocal part added (choose a vocal part that fits well harmonically with the first part).

REPEAT adding another vocal part, etc. In this way the singers can hear how their pitches fit in with the rest of the choir.

Dissonance

Singers have less difficulty with dissonance when they understand how and why dissonance is used.

Activities For Dissonance

i) Divide the singers into four different parts and have them sing:

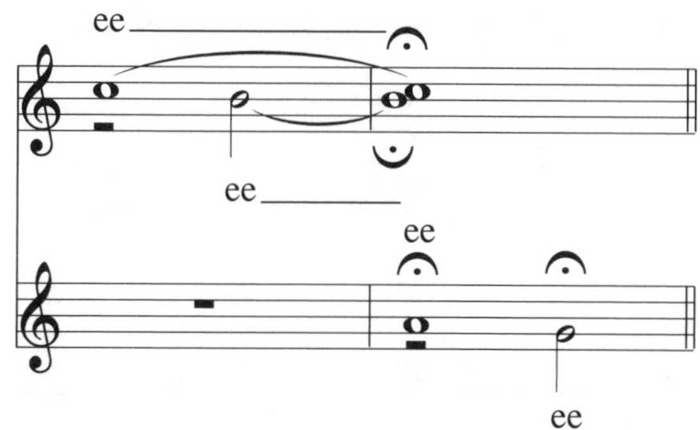

REPEAT using a very bright "ee" and listen for the dissonance – the sound of "knives in the air."

REPEAT on "ah."

REPEAT using a very warm "ah" and listen for the "halo effect" in the air.

NOTE: "Knives in the air" is not always loud; sometimes the scariest part of a horror show has very soft, spooky dissonance. The "halo effect" is not always soft; the climax of an exquisitely beautiful piece may be loud and dissonant but gorgeous.

ii) For warmups, form clusters in 4 parts by adding one pitch at a time:

1) "do[1] ti la so"
2) "do re mi fa"
3) four semi-tones

REPEAT each pattern starting on different pitches.

II. BEAT, PULSE AND RHYTHM

See Book 1 of **Successful Sight-Singing** for activities for beat, changing time signatures, unusual rhythmic patterns and tempo changes.

Activities for Pulse and Changing Meters

i) Have the singers use a slight accent on each beat during changing meters:

When the rhythms are more accurate, remove the accent.

ii) When the time signature changes from simple to compound, have the singers be aware of the eighth note pulse. Mark the transitional measures:

iii) Have half the singers tap the eighth note pulse while the rest sing the music, keeping the voices precisely with the steady tapping.

Check to see if each singer is using just the index finger to tap the pulse. When more than one finger is used, it is almost impossible to tap precisely.

NOTE: In asymmetrical time signatures (i.e. $\frac{5}{8}$ or $\frac{7}{8}$), singers often hold the quarter notes for too long.

iv) With hands on thighs, touch the beat with the wrists and the inner pulses with the fingers:

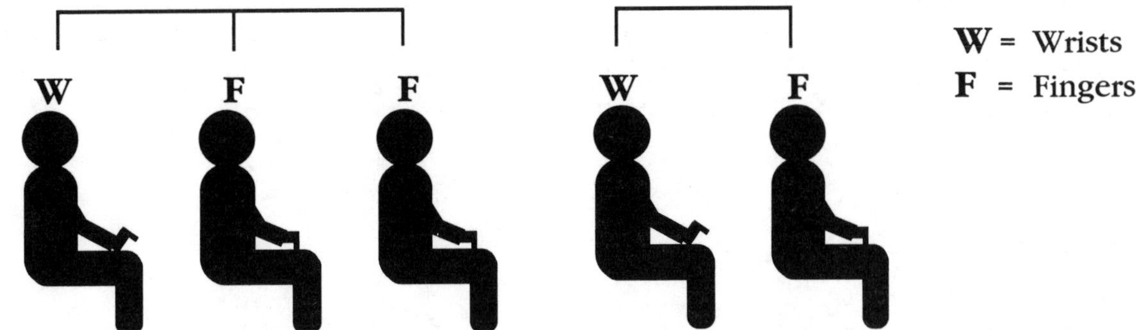

v) With hands together, touch the beat with the wrists and the inner pulses with the fingers:

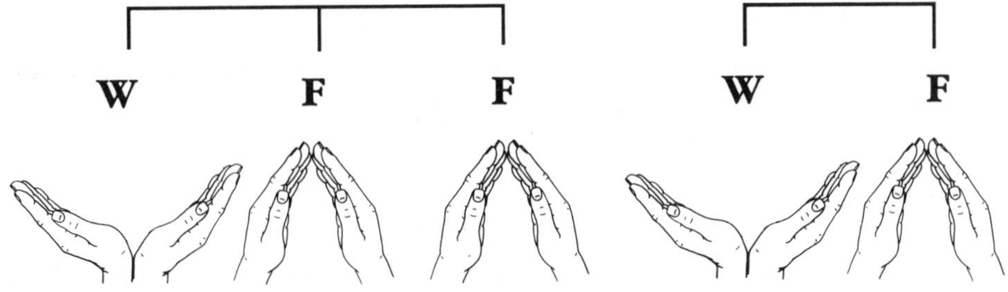

III. PRECISION

It is easier to sight-sing if all the singers sing together precisely. They can concentrate on the music without a clutter of sound to distract them.

Activities For Precision

i) When the body is balanced on two feet and the head is not leaning to either side, the success rate for beat and rhythm is much higher. **See page 11** in the Teacher's Edition for activities for balanced posture.

ii) Have the singers sing "Twinkle, Twinkle, Little Star" using "doo" for each note. When "d" is the initial consonant, it becomes more obvious if the singers are not precisely together.

REPEAT using "oo." Ask the singers to concentrate on starting the vowel exactly in time.

REPEAT using "loo." Ask the singers to go quickly through the "l" to start the vowel sound right on the beat. The "l" should be pitched the same as the vowel sound which follows it. No swooping!

REPEAT using "noo" with a new tempo.

Use a different well known melody (including current repertoire) at each session.

iii) Ask the singers to sing a "doo" every time the conductor gives a downbeat:

1) In $\frac{4}{4}$ time;
2) In $\frac{3}{4}$ time;
3) With changing time signatures:

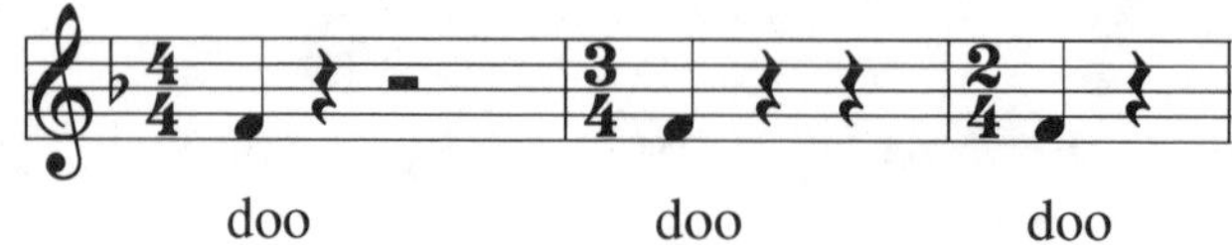

The conductor should make sure the downbeat is much larger then the intermediary beats.

4) For every quarter note <u>and eighth note</u> in Part 1 of Exercise 4, waiting for each rest. Singers must follow the conductor and are not permitted to look at the music. Use a slow tempo and encourage the singers to keep exactly with the conductor.

NOTE: Only use one or two short activities with "doo" in each session. With too much repetition, the muscles of the tongue and the mind tighten.

iv) Use the same system for cut-offs in all repertoire. The singers should be responsible for remembering the rules and marking the cut-off, if necessary.

If the phrase is followed by a rest, place the final consonant(s) at the beginning of the rest:

If the phrase is not followed by a rest, cut off on the last eighth pulse before the next phrase:

The singers may wish to use a half beat marking (1/2 with the 2 removed) for a cut-off on the last eighth pulse:

NOTE: In some music, the conductor will indicate the cut-off on the last quarter note beat before the next phrase.

v) For better precision with rhythmic music, demonstrate an imaginary game of catch with a singer:

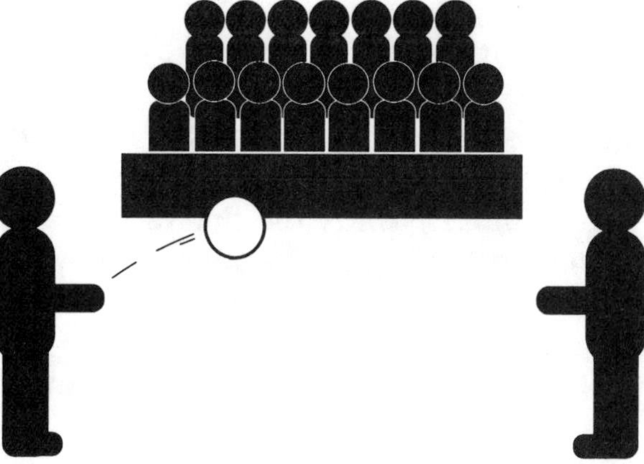

Teacher and singer stand sideways in front of the choir, tossing the imaginary ball slowly back and forth.

The teacher says, "Throw, catch. Throw, catch..." as the imaginary ball is thrown or caught by the teacher or singer. This helps the observers to feel the steady rhythm of the game. All throws should be underhand, smooth and slow.

When the pace is established, the teacher will turn toward the choir and throw the imaginary ball to the entire choir and the entire choir will catch "it."

The entire choir will throw the ball back to the teacher. The teacher will continue to say, "Throw, catch..." to keep a relaxed, even pace as the ball goes back and forth between the teacher and the choir.

NOTE: Let the singers know that you can see whether they are throwing and catching the ball properly. The ones who do it well will have no difficulty singing difficult rhythms precisely in the music to follow.

Continue the game for a minute or two aiming the ball at various sections of the choir.

In subsequent rehearsals, omit the demonstration. Play imaginary catch for a minute or two during the warmup or before practicing a difficult piece.

NOTE: A game of catch or juggling stimulates the brain to think better. Difficulties in precision can completely disappear after a short session of catch. The effect will continue throughout the entire rehearsal and can make a dramatic difference in the concentration of the singers and the productivity of the rehearsal.

IV. SILENT SINGING

In sight-singing, the singer must be able to hear each pitch and rhythm in the mind before singing aloud. Silent singing is one of the best ways for singers to become more independent with this skill. Silent singing takes concentration and develops keen hearing. Every singer has an opportunity to develop sight-singing skills without hearing the music from someone else first.

At first the singers may not hear any music in their own minds. To the conductor, it will seem as if there is a great vacuum in the room. Gradually the singers will start to hear shapes of sound moving up and down, then definite pitches and rhythms and finally a complete, accurate sound of the music (complete with lyrics and dynamics). Then the conductor may notice that the rehearsal room, although silent, has a sense of music flowing through it.

Immediately after each attempt at silent singing, ask the singers to sing the same exercise aloud so that they will:

i) Know how well they have done and will be encouraged by any success;
ii) Note the specific problems they have experienced;
iii) Determine strategies to correct the problems.

Activities for Silent Singing

For sight-singing exercises, sing silently:

i) The entire exercise;
ii) Alternate measures;
iii) Alternate systems;
iv) Alternate beats in slow music.

NOTE: When alternate measures are sung silently, the singers learn different sight-singing skills than they would if they sang the entire exercise silently. It is helpful to use many variations of silent singing to improve different types of skills.

During rehearsal:

i) Occasionally alternate measures aloud and silent to improve precision and independence of singers or to help memorize the music.
ii) Occasionally use silent singing to have the singers imagine the best quality tone or musical phrasing. This "imaging" can make dramatic changes in a short time.

V. TRAINING THE EYES

The singer's eyes should move continuously from left to right across the page in a bouncing motion. At first the eyes learn to bounce beat by beat and then word by word, measure by measure or phrase by phrase. Gradually the eyes begin to move ahead of the voice to anticipate problems in the measures ahead.

Many singers let their eyes get stuck on long notes or difficult rhythms. When the eyes stop moving, the singer loses all sense of time and space. Then their eyes suddenly move on to the next note but it often takes them a measure or two to regain a steady beat and accurate rhythms. It is important to keep the eyes moving steadily so that the singer can keep a steady beat and sing accurate rhythms.

Activities for Training the Eyes

i) Ask the singers to mark the first page of one of their scores with vertical lines evenly spaced out for the beats. Quickly check the singers' markings:

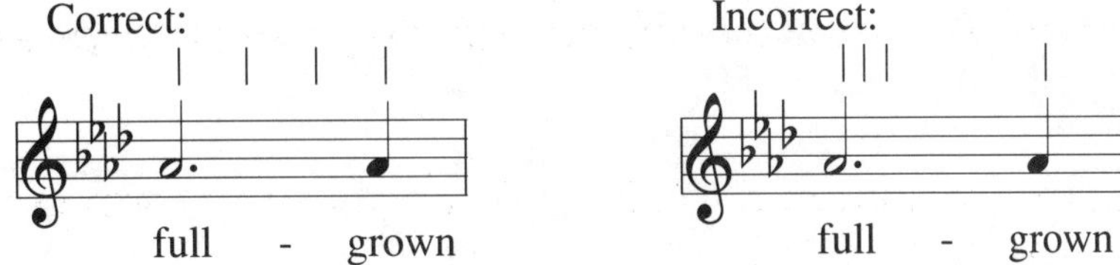

As the singers sing through the marked page, have them bounce their eyes continuously from line to line across the music. By the end of the page the eye muscles are more warmed up and in the habit of moving correctly; often the singer can retain the correct eye movement to the end of the piece even if the vertical lines are not marked after the first page.

REPEAT with a few other pieces with different tempi and with a different duration for the beat (i.e. 𝅗𝅥 = one beat or 𝅗𝅥. = one beat).

NOTE: As the singers' eyes become trained, each singer will need these vertical lines only in parts of the music which are rhythmically difficult for them.

ii) As the singers become more successful with eye movement, start encouraging the singers to keep their eyes moving continuously slightly ahead of their voices.

iii) Have the singers practice whipping the eyes down quickly to the next line. Use an arrow at the end of a line whenever necessary:

Practice the page turns the same way.

NOTE: Because so many elementary music textbooks and hymnaries have been published with one phrase to a line, most singers' eyes have had intensive training to stop at the end of each line. This handicap works against the continuous flow of the music and makes it very difficult to read music at a more advanced level when it is printed continuously on the page. The eyes need to be retrained by practicing the whipping motion.

iv) To help the eyes become more competent at switching from the music to the conductor, choose a singer to conduct. Inexperienced conductors are less predictable and must be watched closely by the singers.

Have the conductor use a *ritard.*, *accel.* or fermata at unusual places in the music.

v) See Book 1 of **Successful Sight-Singing** for more activities for training the eyes.

VI. CONCENTRATION

TIPS:

i) Singers stay fresh (and sight-sing better) if the rehearsal is paced with a variety of music. Alternate different types of music:

fast/slow
loud/soft
serious/amusing
difficult/easy
rhythmic/melodic/harmonic
familiar/a bit familiar/new

ii) During each rehearsal give the singers an opportunity to move about physically even if it is just to sing while standing. A physical break will help their concentration.

Activities for Concentration

i) Have the singers:

1) Stretch their right arms, left arms;
2) Stretch one leg, then the other;
3) Stretch their faces (i.e. make grotesque faces to stretch the face muscles).

ii) Have the singers imitate the movements of the conductor as he or she does a series of slow movements with arms (and legs if they can be seen by all the singers). Use movements that switch from two to three dimensions to get the mind to think in different ways:

1) Move one fist high above the head and slowly to the right. Stop.
2) Move that fist slowly to the left. Stop.

3) Move the fist slowly to the right again. Stop.
4) Open up the hand and separate the fingers in one gesture.
5) Continue with other movements.

Try sequences which are rhythmic and repetitive, too, but keep introducing new ideas.

iii) While the singers sing a familiar piece, have them focus their eyes on the conductor's pencil as it moves to different locations:

1) Right;
2) Left;
3) On top of the head;
4) Bouncing on one arm.

See if the singers can keep focused as the conductor moves to different locations in the rehearsal room as they sing. As the conductor moves about the room, he or she should change direction frequently.

iv) During warmups, use gradual tempo changes (i.e. conduct a *ritard.* or *accel.*):

1) Announced in advance;
2) At unexpected moments.

Occasionally use several unexpected fermatas in a warmup or rehearsal piece.

v) To energize the bodies and get the concentration focused, have the singers follow the directions of the conductor:

"Rub, rub, rub, rub,	(hands rubbing rhythmically together)
Show me your hands.	(conductor's palms facing the singers)
Rub, rub, rub, rub,	(hands rubbing)
Show me your eyes.	(conductor's eyes scan the choir)
Rub, rub, rub, rub,	(hands rubbing)
Show me your faces."	(conductor's face communicates a message to the singers)

For middle school or young singers only:

"Rub, rub, rub, rub,	(hands rubbing)
Show me an ugly face."	(conductor makes an ugly face)

Notice how much more alive the singers feel when they have been rubbing their hands. **Warning:** Never do this activity with singers who tend to be too excited and difficult to control.

vi) When beginning a new piece, ask the singers to:

1) Memorize a phrase or two before they are familiar with the music;
2) Sing without looking at the music;

3) Check the details of the music again to see how well they have done.

This activity trains the eyes to look intensively at all the details.

VII. DEVELOPING INDEPENDENCE

Confident Part-Singing

See Book 1 of **Successful Sight-Singing** for activities for confident part-singing.

Location and Acoustics

Group 1 (Natural Sight-Singers)	Group 2 (The Vast Majority)
- react quickly to changes in acoustics	- have difficulty with changes in acoustics
- naturally listen to details in the sound	- naturally listen to the overall sound
- can concentrate easily on own part	- become distracted by overall sound (which is impossible to sing)
- can sing despite poor singers or voices on other parts right beside them	- may stop singing or go off onto someone else's part

The more practice the singers have with changing acoustics, the better they become at sight-singing. When you change the acoustics, it is more difficult for the singers to inadvertantly follow along with someone singing their own part (they know if they are trying to listen for someone else on their own part). Encourage them to sight-sing independently.

Regularly change the acoustics for:

i) Warmups.
ii) Sight-singing exercises.
iii) A rehearsal piece.
iv) An entire rehearsal.

Activities for Changing Acoustics

i) Direction of sound:
- Face one side of the room; then the opposite side.
- Face the back of the room.
- Back singers face the front singers, regardless of how the parts are allocated.

ii) By rows:
- Parts for warmups or sight-singing exercises divided row by row.
- First and third rows stand while second and fourth rows sit; reverse.

iii) From side to side:
- Singers in the middle of the choir on one part; singers at the sides sing a different part.
- One vocal part sitting while the others stand.
- Change the position of an entire vocal section (i.e. move sopranos from conductor's left to right).

NOTE: The singers will listen for their cues from the other ear. Antiphonal and double choir music helps to improve the singers' ear-training.

iv) By random:
- Singers form two or three circles. This works particularly well for madrigal-style music.
- Parts divided by preference for different flavors (i.e. lemon/orange/cherry).
- Parts divided by preference for different colors.
- Parts divided by preference of seasons.
- Parts divided by birthdays of the singers:

Two-part - January to June; July to December
- Months spelled with the letter "e"; all other months

Three-part - January to April; May to August; September to December
- Months beginning with "J" or "O"; months beginning with "M" or "A"; all other months

- Regularly switch the seating position of each singer within a vocal section (i.e. each alto).

NOTE: The ideal seating plan to help the singers learn the music quickly in rehearsal is not the same seating plan that is needed to provide the best quality sound, balance and musical energy for a concert. If you rarely make seating changes, the singers become very resistant to change. If you make seating changes regularly, the singers soon become accustomed to the constantly changing seating plan and become more flexible and more independent.

v) See Book 1 of **Successful Sight-Singing** for more activities for location and acoustics.

TIPS:
i) When changing formation, save time by doing a warmup during the change.
ii) Introduce acoustical changes gradually as the singers are ready for each new possibility.
iii) Do not change the acoustics so often in a rehearsal that it disrupts the flow of the rehearsal.

Solos

The use of solos or duets encourages independence. Even the ones listening to the solos start to think of themselves more as distinct individuals. They start to realize that the conductor listens to all the voices individually while the choir is singing as an ensemble.

As one singer sings solo, the others sing along silently (in their own hearts, they "know" they could do better than the soloist if they were only given a chance!). Everyone else has intense practice at silent solo singing while the real soloist continues on. Because they are not under stress and because they are dreaming they are doing their very best work as soloists, the silent singers may very well be getting better practice at sight-singing than the real soloist.

Include solo singers with mediocre voices who would not have other opportunities to do solos.

See Book 1 of **Successful Sight-Singing** for activities for solos.

Other Activities for Independence

i) Frequently rehearse without piano accompaniment.

ii) During warmups, use gradual tempo changes (i.e. conduct a *ritard.* or *accel.*):

1) Announced in advance;
2) At unexpected moments.

iii) Occasionally use several unexpected fermatas in a warmup or rehearsal piece.

NOTE: Vocal Edition Page 42 = **VE42**

Appendix A

Preview Checklist

VE42

1. Key signature, key signature changes.
2. Time signature.
3. Texture and cues.
4. Imitation.
5. Tempo and expression markings.
6. Posture.

Appendix B

Tuning

Seating Plan

In most situations it is best to seat your choir in this formation:

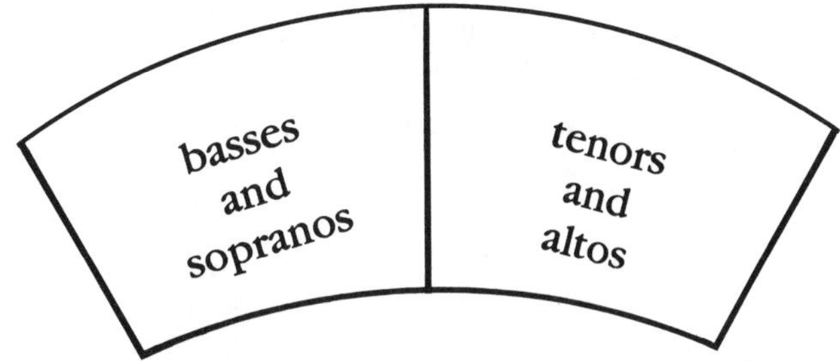

There are several reasons for placing basses and sopranos together:

1) Better Tuning - Because of the natural makeup of the different voices, sopranos and tenors have a tendency to sing a bit sharp; altos and basses have a tendency to sing a bit flat. Sopranos and basses tune well together.

2) Better Blend - The bass and alto sections tend to have a predominance of "soakers" (singers who "soak" in harsh tones around them). The soprano and tenor sections tend to have a predominance of "hard shells" (singers who pierce through the fabric of the sound). The "soakers" in the bass section can help to filter the "hard shells" in the soprano section; the sopranos bring out the bass sound so that it does not become lost. It is always easier to tune if your voice blends well with surrounding voices.

3) Greater Range of Dynamics - Because the voices fit better together acoustically, one section is not "cancelling out" the sound of another section and making them sound softer.

The same principles apply for placing altos and tenors together.

The tuning is better if the basses and sopranos are to the left of the conductor. Singers learn to tune to the basses and sopranos because these outer parts are easier to hear, being the highest and lowest pitches. A choir will often balance their tuning with the bass line since it usually presents the harmonic foundation of the music.

Most singers have better discrimination for tuning in their right ears. When the altos and tenors are on the conductor's right, they are able to use their right ears to tune with the sopranos and basses. The sopranos and basses should tune with each other.

NOTE: In some choirs, the voices are staggered with basses and sopranos mixed together rather than singing in two separate sections. This can enhance the results with tuning, blend and dynamics.

Breathing

Poor tuning may be caused by poor breathing habits. Teach your singers to:

i) Stand with correct posture.
ii) Breathe in with the entire body. Feel the air come up through the "holes in the soles of the feet."
iii) Keep the shoulders down and expand the ribcage.
iv) Build up the tummy muscles with hissing exercises.
v) Practice pacing the breath for a variety of short and long phrase lengths.
vi) Spin the sound forward through the air.

Warmups

When the voices are warmed up, the tuning is better. Take the time for a good warmup at the beginning of each rehearsal. Remember that changing and changed voices take longer to warmup than unchanged voices; humming warms up the voice quickly.

Vowel Formation

When the vowel sounds are uniform, the tuning improves and it is easier for the singers to tell quickly whether they are singing the right pitches.

NOTE: When singers are instructed to make each vowel sound pure, they tend to unconsciously model their sound after the best natural or trained voices in the group. Even when the teacher is unable to demonstrate a good vowel sound, the singers will be able to improve the purity of their own vowel sounds.

A teacher who does not have a "model" voice should not demonstrate a pure vowel sound. Use descriptive words or images instead.

Ask the singers to:

i) Think of the sound shaped as a circle. If they sing only the top half of the circle, it will sound sharp. The bottom half alone will sound flat. When they sing in the center of the pitch, the music will be in tune and it is easier to sing the correct intervals.

 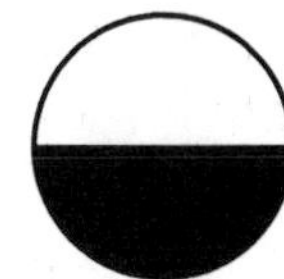 

ii) Concentrate on pure vowel sounds when working on pieces with:
- A slow tempo;
- Long, held notes.

The singers will have more time to concentrate on pure vowels and the voice will get a better workout with sustained vowels. The singers will start to form a habit of using pure vowels all the time and gradually transfer this habit to music with a faster tempo or short notes.

Ear-Training

Poor tuning may be caused by singers who are not listening to their own voices.

TIPS:

i) Simply remind them to listen to their own tuning. They may be selectively listening to tone quality, expression, etc. instead and may not realize that they are singing out of tune at that particular moment. A reminder may be the easiest and best solution.

ii) Have the singers sing softly enough so that they can hear the other singers to tune with them.

iii) Frequently change the acoustics. Singers tend to listen more carefully when the acoustics have been changed.

iv) Be aware of passages where the tuning is likely to cause trouble:

Sopranos and tenors have a tendency to go sharp on repeated pitches; altos and basses have a tendency to go flat.

Everyone has a tendency to go flat in music that has a lot of falling patterns and sharp in music that continually rises.

Ask the singers to listen carefully and keep the energy alive in their voices.

Appendix C

Breathing

Where to Breathe

At the beginning of the music, breathe in rhythm with the conductor's upbeat:

After rests, breathe in rhythm a few beats before the entry:

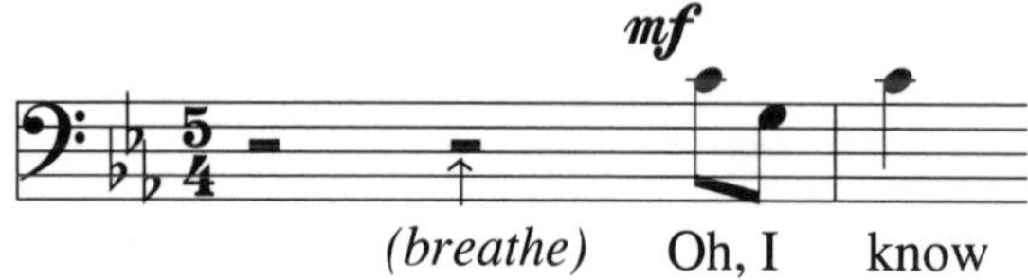

Between phrases, breathe quickly in rhythm with the music:

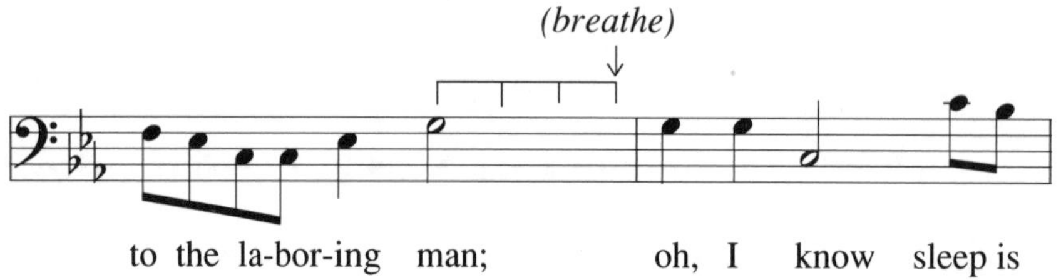

In some music the singers should take a full beat to breathe between phrases.

NOTE:

i) The singers should breathe through the mouth quietly; the first sound the audience should hear is the music. Noisy breathers are not listening.

ii) Have the singers mark a comma above the music as a breath mark:

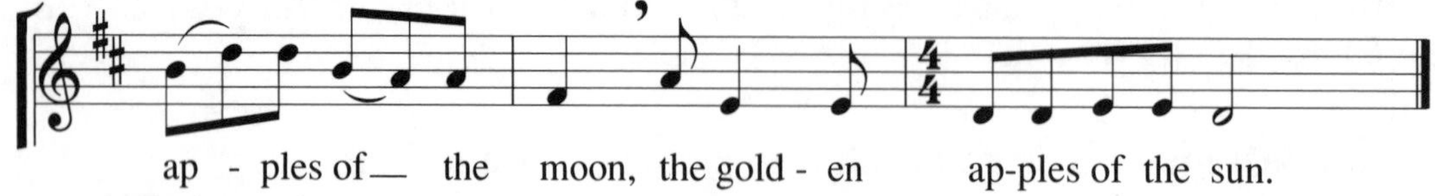

Conducting an Early Breath

During an introduction or interlude, show by your conducting when you want the singers to start breathing early (i.e. raise your left hand slowly with the palm up as they breathe in).

Good breathing habits steady the singer for sight-singing the correct pitches with a steady beat.

See page 194 for more information on breathing.

Appendix D

Cues

Most singers are fine as long as they are singing continuously but if they have a few measures or a page rest, they have great difficulty with the next entry. It takes them several measures before they start singing musically again. It is important for singers to feel confident with entries after rests.

TIPS:

i) Whenever a singer misses an entry, they should mark the cue.
ii) Two singers on the same vocal part may choose different cues depending on where they are sitting or their own particular preference. Singers should learn a variety of strategies for cues. On some days their cue may be absent (i.e. the reliable tenor is sick) and so they must choose an alternative cue.
iii) Each singer should be responsible for marking the cues in their own score.
iv) If the singers are generally having difficulty with cues, teach a complete unit on cues using the information in Appendix D as the singers follow along with their own books for the corresponding information (i.e. VE13).

Types of Cues:

i) Same Pitch Cue From Another Vocal Part or the Accompaniment

Focus your ear on the melody and sing along silently until you reach the cue. Remember the cue until you need it for your entry.

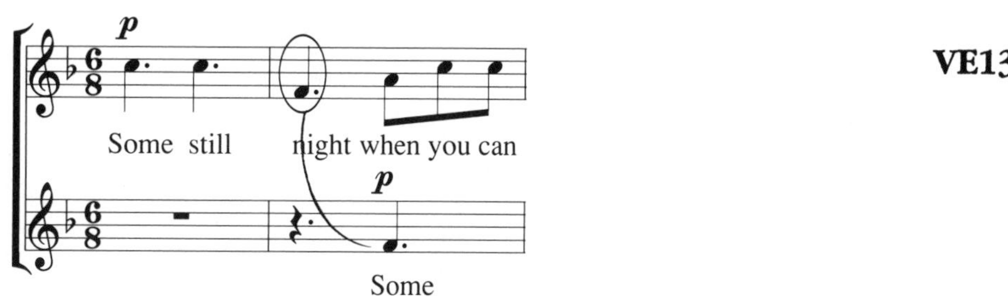

VE13

Always circle the cue and draw a line to your entry.

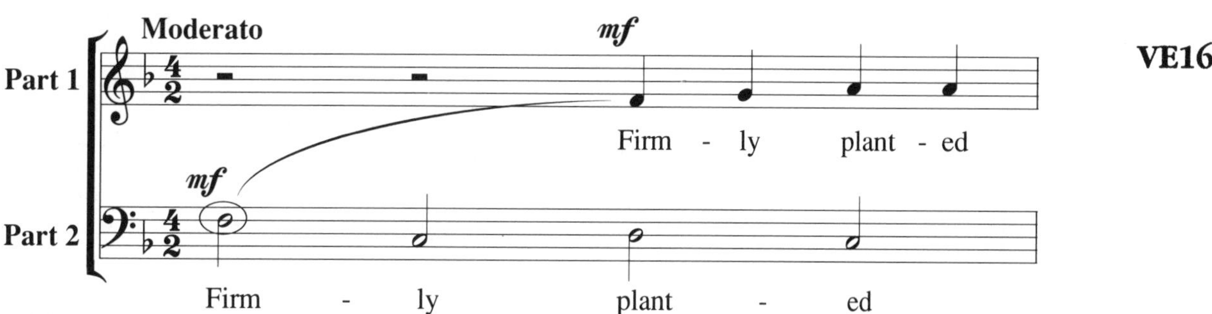

VE16

If the cue is an octave lower, sing along silently an octave above.

ii) Cue From Memory

If the entry is on the tonic, think "home": **VE65**

A. W. E. O'Shaughnessy

Intensely

Part 1

mf

For each age is a dream — that is dy -

Part 2

mf

is a dream that is

Intensely

Key-board

mf

If the same pitch is used frequently in one piece, memorize it for entries:

VE15

If the entry is on "ti," think "leading tone" leading up to the tonic:

VE43

iii) <u>Cue is a Different Pitch Than the Entry</u>

Sing silently with a part which ends close to your entry pitch:

VE16

Find your entry pitch down a third from the last pitch of the other part.

When you mark the cue, draw two strokes through the line to show that the cue and the entry pitch are not the same.

iv) Unusual Introductions

When you cannot sing along silently with another part to find your cue: **VE27**

1) Mark the beat with vertical lines.
2) Follow the beat with your eyes and ignore the sounds of the pitches until you reach the cue. Start a long, slow breath a few beats before your entry.
3) Quickly focus your ears on the pitch of the cue and remember that pitch until your entry.

v) Long Introduction

During a long introduction or interlude: **VE84**

1) Follow the shape of the melody;
2) Look for outstanding features in the score as landmarks:

If the music in the introduction or interlude all looks the same:

1) Count the measures:

1 2 3 4, 2 2 3 4, 3 2 3 4, 4 2 3 4, etc.

2) Mark the number of the measure above the staff:

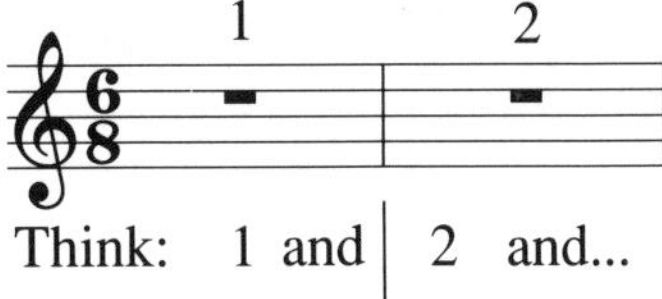

vi) A Choice of Cues

If possible it is better to choose a cue: **VE40**

1) From a reliable source (the accompaniment or another vocal part which you can hear clearly and which is usually right!);
2) As close as possible in time to your entry;
3) At the same pitch as your entry or an octave from your entry.

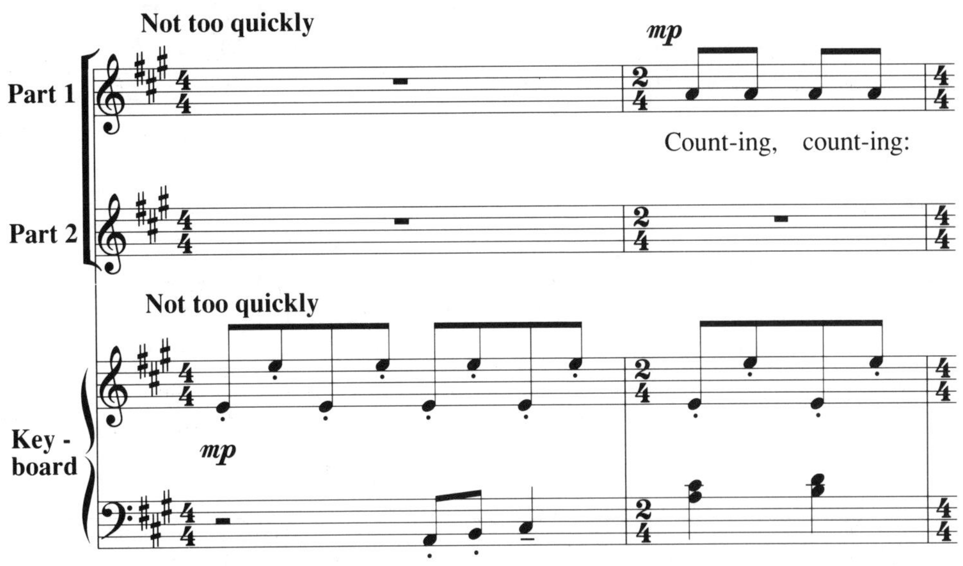

Appendix E

Useful Ways to Mark Scores

Appendix E shows the markings used by good sight-singers. Many of these markings are also used by world-class conductors of orchestras, bands and choirs.

TIPS:

i) At the beginning of each rehearsal, check that every singer has a pencil.

ii) If the singers do not always have a pencil:
   1) Ask them to keep a sharpened pencil in their choir folders; or
   2) Pass around a box of sharpened pencils at the beginning of each rehearsal. At the end of the rehearsal they can leave the pencils in the box as they leave.

iii) Singers should keep their pencil ready in one hand throughout the rehearsal so that they can mark their scores as they sing. It is amazing how quickly they learn how to manipulate the page turns while holding a pencil.

iv) Encourage the singers to mark their scores carefully with pencil and use these markings later.

v) If the singers are generally having difficulty with marking their scores, teach a complete unit using the information in Appendix E as the singers follow along with their own books for the corresponding information (i.e. VE25).

Pitch

i) Before beginning each new piece, have the singers mark the tonic in pencil and sing "do so do" (minor keys: "tonic dominant tonic"). **VE2**

ii) If a singer continually sings a pitch incorrectly, something could be confusing their ears (i.e. the memory of a similar melodic line from another piece, etc.). Have them circle the incorrect pitch and mark it with an arrow to show that the pitch should be higher (or lower) than they are hearing it:

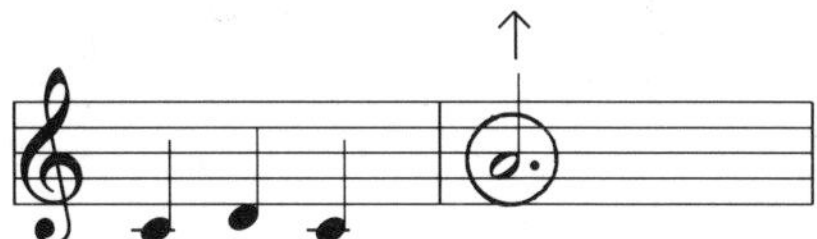

iii) Notice any enharmonic changes where it would be easier for the singers to rename a pitch (i.e. A♭ to G♯). Mark the score:

A♭ to B is a third but does not look like a third. G♯ to B does look like a third and may be easier to read.

Time Signature

i) For measures of rests, have the singers circle the time signature each time it changes:

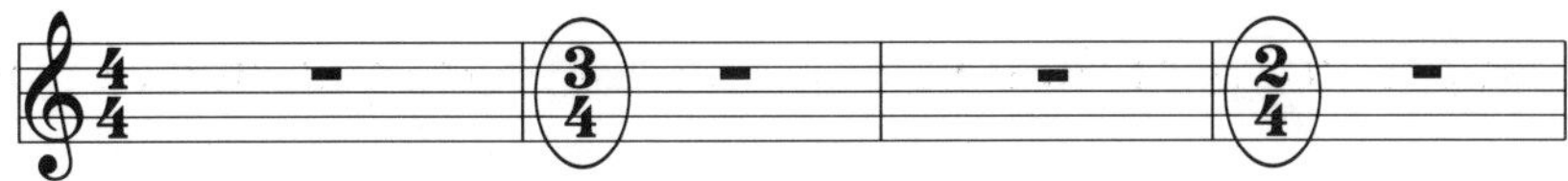

or mark vertical lines above the beats:

ii) Before starting music in duple time, ask the singers to notice that the half note gets one beat. Circle the bottom 2 as a reminder. If singers have difficulty remembering, have them draw half notes (instead of vertical lines) over the first two beats in each system: VE8

Ev -'ry -one has seen the sign

<u>**Beat and Rhythm**</u>

Use vertical lines in any kind of music when:

i) The beat is not easy to see;
ii) The rhythms are difficult;
iii) Your eyes need help to keep moving continuously to the right.

Each singer should mark in vertical lines only when they need them. Some singers will need them frequently at first but less often as their skills improve. These markings continue to be valuable as the singers work with more difficult music.

The lines should be exactly above each beat and evenly spaced so that the eyes will move forward more steadily.

Align the marks with the other vocal parts: VE23

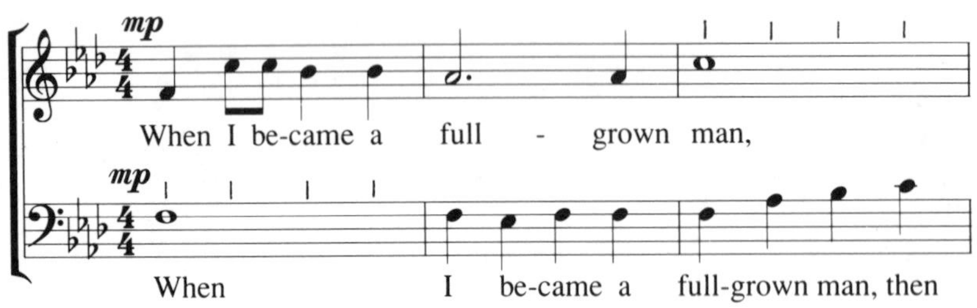

Typical situations for vertical lines:

i) $\frac{3}{2}$ or $\frac{2}{2}$ time: VE8

The singer may wish to draw half notes over each beat:

ii) Compound time: **VE30**

iii) Eighth and sixteenth notes printed separately: **VE20**

iv) Transitional measures of changing time signatures: **VE35**

Finding Their Part

i) If the singers have difficulty finding their part, have them mark their part with an arrow at the beginning of each system: **VE86**

ii) Whenever the singers have difficulty moving down to the next line, mark an arrow (→) at the end of the line as a reminder to whip the eyes down quickly.

iii) For a difficult page turn, mark an arrow (→) above the music at the bottom of the page and mark your next pitch in pencil:

VE10

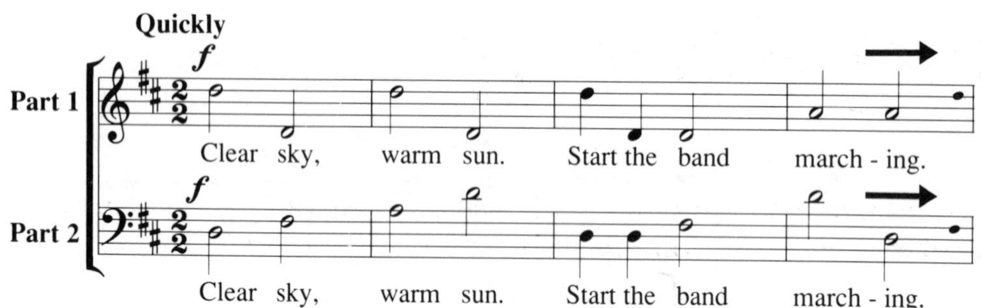

Practice the measures before and after the page turn.

Full Score

Encourage the singers to let their eyes quickly scan the other parts while they sing their own part.

i) If the music suddenly changes texture, mark it with a bracket:

VE37

ii) If the singers get lost, they can check the texture of the full score for signposts:
- Sudden switch to harmony, counterpoint or unison;
- A distinctive melody;
- A distinctive rhythm.

The beat for all parts is aligned vertically on the page in all published music. You can quickly move your eyes up or down to another part to see what they are doing at the same time:

VE23

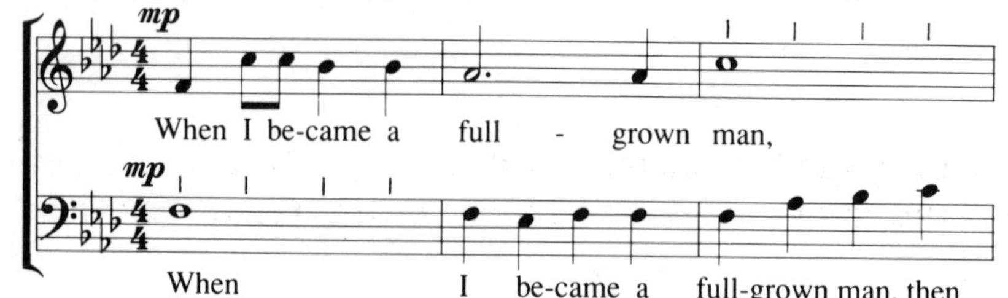

iii) **See pages 197 and 199** for information on marking cues.

Other Markings

i) Have the singers mark a comma above the music as a breath mark:

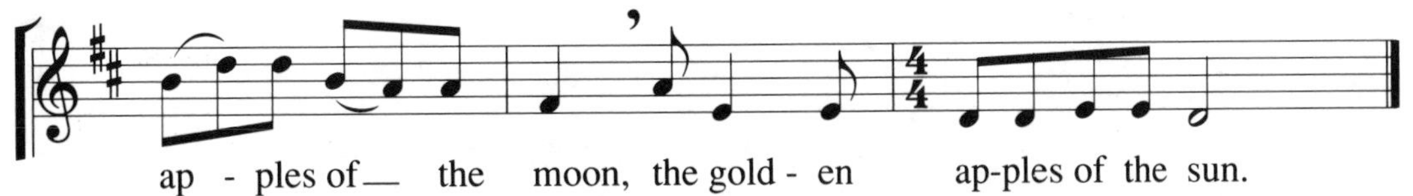

ii) Whenever the singer has a problem while sight-singing, they should quickly mark the top corner of that page and continue singing without a break:

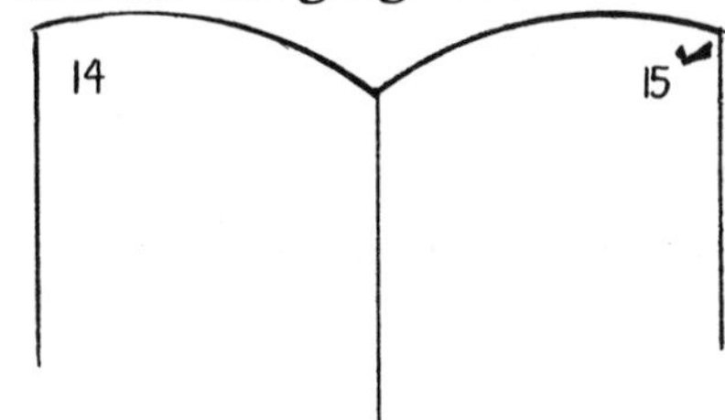

When the singer has time, they can find the problem page easily and determine a strategy to correct the problem.

Appendix F

Conducting Tips

i) **The downbeat should always be bigger than the other beats.** Conduct a few measures of an exercise as you speak the lyrics. Ask the singers to notice how the barlines correspond with the conductor's downbeat: VE2

ii) For a fast tempo, keep the beat pattern small and light. Dynamics may be shown by the left hand and the amount of room between the two hands (leave more space for louder dynamics).

iii) When the music begins with a pick-up, tell the singers how many preparatory beats you will be conducting before their entry: **VE34**

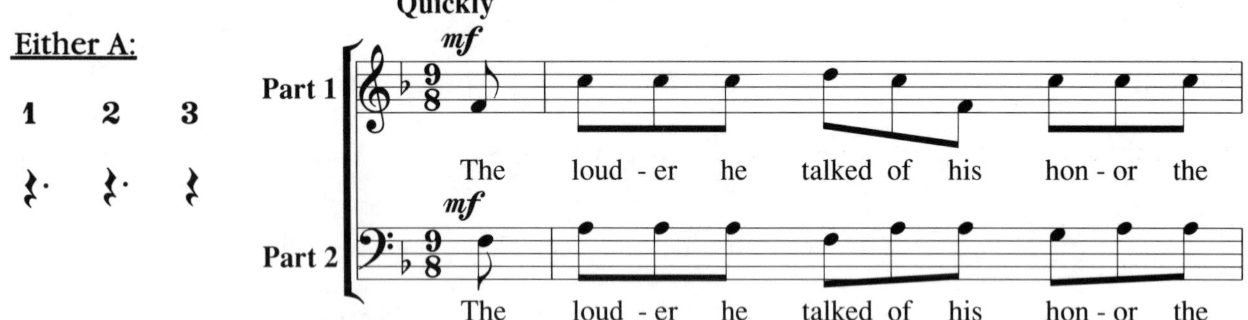

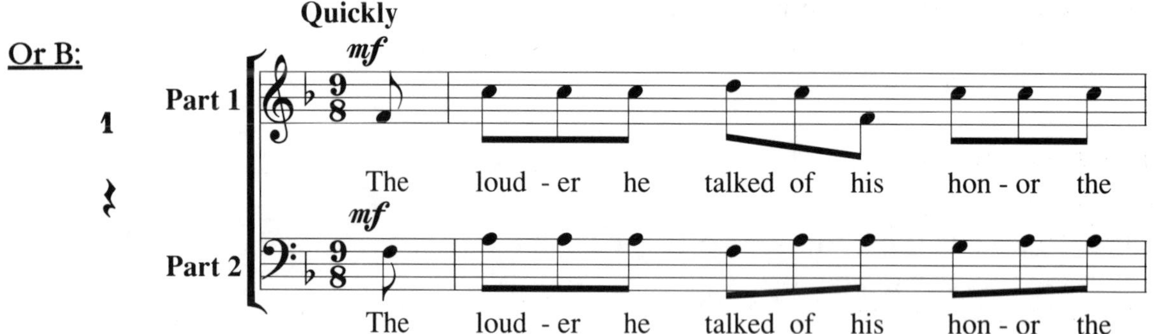

iv) Sometimes the conductor will decide to conduct $\frac{4}{4}$ music with two beats to the bar rather than four. Inform the singers about the change in conducting pattern and ask them to change the time signature to cut time.

v) During an introduction or interlude, show by your conducting when you want the singers to start breathing early (i.e. raise your left hand slowly with the palm up as they breathe in).

vi) **Let your eyes make contact with each singer sometime during the rehearsal.** This helps to give the singers the courage to think of themselves as individuals (rather than just part of an ensemble) so that they will become more independent in their sight-singing.

vii) Use neutral conducting for sight-singing exercises. Do not show when each entry comes by your breath or any other movement. Use a large downbeat and clear intermediary beats and look supportive! When the singers see the conductor using neutral conducting, they quickly realize that they must learn to rely on their own skills to sight-sing.

Appendix G

General Teaching Strategies

Warmups

It saves rehearsal time if you begin with warmups.

When the voice is properly warmed up,
it is easier to sing correct pitches.

When the ears are warmed up,
it is easier to sing in tune, sing precisely together
and hear whether you are singing your own part
correctly.

When the mind is warmed up,
it is easier to follow the music
and to sing with intelligence and musicality.

Adult and changing voices take much longer to warm up than unchanged voices. Just as athletes begin their day with a warmup, singers should begin their day with a vocal warmup. Humming is the fastest way to warm up a voice and may be done while the singer is engaged in other early morning activities. Singers sight-sing much better when their voices are warmed up.

Keeping the Rehearsal Productive

i) After the warmup, rehearse a familiar piece or two while the singers adjust to the rehearsal situation. Then sight-sing new music while the singers are warmed up but still fresh. If the entire rehearsal consists of new repertoire, start with an easy piece or one in a style to which the singers are accustomed.

ii) If the music is sectional, sight-sing part of the piece; then rehearse that section for a few moments. Then sight-sing a new section of the piece.

iii) If the music is difficult to sight-sing, only sight-sing part of it. Teach part of it by rote or sight-sing more of it at a later rehearsal. Stop sight-singing while the singers are still feeling successful (before the singers become discouraged).

iv) Singers stay fresh (and sight-sing better) if the rehearsal is paced with a variety of music. Alternate different types of music:

fast/slow
loud/soft
serious/amusing
difficult/easy
rhythmic/melodic/harmonic
familiar/a bit familiar/new

v) Check the lighting in your rehearsal area as the seasons change. Good lighting is essential for good sight-singing.

vi) If possible, keep the temperature fairly cool so that the singers can concentrate better.

vii) Singers who drink plenty of water have more energy, are less vocally stressed and tend to sight-sing better. For small choirs, a set of glasses and a pitcher of water is a welcome addition. For large choirs, remind the singers to drink sufficient amounts of water before the rehearsal and during the break.

viii) Singers are more relaxed and more productive right after a good laugh. Welcome humor in your rehearsal.

Individual Achievement

Each singer should be encouraged to work at their own ability level, sight-singing as much as they are able with each exercise. Some singers will read the pitches well, others the rhythms, others the dynamics and phrasing as well as the right rhythms and pitches. Within the group each singer continues to progress at their own individual pace.

Whenever the singers have difficulty with an exercise, give them a few moments afterwards for each singer to determine where they had difficulty and to decide on a strategy to correct the problem. Then repeat the exercise.

Meaningful Integration of Sight-Singing

i) **Have the singers memorize the preview checklist and use it for each new piece.** A preview takes time in rehearsal but the singers will sight-sing so much better that it actually saves rehearsal time. With practice, the singers can do the preview quite quickly.

ii) Introduce the terms for new tempo or expression markings as they appear in the repertoire. The singers will understand and remember their meanings better if they connect them with specific pieces of music rather than a list of terms.

iii) If the singers are generally having difficulty with cues or do not mark their scores well, teach a complete unit on cues or useful ways to mark scores (see pages 197 and 202).

iv) Use the "In Rehearsal" information at every rehearsal!

Musical Singing

i) Encourage the singers to **think of music as a total art form.** The music always begins with the first sound whether it is the sound of the piano or the singers. The singing should naturally continue on from the introduction.

ii) For accompanied music, play the piano part along with the choir the first time through. Do not play the choral parts. The piano accompaniment will help to give the singers the overall picture of the music; it is easier to sight-sing when you hear your own part in context with the overall picture and the singers will get to the heart of the music more quickly.

iii) Each time you repeat a passage in the music, give the singers something different on which to concentrate (i.e. dynamics, phrasing, etc.) so that the singers will be thinking about the music itself instead of just "singing along." The better they understand music intellectually and emotionally, the more their sight-singing will improve.

iv) If the rhythms are mechanical-sounding, ask the singers to put a slight emphasis on:

1) The important words;
2) The first eighth note of each group: 

Working On Details

i) Occasionally ask a quartet to sing a small section of the rehearsal music while the rest of the singers listen for phrasing, tuning or balance.

REPEAT the same section of music with the entire choir. Each singer should try to implement what they have learned while listening to the quartet.

ii) It is not necessary for the singers to analyze every temporary shift of key or mode. Sometimes it is better that they simply sing the accidentals as marked and recognize a change in the sound.

iii) Occasionally use a metronome to set the tempo before you begin a piece. Tell the singers what number setting you are using on the metronome.

iv) It is easier to sight-sing music at a fast tempo if you sing lightly because then the voice is more flexible for changing rhythms and pitches.

Appendix H

Adjusting A Sight-Singing Program to Fit Your Situation

Is it Possible to Change The Sequence of Rhythm and Pitch?

All singers should be competent with:

i) Tonic/dominant and the basic beat before going on to more advanced exercises.

ii) Sight-singing major tonality before proceeding on to minor keys and modes. The framework is the same for major and minor keys:

The pitches between are different. Because the singers are already competent in sight-singing in major keys, they do not have much difficulty switching to the contrasting sound of minor keys.

If you are doing a great deal of concert repertoire which concentrates on a specific element not yet covered (i.e. compound time), skip ahead to the exercises which will be helpful with that repertoire. Then go back and work with the exercises you missed. It is more meaningful for the singers if the information in the sight-singing lessons relates directly to problems in current repertoire.

How Can the Program Be Adapted For Middle School Singers?

Every middle school choir is different and each middle school choir changes from day to day as the voices grow. Because of the unique problems of this age range, the sight-singing program must be adapted slightly from day to day to maximize the benefits. Try the following ideas:

i) **Singers sight-sing much better when their voices are warmed up.** Adult and changing voices take much longer to warm up than unchanged voices. Just as athletes begin their day with a warmup, singers should begin their day with a vocal warmup. Humming is the fastest way to warm up a voice and may be done while the singer is engaged in other early morning activities.

Be sure to give the choir a warmup just before the sight-singing session. A good warmup prepares the voice, the ear and the mind.

ii) Whenever possible, the ranges in the exercises are limited. When teaching the larger leaps (i.e. an octave):

- Have singers with a very limited range sing a repeated note rather than jumping the octave. They will at least hear the sound of the octave sung by other singers and will be able to sing it properly when their range stretches.

- Consider changing the key of some of the exercises to accommodate the ranges of your singers whenever necessary. It is much better if the singers are singing a real A 440 whenever they are looking at an A in the music. However, sometimes compromises are necessary as a temporary measure.

iii) Middle school singers have more difficulty with precision because:
- Changing voices have more difficulty initiating a sound.
- Changing voices are not very flexible.

Use a slower tempo for sight-singing.

What Should You Do When You Have a Mixture of Strong and Weak Sight-singers in the Same Choir?

Each singer should be encouraged to work at their own ability level, sight-singing as much as they are able with each exercise. Each singer has different strengths; even the best sight-singers have weaknesses in some areas. Some of the singers will read the pitches well, others the rhythms; others will read the dynamics, phrasing, rhythms and pitches.

It is not a great handicap to have sight-singers at different levels within the same group. Each singer will continue to progress at their own individual pace. Each singer should monitor their own progress.

What Should I Do When New Singers Join the Choir?

Try one of the following possibilities:

i) An inexperienced sight-singer can be an apprentice and sit beside an experienced sight-singer who can quietly give them survival strategies to get them started.

When inexperienced sight-singers are surrounded by competent sight-singers, they can learn the skills and habits at an accelerated pace.

ii) If half the singers are new but the rest are ready for Book 2 of **Successful Sight-Singing**, start into Book 2 slowly and supplement with Book 1 as needed.

iii) If it is possible to split up the singers, you may wish to try one of the following:
- Singers divided into groups by sight-singing expertise. Each group could have their own "teacher."

- Each good sight-singer paired with a poorer sight-singer. The good sight-singer teaches and tests the poorer sight-singer. The good sight-singer will also improve in this type of program just as a regular teacher's skills improve when they teach a new topic. The conductor moves from pair to pair monitoring the general progress.

Appendix I

Performance Selections

As singers improve their sight-singing skills, they quickly become able to sing:

i) A greater quantity of concert repertoire during each season; and

ii) Repertoire at a higher level of difficulty.

The **Successful Sight-Singing Performance Selections** are concert pieces which co-relate with the Milestones in the **Successful Sight-Singing** books (Milestone 1 is the easiest; Milestone 8 the most difficult). When the singers reach Milestone 6 in Book 2 of Successful Sight-Singing, they will be ready for Performance Selections at the Milestone 6 level.

This series includes selections from Renaissance to Twentieth Century (both sacred and secular) and multi-cultural music for a variety of voicings.

Suggested Milestone Levels for Choirs:

Elementary	- Milestones 1-5 (Unison, SA, SSA)
Middle School	- Milestones 1-6 (Unison, SA, SSA, SATB)
High School	- Milestones 1-7 (SA, SSA, TTBB, SATB)
University, College	- Milestones 3-8 (SA, SSA, TTBB, SATB)
Community Choirs	- All Milestones, All Voicings
Church Choirs	- All Milestones, All Voicings

At the front of each Performance Selection are written notes for the singers; this information is designed to help them understand the music better and to perform it better. The pages are illustrated and each Performance Selection has information which will help with that particular piece of music:

COMPOSERS ARE REAL PEOPLE

- what the composer looked like
- the nationality and era of the composer
- how the composer became involved with music
- other famous music by the same composer

A SIGN OF THE TIMES

- a description of typical performance practices of the time
- information about the original instrumentation of the accompaniment
- time line to fit the composer into an historical timeframe with other composers and other musical time periods
- characteristics of music of this time period

THE LYRICS

- relevant historical background for traditional lyrics
- insight into the meaning of contemporary lyrics
- word by word easy-to-read pronunciation guide with stressed syllables underlined
- phrase by phrase translation

THE MUSIC BETWEEN THE NOTES

- getting to the heart of the music: form, vocal production, dynamics, phrasing, etc.

INTRODUCTION FOR THE AUDIENCE

- for a more enjoyable and enlightened listening experience for the audience, one of your singers may read this introduction

The teacher may wish to use some of the information in the written notes:

i) To introduce the music at the first rehearsal;
ii) To add one more bit of knowledge during each subsequent rehearsal;
iii) As an opportunity for the singers to discover new insight into the music on their own time;
iv) As a study source to be used by one vocal section while the other sections are rehearsing a difficult part with the conductor.

At the end of each piece are rehearsal tips for the conductor. Topics include:

- vocal production
- rehearsal techniques
- conducting tips
- teaching strategies
- suggestions for interpretation

Appendix J

Quick Diagnostic Chart

Teacher's Edition Page 178 = TE178

Problem	Solutions	
Pitch: Easy Level	- use pitch framework: blindfold drill, test in mid-rehearsal	TE178-179
	- mark tonic in pencil	TE178
	- memorize major and minor triads	TE19, 47
	- memorize frequent pitches	TE7, 198
	- check position of head	TE10, 12
	- practice variations of silent singing	TE186
	- sight-sing a cappella	TE8
	- have a good warmup	TE209
	- rehearse without piano	TE192
	- check lighting	TE210
Advanced Level	- memorize problem intervals; practice one interval a session	TE179-180
	- use intermediary pitches	TE180
	- use the function of the pitch (i.e. "home")	TE180
	- mark incorrect pitches	TE203
	- mark enharmonic changes	TE203
	- review tips for atonal music	TE145, 157
Tuning	- seating plan: basses with sopranos to left of conductor	TE193-194
	- breathing: correct posture, sing with entire body, expand ribcage, hissing, pace the breath, spin the sound	TE194,196
	- warmups	TE209
	- vowel formation: uniform vowels shaped as a circle, center the pitch	TE194-195
	- ear training: sing softly, change acoustics, repeated pitches, falling or rising pitch patterns	TE195
	- small group demo	TE211
	- doo/oo/loo/noo activity	TE183-184

Cues	- mark the cue	TE62, 197, 199-201
	- sing silently with cue	TE197
	- think the function of pitch (i.e. "home")	TE198-199
	- memorize frequent pitches	TE198
	- breathe early	TE200
	- count measures rest	TE201
	- choose the best cue	TE201-202
	- teach a unit on cues	TE197-202
Dissonance	- think the pitch before you leap	TE107
	- center the pitch immediately	TE110
	- relax for "halo effect"; intense for "knives in the air"	TE106-107, 181-182
	- use clusters for warmups	TE182
Uneven Beat	- check balanced posture	TE11-12
	- use clear conducting patterns	TE207-208
	- sing with entire body	TE194
	- mark vertical lines above beat	TE204-205
	- activities for training the eyes	TE187-188
	- breathe early in rhythm with the beat	TE200
	- practice each exercise at different tempi	TE37
	- practice variations of silent singing	TE186
Precision	- good warmup	TE209
	- check balanced posture	TE11-12
	- use clear conducting patterns	TE207-208
	- sing more softly or lightly	TE131
	- place vowel on the beat	TE66
	- know when to breathe	TE196
	- practice cut-offs	TE184-185
	- activities for training the eyes	TE187-188
	- erratic downbeat activity	TE184
	- doo/oo/loo/noo activity	TE183-184
	- drink plenty of water	TE210
	- play imaginary game of "catch"	TE185-186
Difficult Rhythms	- make sure beat is steady	*see Uneven Beat above*
	- check balanced posture	TE11-12
	- check lighting	TE210
	- use clear conducting patterns	TE207-208

Difficult Rhythms, cont.	- drill the practice examples in lesson where the specific rhythm is introduced	TE22
	- rhythm framework	TE7-8
	- mark vertical lines above beat	TE204-205
	- activities for training the eyes	TE187-188
	- emphasize first note in each grouping	TE35
	- use a strong beat before change in rhythmic texture	TE61
	- activities for concentration	TE188-190
	- drink plenty of water	TE210
	- play imaginary game of "catch"	TE185-186
Longer Durations and Ties	- mark vertical lines evenly spaced above the beat	TE204
	- practice moving eyes continuously	TE187-188
	- follow along with another part	TE60
	- coordinate bar lines with the conductor's downbeat	TE207
Duple Time	- mark half notes above each beat in first few measures	TE204
	- circle bottom 2 in time signature	TE30
Simple Time	- read one beat at a time	TE26
	- count beats only during rests	TE201
Changing Meters	- feel a steady eighth note pulse	TE76-77, 205
	- use slight accent on beat	TE182
	- use a large downbeat	TE207
	- mark pulse at transitions	TE182
	- have half the singers tap the pulse	TE182-183
	- tap wrists and fingers for beat and pulse (on knees, in air)	TE183
Change of Rhythmic Texture	- be aware of strong beat just before change	TE61
Beginning a New Line	- mark an arrow at end of previous line	TE206
	- practice whipping eyes down	TE24
	- mark vocal part with an arrow at beginning of each system	TE205

Topic	Strategy	Reference
Page Turns	- mark an arrow and your next pitch at end of previous page	TE206
	- practice page turn	TE33
	- keep eyes moving ahead of voice	TE187-188
Getting Lost	- use preview checklist	TE89
	- mark vocal part with an arrow at the beginning of each system	TE205
	- coordinate barlines with conductor's downbeat	TE207
	- mark landmarks: changes of texture or tempo, distinctive rhythms or melodic lines in other voices or the accompaniment	TE201
Concentration	- physical breaks	TE65
	- use a variety of music	TE188
	- alternate types of music	TE188
	- stretch arms, legs, faces	TE188
	- imitate movements of conductor	TE188
	- focus on conductor's pencil	TE189
	- warmups with tempo changes	TE189
	- unexpected fermatas	TE189
	- rubbing energizer	TE189
	- memorize phrase in new music	TE189-190
	- imaginary game of "catch"	TE185-186
	- use short sight-singing sessions	TE5
	- sight-sing when warmed up but still fresh	TE209
	- check lighting	TE210
	- check temperature	TE210
	- drink plenty of water	TE210
Lack of Independence	- change direction of sound	TE190
	- parts by rows sitting/standing	TE191
	- switch parts	TE191
	- parts by flavors, colors, seasons, birthdays	TE191
	- sing standing in circles	TE191
	- change seating plan	TE191
	- silent singing	TE186
	- solo singing	TE191-192
	- rehearse a cappella	TE192
	- warmups with tempo changes	TE189
	- unexpected fermatas	TE189

General Hesitation		
	- use preview checklist	TE89
	- use confident posture	TE10-12
	- activities for precision	TE183-186
	- activities for independence	TE190-192
	- activities for training the eyes	TE187-188
	- activities for silent singing	TE186
	- place vowel on the beat	TE66
	- keep the sound moving forward	TE194
	- activities for solo singing	TE191-192
	- use frequent eye contact with singers	TE208
	- teach a unit on cues	TE197-202
	- teach a unit on useful ways to mark scores	TE202-207

Index

NOTE: **Bold** numbers indicate page numbers where new information is introduced.